Eight Ways

The Artistry of Teaching with Multiple Intelligences

David Lazear

of Teaching

SkyLight
Professional
Development

Eight Ways of Teaching: The Artistry of Teaching with Multiple Intelligences
Fourth Edition

Published by SkyLight Professional Development
1900 E. Lake Ave., Glenview, IL 60025
800-348-4474 or 847-657-7450
Fax 847-486-3183
info@skylightedu.com
http://www.skylightedu.com

LCCCN 2002114225
ISBN 1-57517-852-4

V

ZYXWVUTSRQPONMLKJIHGFEDCBA
06 05 04 03   20 19 18 17 16 15 14 13 12 11 10 9 8 7 6 5 4 3 2 1

There are
one-story intellects,
two-story intellects, and
three-story intellects with skylights.

All fact collectors, who have no aim beyond their facts, are

one-story minds.

Two-story minds
compare, reason, generalize,
using the labors of the fact collectors
as well as their own.

Three-story minds
idealize, imagine, predict—their best illumination
comes from above,

through the **skylight**.

—Oliver Wendell Holmes

SkyLight
Professional
Development

Table of Contents

Foreword vii

Preface xi

Introduction 1

Section I   THE 8-IN-1 LESSON PLANNING STRATEGY 11

Section II   THE INTELLIGENCE-FOCUSED LESSON PLANNING STRATEGY 33

1   TEACHING WITH **Verbal/Linguistic** Intelligence 45

2   TEACHING WITH **Logical/Mathematical** Intelligence 59

3   TEACHING WITH **Visual/Spatial** Intelligence 75

4   TEACHING WITH **Bodily/Kinesthetic** Intelligence . . . 91

5   TEACHING WITH **Musical/Rhythmic** Intelligence . . . 107

TEACHING WITH
6 Interpersonal Intelligence 121

TEACHING WITH
7 Intrapersonal Intelligence 135

TEACHING WITH
8 Naturalist Intelligence 151

Epilogue 167
Appendix A: Lesson Processing Blacklines 171
Appendix B: Lesson Procedure Blacklines 189
Appendix C: Graphic Organizer Blacklines 201
Glossary 215
Bibliography 219
Index 225

Foreword

In 1967, a Harvard study of how artistic knowledge develops and functions began. At this time Howard Gardner and David Perkins, currently the project's codirectors, were first-year graduate students. In 1981, Howard Gardner was awarded a MacArthur Prize to fund a shift to an educational emphasis in the work of Project Zero. In the APA Monitor article about the award, the author noted that "early in his career, Gardner had been a committed Piagetian, but as he pursued his own studies, Gardner came to view Piaget's theories as too narrow a notion of how the human mind works."

Gardner was already formulating his multiple intelligences theory based on his belief that there is not just one form of cognition that cuts across all human thinking. His theory proposed that there are multiple intelligences with autonomous intelligence capacities. A book was forming in his mind in the late 1970s, and through a large grant from the Bernard Van Leer Foundation, he began to write *Frames of Mind*, which he described as a "contemporary, empirically-based effort to answer long-standing philosophical questions about Psychology's theoretical underpinnings."

Frames of Mind was published in 1983. In 1984, Howard Gardner presented his new theory to a large number of educators who attended The Coming Education Explosion conference in New York, designed by New Horizons for Learning. The conference program was featured leading-edge educational theorists and practitioners—all of whom were finding successful, innovative ways to foster learning and human development. As soon as Gardner spoke, it became clear that his theory provided a framework for all of the other presentations. The implications for education at all levels and in every setting were evident.

That conference touched off a wave of educational innovation throughout the country and was the beginning of a series of eight international conferences that New Horizons for Learning produced with the multiple intelligences (MI) theory as a framework. Each of those conferences presented information through many kinds of intelligences in a specially created environment filled with music, colorful mind maps, exercises and other physical activities, and dancing into the night.

Attendees reported that they were able to absorb more information than they ever thought possible, and, moreover, during the conference, rather than being tired, they became energized. After each of these events, teachers and school administrators could hardly wait to go back to their classrooms and schools to apply what they had learned. From many different parts of the country letters poured in with enthusiastic reports about students who were learning in new ways, about new curriculum that was being designed, and about classrooms and schools taking on a new look.

In 1984, eight Indianapolis public school teachers submitted a proposal to the Indiana Department of Education for a grant to plan a curriculum for the creatively gifted and talented. During the next school year the teachers met on a voluntary basis to complete their project, and in 1985 they approached the superintendent to ask for their own school. That fall they met with Howard Gardner to share the results of their work based on his multiple intelligences theory and to discuss their plans to develop their own school around the theory. The "Indianapolis Eight" set up a steering committee of experts to advise them, and by 1986 they submitted their proposal to begin the Key School, which opened its doors the next year.

At the present time, the Key School has grown into The Key Learning Community, a unique urban K-12 public school. Pat Bolonos, principal, notes that "The purpose of this school is to be a vibrant learning community where the arts, sciences, and humanities are equally valued and the students are educated to actively participate and thrive in a diverse society. The curriculum, instruction, and assessment of students' progress and motivation continue to be a systemic synthesis of the Theory of Multiple Intelligences." The Key Learning Community gives equal emphasis for each student on each of the eight areas of intelligence.

In 1987, Thomas Armstrong, a psychologist and learning specialist, wrote *In Their Own Way*, an important parenting guide based on Gardner's theory. Armstrong's book continues to help parents and teachers understand complex differences among children and how to create a stimulating and nurturing environment to foster the development of all their intelligences. It has done much to further the understanding and appreciation of an expanded view of intelligence.

In 1988, The New City School, located in St. Louis, Missouri, began implementing MI theory. Tom Hoerr, director of the school, notes that, "Multiple intelligences is more than a theory of intellect, it has become a philosophy of education." The school includes students from age three through grade six, and has hosted four MI conferences. A particular feature of the school is the belief that the personal intelligences are the most important facet of the education, signified by "Who you are is more important than what you know." The teachers have worked from the beginning as colleagues to develop curriculum materials, instructional approaches, and assessment techniques that value all of the intelligences, and they have also published two books on the subject. Tom Hoerr wrote *Becoming a Multiple Intelligences School*, which has not only been used to transform existing schools in this country, but has also been translated into French and Chinese.

In 1993, Howard Gardner updated his theory with another landmark book, *Multiple Intelligences: The Theory in Practice*, and in 1999 his book, *Intelligence Reframed*, described how his theory has evolved and has been revised. These books, along with the work of numbers of practitioners and consultants have helped students throughout the world to be more successful at learning.

It is into this context of pioneering efforts in education that David Lazear offers his comprehensive book of teaching and learning strategies to further the practical application of the theory of multiple intelligences. This updated edition of *Eight Ways of Teaching* offers expanded, useful, creative, and stimulating strategies to vitalize classrooms and help students to learn in exciting new ways.

In the last ten years David Lazear has conducted workshops throughout the United States and Canada, as well as in Iceland, Australia, and New Zealand. He has worked with the Ministry of Education in Singapore for five years, and has trained a cadre of local trainers to teach school staff how to use MI in the classroom. He has now written seven books on the practical applications of MI and is working on two others.

Lazear observes that one of the biggest changes he sees as people work with MI in the classroom is that teachers and principals are looking at students in very different ways. He notes, "They have a more holistic view of children—and of themselves. Much of the labeling of the past has fallen by the wayside, and teachers are more concerned with finding the doorways that will unlock a student's learning, rather than assuming that something is wrong with nontraditional learners."

In this new edition, Lazear includes specific examples of authentic assessment that go far beyond what standardized tests are capable of revealing. Portfolios of student work, student projects, and journals are not only useful measures of student progress, but offer students insight about their own work. Furthermore, they provide rich opportunities for students to engage in the reflective thinking that is often neglected by teachers in their haste to cover more subject matter. Lazear has also added new materials on the uses of technology in the applications of MI theory.

At a time of high accountability to meet increasing standards of academic achievement, this book provides ways teachers can reach all students more effectively as they focus on identifying and helping their students to learn through their strengths. Every teacher will find numerous examples of how to motivate students, teach material in a variety of ways, and offer opportunities for practical and creative application of what has been learned.

Dee Dickinson
CEO/Founder, New Horizons for Learning
www.newhorizons.org

Preface

My interest in the theory of multiple intelligences and its application in the classroom comes from a number of experiences, one of which is having mentored two daughters through grade school and junior high. Two events stand out in my mind as I begin this companion volume to my first book on this subject, *Eight Ways of Knowing: Teaching for Multiple Intelligences.*

The first experience was an encounter with my youngest daughter's fifth-grade teacher. Naomi was having difficulties in a number of subjects, mostly those in which understanding the relationships of ideas, events, and people were important (history, social studies, literature, and the like). In a parent-teacher meeting the teacher explained that Naomi simply didn't have the capacity for grasping complex relationships and intricacy of detail and that she probably needed to be placed in a lower-level class.

Almost in the same breath the teacher pointed to a piece of Naomi's artwork on the wall. It was near Valentine's Day and she had created a large heart poster. It looked like a simple valentine with lace decorations. But as I got closer I discovered that she had created a multilayered, three-dimensional heart from construction paper that had hearts within hearts within hearts all forming an intricate maze of pathways to a central heart chamber where, in raised, multicolored letters, made from hundreds of miniature hearts (much like the flower petals on floats in the Rose Parade), she had created the message: Be mine, Valentine! I was stunned, especially in light of the fact that I had just been told that my daughter did not have the capacity for dealing with complex relationships and intricate detail!

Almost immediately I said to the teacher, as I pointed to the valentine on the wall, "If she could learn her history, social studies, and literature this way, she'd get it!" To which the teacher replied, "Mr. Lazear, art is art and history is history. History is not art. History involves learning facts, dates, people, and events and how they are all related. Your daughter isn't learning these things."

While I did not know then what I know now about multiple intelligences, I knew this teacher was wrong about the separateness of the disciplines. I, perhaps instinctively, knew that somehow Naomi's highly developed visual/spatial capacities could be tapped to help her with her studies. It was many years later that I discovered how.

The second experience involved my eldest daughter, Esther. Esther is very much a bodily/kinesthetic knower and learner. In fact, over the years many teachers have called me with what was supposed to be alarming news—that she was hyperactive. In any event, when she was in junior high school, she came home from school one day with a list of twenty vocabulary words to learn for a test the next day. I sent her to her room to memorize the words and to come back to me when she had learned them.

After a period of time she came to me and said, "Okay Daddy, I'm ready. Test me." I proceeded to do just that. She got less than fifty percent of the words right. So I said to her, "Esther, you're an intelligent girl. You're just not thinking. Back to your room and write each word and definition five times, and this time pay attention to what you are doing!" Reluctantly she wandered off to her room. After a reasonable amount of time, she brought her work to me and I was sure she would have them this time; after all, *I would have if it had been me*! I tested her again, and to my dismay, she had improved very little. Finally, totally exasperated, she said to me, "Daddy, I can't learn this way. I've got to be moving around. I've got to learn with my body!"

Well, for the next twenty to thirty minutes very strange and wonderful things transpired in my study. We proceeded to "embody" the meaning of the words—that is, learn them with our bodies. I would say the word and its definition and she would create body movements and physical gestures that somehow communicated the meaning of the word to her. We were crawling on the floor, leaping in the air, jumping off furniture, doing all manner of strange and bizarre things. But at the end of this time, to my amazement, she had the list down perfectly *with her body!* I would say the word, the word would remind her of the body movement, which she would then perform, and, the body movement helped trigger the verbal definition.

This book is dedicated to Esther and Naomi, and to all children in our schools who have other ways of knowing and learning than our current systems of education take into account. It is my hope that educators will use this book, and *Eight Ways of Knowing,* to begin a very important educational experiment in teaching *for, with,* and *about* multiple intelligences. I have called this book *Eight Ways of Teaching* in order to suggest that our instructional methods must undergo a revolution if we are to reach all students sitting in our classrooms, who have at least eight ways of knowing and probably many more! I often wonder how many kids are in special education classes simply because we have not known how to approach their knowing and learning through a different set of doorways than the verbal/linguistic and logical/mathematical, which dominate all systems of education in the Western world today. In a time when programs for the gifted flourish in many schools, I find myself an advocate for the giftedness of every child, if only we as teachers can find the keys to unlock their full potential.

This edition of *Eight Ways of Teaching* marks the ten-year anniversary of the book's first publication. During these ten years, I have spent an immense amount of time conducting professional development workshops for teachers and administrators on how to plan lessons that incorporate multiple intelligences into the daily teaching and learning process. I have often used this book as the textbook for these workshops. Frequently, I have wished that I could add many, many more chapters to this book to share the creative lesson ideas generated during these workshops. I am thankful for all who have supported and continue to support my work. I am even more grateful for the transformation that you are bringing about in classrooms and in the lives of students around the world as you teach with multiple intelligences.

David G. Lazear
Maui, Hawai'i, 2002

Introduction

The Artistry of Teaching *For,* *With,* and *About* Multiple Intelligences

---

What is intelligence? How can we measure it? And once it's been measured, what should we do with it?

For many centuries humankind has been trying to understand the workings of the mind—sometimes through magic, sometimes through psychology, sometimes through sociology and anthropology, sometimes through religion, and sometimes through medicine. In the last thirty to fifty years, researchers from every walk of life, and from virtually every profession and academic discipline, have begun a new set of explorations of a new frontier—the human mind and how it works. And they have been coming up with some astonishing discoveries, many of which have called into question all previous understandings about humanity and its potentials:

- **Left brain, right brain, and whole brain.** In 1981 Dr. Roger Sperry received a Nobel Peace Prize for his research into the different ways the left and right hemispheres of the brain process information. His research suggested that the left brain's processing is more logical, analytical, linear, and sequential, while the right brain's processing is more simultaneous, nonlinear, and holistic. However, current research suggests that the brain is not nearly as split as we used to think. While the left and right hemispheres *do* have special functions, they almost always work together in an integrated manner as the whole brain. However, this does not negate Sperry's research—it simply corrects his previous ideas that the left and right hemispheres act in isolation from each other.

Left, right, and whole brain research is especially interesting when working with multiple intelligences. The neurological processes of some intelligences are more localized in the right hemisphere, others are more localized in the left hemisphere, and some are more whole brain, integrating information processing from the left and right sides of the brain. For example, the visual/spatial intelligence is primarily focused in the right brain, especially in the occipital and parietal lobes (see fig. 0.1). This does not mean, however, that visual/spatial intelligence is an exclusively right brain intelligence. It simply means that more neurological activity occurs in the right hemisphere when one is using this intelligence. In the case of verbal/linguistic intelligence, more activity is present in the left hemisphere in Broca's area, Wernicke's area, and the temporal lobes (see fig. 0.1). However, using the verbal/linguistic intelligence to form creative and expressive language also accesses the right hemisphere.

- **Triune brain.** Dr. Paul MacLean (1977), Chief of the Laboratory of Brain Evolution and Behavior at the National Institute of Mental Health in Washington, D.C., has done an important research study that suggests that within our one brain there are three separate brains that come from our earlier development as a species. As humans developed, and the need for more involved levels of thinking and mental processes were required, the brain simply grew new layers, each more complex and more intricate than its predecessor. While all three brains are still present in humans, they operate as a unified whole giving us the wisdom and potentials from our evolutionary past.

- **Intelligence can be enhanced and amplified.** In the past intelligence was viewed as a fixed, static entity. It was something you were born with and were stuck with for life. However, contemporary brain-mind researchers, such as Dr. Jean Houston (1980, 1982), Dr. Robert Masters (Masters and Houston 1972, 1978), Dr. Willis Harman (1988), and Dr. Luis Machado (1980), are suggesting that possibly the only limits to our intelligence are self-made and are related to our beliefs about what is possible. What is more, Israeli psychologist and researcher, Dr. Reuven Feuerstein (1980), along with a number of others, suggest that at any age, and at almost any ability level, one's mental functioning can be improved. We can, apparently, all learn to be more intelligent by consciously activating perception and knowing on more levels than we usually use!

- **The brain is a like a hologram.** Dr. Karl Pribram (1971, 1974) of Stanford University proposed a fascinating theory of the brain as a hologram. In a hologram, all of the basic information of the whole is stored within each part of the hologram, so that if it is in some way shattered, each piece contains and is capable of reproducing all of the information of the former whole. Pribram suggests that memory storage may work like this in the brain. Think for a moment about times when a very

Views of the Brain

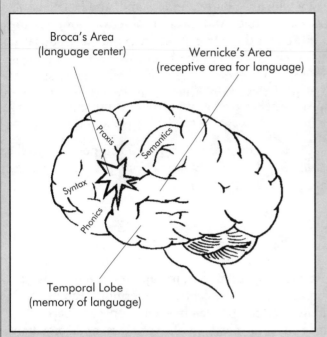

Broca's Area
(language center)

Wernicke's Area
(receptive area for language)

Praxis

Semantics

Syntax

Phonics

Temporal Lobe
(memory of language)

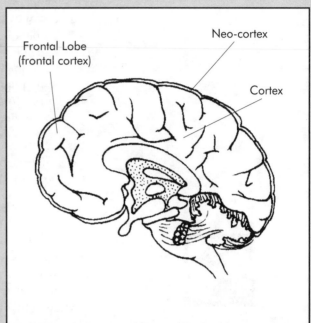

Frontal Lobe
(frontal cortex)

Neo-cortex

Cortex

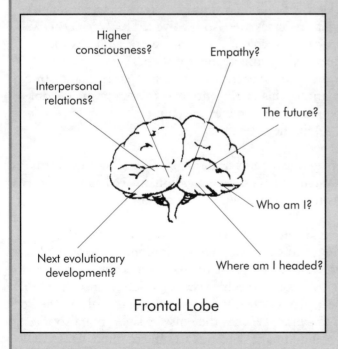

Higher
consciousness?

Empathy?

Interpersonal
relations?

The future?

Who am I?

Next evolutionary
development?

Where am I headed?

Frontal Lobe

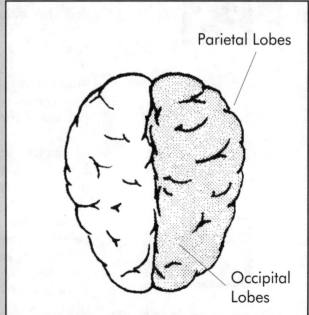

Parietal Lobes

Occipital
Lobes

Figure 0.1

small fragment of a memory is able to bring back a full-sensory experience of something that may have happened in your childhood.

- **Intelligence is a multiple reality.** Dr. Howard Gardner (1983) and his team of Harvard researchers involved in Project Zero have postulated that there are many forms of intelligence—many ways by which we know, understand, and learn about our world—not just one. And most of these ways of knowing go beyond those that dominate Western culture and education, and they definitely go beyond what current IQ tests can measure. He proposed a schema of eight intelligences and suggests that there are probably many others that we have not yet been able to test!

It is the research of Howard Gardner on which this book, as well as *Eight Ways of Knowing* (Lazear 1998a), is primarily based. Let me briefly summarize the eight intelligences Gardner identified:

Verbal/linguistic intelligence is responsible for the production of language and all the complex possibilities that follow, including poetry, humor, storytelling, grammar, metaphors, similes, abstract reasoning, symbolic thinking, conceptual patterning, reading, and writing. This intelligence can be seen in such people as poets, playwrights, storytellers, novelists, public speakers, and comedians.

Logical/mathematical intelligence is most often associated with what we call scientific thinking or inductive reasoning, although deductive thought processes are also involved. This intelligence involves the capacity to recognize patterns, work with abstract symbols (such as numbers and geometric shapes), and discern relationships and/or see connections between separate and distinct pieces of information. This intelligence can be seen in such people as scientists, computer programmers, accountants, lawyers, bankers, and of course, mathematicians.

The logical/mathematical and verbal/linguistic intelligences form the basis for most systems of Western education, as well as for all forms of currently existing standardized testing programs.

Visual spatial intelligence deals with the visual arts (including painting, drawing, and sculpting); navigation, mapmaking, and architecture (which involve the use of space and knowing how to get around in it); and games such as chess (which require the ability to visualize objects from different perspectives and angles). The key sensory base of this intelligence is the sense of sight, but also the ability to form mental images and pictures in the mind. This intelligence can be seen in such people as architects, graphic artists, cartographers, industrial design draftspersons, and of course, visual artists (painters and sculptors).

Bodily/kinesthetic intelligence is the ability to use the body to express emotion (as in dance and body language), to play a game (as in sports), and to create a new product (as in invention). Learning by doing has long been recognized as an important part of education. Our bodies know things our minds do not and cannot know in any other way. For example, our bodies know how to ride a bike, rollerskate, type, and parallel park a car. This intelligence can be seen in such people as actors, athletes, mimes, dancers, and inventors.

Musical/rhythmic intelligence includes such capacities as the recognition and use of rhythmic and tonal patterns, and sensitivity to sounds from the environment, the human voice, and musical instruments. Many of us learned the alphabet through this intelligence and the A-B-C song. Of all forms of intelligence, the consciousness altering effect of music and rhythm on the brain is probably the greatest. This intelligence can be seen in advertising professionals (who write catchy jingles to sell a product), performance musicians, rock musicians, dance band members, composers, and music teachers.

Interpersonal intelligence involves the ability to work cooperatively with others in a group as well as the ability to communicate, verbally and nonverbally, with other people. It builds on the capacity to notice distinctions among others such as contrasts in moods, temperament, motivations, and intentions. In the more advanced forms of this intelligence, one can literally pass over into another's perspective and read his or her intentions and desires. One can have genuine empathy for another's feelings, fears, anticipations, and beliefs. This form of intelligence is usually highly developed in counselors, teachers, therapists, politicians, and religious leaders.

Intrapersonal intelligence involves knowledge of the internal aspects of the self, such as knowledge of feelings, the range of emotional responses, thinking processes, self-reflection, and a sense of or intuition about spiritual realities. Intrapersonal intelligence allows us to be conscious of our consciousness; that is, to step back from ourselves and watch ourselves as an outside observer. It involves our capacity to experience wholeness and unity, to discern patterns of connection within the larger order of things, to perceive higher states of consciousness, to experience the lure of the future, and to dream of and actualize the possible. This intelligence can be seen in such people as philosophers, psychiatrists, spiritual counselors and gurus, and cognitive pattern researchers.

Naturalist intelligence involves the ability to discern, comprehend, and appreciate the various flora and fauna of the world of nature as opposed to the world created by human beings. It involves such capacities as recognizing and classifying species, growing plants and raising or taming animals, knowing how to appropriately use the natural world (e.g., living off the land), and having a curiosity about the natural world, its creatures, weather patterns, physical history, etc. In working with and developing the naturalist intelligence, one often discovers a sense of wonder, awe, and respect for all the various phenomena and species (plant and animal) of the natural world. This intelligence can be seen in such people as farmers, hunters, zookeepers, gardeners, cooks, veterinarians, nature guides, and forest rangers.

On the following pages are a summary of the multiple intelligences (fig. 0.2) and the Multiple Intelligences Capacities Wheel (fig. 0.3). I created the wheel for *Eight Ways of Knowing* to show some of the specific capacities (what Gardner sometimes calls subintelligences) that are related to the eight ways of knowing.

The good news is that each of us have all of these intelligences, but not all of them are developed equally and thus we do not know how to use them effectively. In fact, it is usually the case that one or two intelligences are stronger and more fully developed than the others. But, this need not be a permanent condition. *We have within ourselves the capacity to activate all of our intelligences!*

What are possibilities of teaching *for, with,* and *about* multiple intelligences in the classroom?

There are at least three different types of lessons that are needed:

1. **Intelligence as a subject unto itself** *(teaching for multiple intelligences).* Each of the intelligences can be taught as a subject in its own right: music skills, language, art as a formal discipline, mathematical calculation and reasoning, skillful body movement (as in physical education, dance, and drama), and various social skills necessary for effective functioning in our society. Teaching these subjects requires a grasp of the developmental stages of each intelligence as well as an understanding of the accumulated cultural wisdom on the subject, the formal knowledge base, and the practical methods, skills, and techniques of the intelligence.

2. **Intelligence as a means to acquire knowledge** *(teaching with multiple intelligences).* Each of the intelligences can be used as a means to gain knowledge in areas beyond itself: using body movement to learn vocabulary words, music to teach math concepts, art (drawing, painting, and sculpture) to bring to life different periods of history and different cultures, debate to

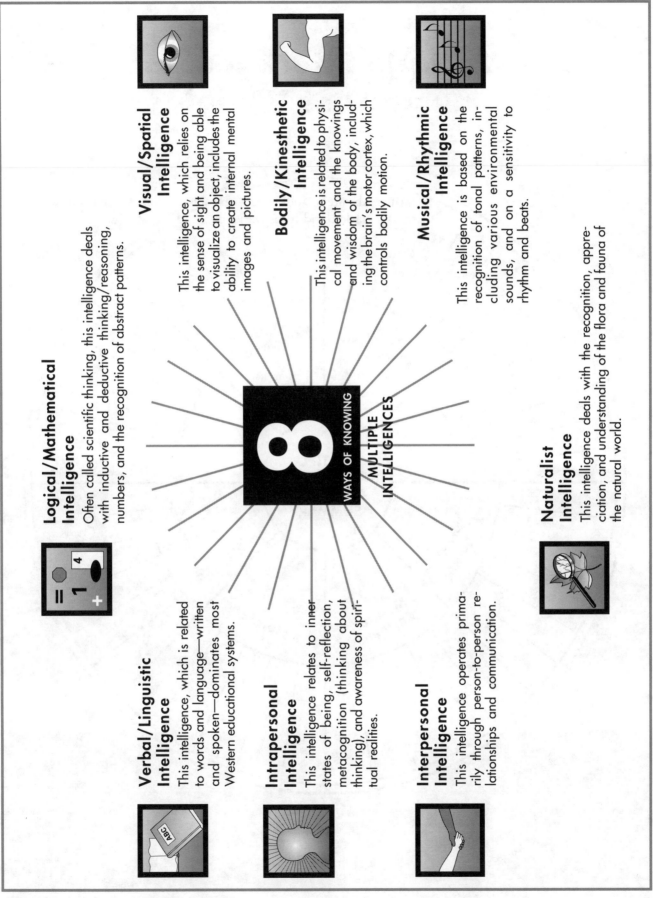

Figure 0.2

Multiple Intelligences Capacities Wheel

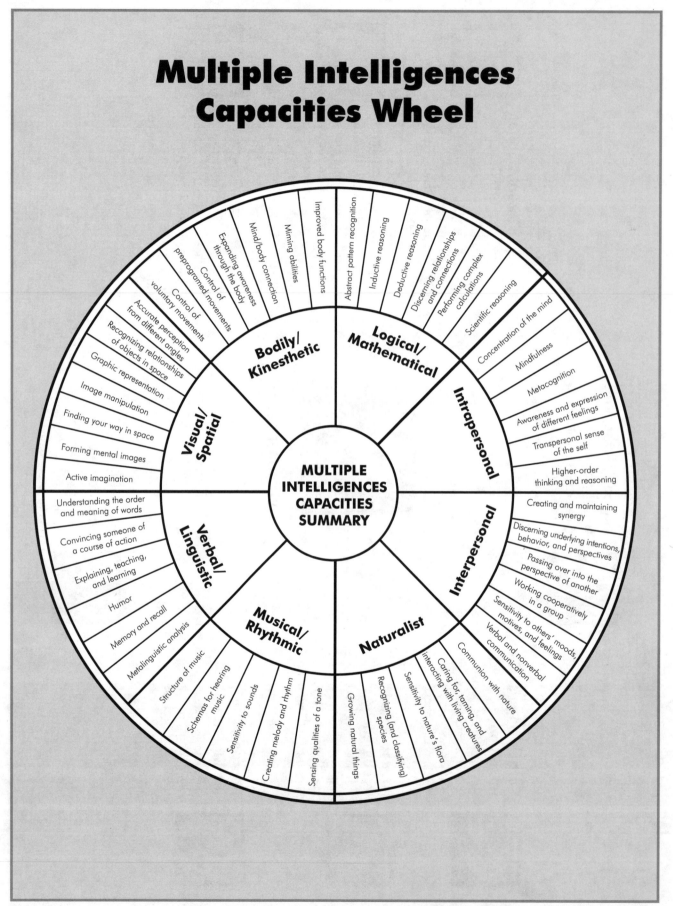

Figure 0.3

SkyLight Professional Development

explore various perspectives on current events, and the skill of comparing and contrasting to analyze characters in a Shakespearean play.

3. **Metaintelligence—intelligence investigating itself (*teaching* about *multiple intelligences*).** Lessons that deal with metaintelligence processes teach students about their own multiple intelligences— how to access them, how to strengthen them, and how to actively use them in learning and in everyday life.

OK, I buy the eight ways of knowing! What does it take to teach in this way? What's involved in lessons that take into account the reality of multiple intelligences in the classroom?

One of the exciting things about teaching with multiple intelligences is that there is not just one right way to do it. There are many right ways! In fact, the only limits in planning lessons that incorporate multiple intelligences are your own creativity and willingness to experiment with the teaching/learning process in your classroom.

This book presents two ways to structure lessons for multiple intelligences: 8-in-1 lessons and intelligence-focused lessons. 8-in-1 lessons incorporate all eight intelligences into a single teaching/ learning experience, while intelligence-focused lessons incorporate the tools and techniques of one intelligence into a given learning experience. (As I will explain later, from a neurological standpoint you cannot do a lesson that uses only one intelligence—the brain is simply not "wired" in this fashion. In everything we do, all eight intelligences are somehow involved. However, in teaching and learning, you can focus your instruction and students' learning on one intelligence.) This book guides you through the process for creating both 8-in-1 and intelligence-focused lessons and gives many examples for both types of lessons. Section I features 8-in-1 lessons and Section II features intelligence-focused lessons.

SECTION

1

The 8-in-1 Lesson Planning Strategy

The 8-in-1 Lesson Planning Strategy

Imagine the following scenes:

A classroom of first and second graders are lying on the floor, curled up like little balls. Some soothing music is playing. The teacher tells the students that they are all little seedlings who want to become mature plants. The music changes to a subtle beat. Suddenly the little balls begin to wiggle and slowly start to stretch. The music changes to a lively rhythm and the children rise to their feet, sway back and forth, and stretch towards the sky. Many of them are making sounds of contentment and pleasure. The teacher tells the students to stop and go to their tables. Lumps of clay are placed on the tables. The teacher instructs the students to sculpt the journey of a plant from seedling to mature plant. Pictures of each stage of the journey guide them in their creations. The classroom also includes a growing project. Under a fluorescent light at the back of the class are paper cups filled with dirt. Students have planted seeds in the cups. The word *germination* is posted on the wall above the cups. As the seeds sprout and grow, the word posted on the wall will change to match the stages of plant growth.

A class of middle school students is reviewing the parts of speech. The class has been divided into expert groups. Each group is to become an expert in their assigned part of speech and then lead the whole class in a review of their part of speech. First, the expert groups study the definitions of their assigned parts of speech in the dictionary and rewrite the definitions in their own words. Second, they create a song that explains what role their part of speech plays in a sentence. Third, they demonstrate this role through physical movements such as gestures, role play, posture, facial expressions, physical exercise, etc. Fourth, they create an advertisement for *USA Today* to promote their part of speech. Fifth, they present their definitions, songs, physical movements, and newspaper advertisement to the whole class. They try to convince the class, via the newspaper advertisement, that their part of speech is the most important.

A high school history class is singing Gregorian chants. The classroom windows are made to look like stained glass windows: they are covered with cellophane paintings of scenes from twentieth and twenty-first century life. The students are sitting at tables. Each table is labeled with a medieval role—peasants, serfs, lords, etc. The teacher explains that students will learn about the social hierarchy and structure of the Middle Ages in this lesson. She asks each group to research their assigned social role by reading information in the textbook or encyclopedia. After the groups have completed their research, the teacher tells the class that they are going to dramatize a typical scene from twenty-first century life, such as shopping at a mall, participating in a public meeting, or attending the theatre. Each group must play their assigned medieval role in the drama, trying to fully embody how this segment of society would behave. Students are given time to discuss how they will act and they make simple costumes that would be typical of their social class. The teacher acts as the king or queen and orchestrates the drama.

In all three scenarios, you witnessed an imaginary journey of classrooms immersed in teaching and learning with multiple intelligences. One of the strategies for incorporating multiple intelligences into lessons is one that I have called the 8-in-1 strategy. The goal of the 8-in-1 strategy is to incorporate all eight intelligences in a single learning experience for students. This strategy is not only exciting, it also promotes deep and lasting understanding in students. I am not an advocate of using the 8-in-1 strategy with *every* lesson, although I am a firm believer that, in principle, every lesson *could* incorporate all eight intelligences. I will make some comments later about when is the best time to use this strategy. But for now, let's look at the basic procedures for designing the 8-in-1 lesson.

How to Design 8-in-1 Lessons

Before creating an 8-in-1 lesson, consult the Multiple Intelligences Toolbox (fig. I.1; for a detailed explanation and technology tips for each tool, see appendix A, pp. 172–180). Use the toolbox as a quick reference for a plethora of ideas, strategies, methods, and techniques that you can incorporate into your current lessons. The toolbox gives ten teaching and/or learning tools for each intelligence. These tools help students access each intelligence.

While the toolbox is not an exhaustive list of all the possible tools, it does delineate the distinct capacities of the different intelligences. Gardner (1983) calls these capacities the "core operations" of an intelligence. Each intelligence encompasses a set of clearly defined bio-neurological and cognitive capacities. The toolbox simply offers

Logical/Mathematical

- Abstract Symbols/ Formulas
- Calculation
- Deciphering Codes
- Forcing Relationships
- Graphic/Cognitive Organizers
- Logic/Pattern Games
- Number Sequences/ Patterns
- Outlining
- Problem Solving
- Syllogisms

Verbal/Linguistic

- Creative Writing
- Formal Speaking
- Humor/Jokes
- Impromptu Speaking
- Journal/Diary Keeping
- Poetry
- Reading
- Storytelling/Story Creation
- Verbal Debate
- Vocabulary

Visual/Spatial

- Active Imagination
- Color/Texture Schemes
- Drawing
- Guided Imagery/ Visualizing
- Mind Mapping
- Montage/Collage
- Painting
- Patterns/Designs
- Pretending/Fantasy
- Sculpting

MULTIPLE INTELLIGENCES TOOLBOX

Musical/Rhythmic

- Environmental Sounds
- Instrumental Sounds
- Music Composition/Creation
- Music Performance
- Percussion Vibrations
- Rapping
- Rhythmic Patterns
- Singing/Humming
- Tonal Patterns
- Vocal Sounds/Tones

Bodily/Kinesthetic

- Body Language/Physical Gestures
- Body Sculpture/Tableaus
- Dramatic Enactment
- Folk/Creative Dance
- Gymnastic Routines
- Human Graph
- Inventing
- Physical Exercise/Martial Arts
- Role Playing/Mime
- Sports Games

Interpersonal

- Collaborative Skills Teaching
- Cooperative Learning Strategies
- Empathy Practices
- Giving Feedback
- Group Projects
- Intuiting Others' Feelings
- Jigsaw
- Person-to-Person Communication
- Receiving Feedback
- Sensing Others' Motives

Intrapersonal

- Altered States of Consciousness Practices
- Emotional Processing
- Focusing/Concentration Skills
- Higher-Order Reasoning
- Independent Studies/Projects
- Know Thyself Procedures
- Metacognition Techniques
- Mindfulness Practices
- Silent Reflection Methods
- Thinking Strategies

Naturalist

- Archetypal Pattern Recognition
- Caring for Plants/Animals
- Conservation Practices
- Environment Feedback
- Hands-On Labs
- Nature Encounters/Field Trips
- Nature Observation
- Natural World Simulations
- Species Classification (organic/inorganic)
- Sensory Stimulation Exercises

(Note: For a detailed explanation and technology tips for each tool, see appendix A, pp. 172–180.)

Figure I.1

practical and quick ways to tap into these capacities. (See the Multiple Intelligences Capacities Wheel, fig. 0.3 on p. 8, and *Eight Ways of Knowing: Teaching for Multiple Intelligences* [Lazear 1998a] for more information about the distinct capacities for each intelligence.)

After consulting the Multiple Intelligences Toolbox, follow these steps to create an 8-in-1 lesson:

1. **Focus the content.** In your own mind get a clear fix on all aspects of the content involved in the lesson. Remember that you are only creating a lesson, not a whole unit! Aim for a topic that can be covered within a single learning experience, even if it must take a couple of days to complete.

2. **State the lesson objectives and outcomes.** Write down the academic objectives of the lesson. Decide what you want your students to know and understand by the end of the lesson. You may also target certain learning outcomes, such as developing a specific skill, making personal connections, developing or emphasizing a behavioral pattern. In this 8-in-1 strategy, this part of the planning process is critical. If you do not begin with clear objectives and outcomes, 8-in-1 lessons can quickly turn into a string of very fun and interesting activities—everyone has a good time—but at the end of the lesson, you are not sure if students learned anything.

3. **Pick tools from the Multiple Intelligences Toolbox.** Go to the toolbox and select one tool from each intelligence area. Keep your lesson objectives and outcomes in mind as you choose the tools. Be sure that the tools you choose help achieve your objectives and outcomes for the lesson. Do not fall into the trap of avoiding certain intelligences or tools within an intelligence simply because they are difficult for you personally. The tools that seem the most difficult for you may be those that will turn on some students to the learning at hand.

4. **Define how each tool will be used.** Think through how each tool will be used by using a blank palette (see appendix A, p. 181). Beside the icons for each intelligence, write the names of the tools you have selected from the toolbox. Then write a brief description on how you will use each tool to achieve the objectives and outcomes of the lesson. Determine the learning activities in which students will be involved, what products they will produce, how you will use the tools to teach the lesson, how you will assess students' understanding of the material through the tools, etc. (See the example lessons provided on pp. 20–32.)

5. **Sequence the lesson.** Once you are clear on how you and your students will use the tools in the lesson, decide how to order the various learning activities within the lesson. Again,

refer to your objectives and outcomes for guidance. Remember, even though you have chosen eight different tools does not mean that you will necessarily need eight different steps in the lesson. Some activities may happen simultaneously.

Voilà! You have just planned a lesson that incorporates all eight intelligences into a single learning experience. You have figured out how to teach some of the "same old stuff" in a dramatically new way! The last and most important step is to actually do the lesson you have created.

At the end of this section are three examples of 8-in-1 lessons—one each for elementary, middle, and secondary school. (See pages 20–32.) Please use these to guide you through the lesson planning process outlined above.

Comments on the 8-in-1 Strategy

The 8-in-1 strategy is one of the best techniques for getting all students actively involved with the material you are teaching. There is something for everyone in each 8-in-1 lesson. Not all parts of the lesson will appeal equally to all students, but if you are sure to involve all intelligences, you are almost certain to grab each student's interest and involvement at some point in the lesson.

By its very nature, this strategy is extremely student-centered. You, the teacher, assume a facilitator or coaching role as you help students learn the material and perform the learning tasks. As your students become more familiar with multiple intelligences and the 8-in-1 strategy, you may ask students what they would like to do to explore each intelligence. I can promise that students will come up with things they want to do, thereby overcoming one of the biggest hurdles to learning—motivation.

THE 8-IN-1 LEARNING PROCESS

The 8-in-1 process has a profound impact on both learning and the learner. For myself, I have summarized one of the key discoveries of contemporary brain research (Houston 1982; Jensen 1999; Sylwester 2000; Wolfe 2001) as follows:

- The more ways a person learns something, the more he or she really learns it.
- The more ways a person learns something, the more he or she will remember it.

- The more ways a person learns something, the more he or she genuinely understands it and it becomes a part of his or her being.

I know of no strategy that embodies this insight more than the 8-in-1 lesson.

When we consider the impact of the 8-in-1 lesson on the learner, one of the first things we see is students having fun. Contrary to popular belief, students can have fun learning! Contemporary brain research demonstrates the important role that fun plays in learning (Pert 1997).

In the 8-in-1 lesson, students become actively involved with the material, rather than passive recipients of whatever the teacher doles out for the day. Students take responsibility for their own and each others' learning. I know of no better strategy to effectively reach the ultimate goal of education—creating lifelong learners.

STRUCTURING 8-IN-1 LESSONS

When you use the 8-in-1 strategy, it is important to keep in mind the underlying structure of the lesson. First, be sure that all eight intelligences are somehow involved in the lesson. Second, decide which parts of the lesson will require small group work, whole class activities, and individual or group projects. Third, if you use cooperative groups in the lesson, plan to assign appropriate roles and review the rules of cooperative learning (e.g., everyone pulls their own weight, no put-downs, etc.). (See Key Ingredients for Success in Cooperative Learning, appendix A, p. 187, for more pointers.) Fourth, set time parameters for the lesson. Use time effectively to promote on-task behavior in groups and to maximize students' creativity. Finally, determine how you will use your classroom space as well as equipment and supplies. Be sure to make room for students to do their learning activities and take care to make readily available the necessary equipment and supplies students need to use during the lesson.

WHEN TO USE 8-IN-1 LESSONS

You may use 8-in-1 lessons anytime, but 8-in-1 lessons are especially powerful when they are used to introduce a lesson, unit, or theme; teach difficult topics; review a unit; or enliven bored students.

Using the 8-in-1 strategy to introduce a lesson, unit, or theme builds students' anticipation for what is to follow. It also gives you, the teacher, an opportunity to assess students' prior knowledge of the material. Many students already know a great deal about what we are teaching, but they may not be good at expressing it in a more traditional, verbal/linguistic way. However, you can often observe students in an 8-in-1 lesson and discover that they know and understand more than you expected.

The 8-in-1 strategy tends to be very effective in teaching complex or abstract concepts that are very difficult for students to grasp. Instead of going over and over and over a complex concept in the same way (and students still not "getting" it), you may employ the 8-in-1 strategy to approach the concept through a wide variety of doorways (so that students can grasp the concept). 8-in-1 lessons also help you transform abstract concepts into ideas that students can see, touch, feel, taste, hear, etc. Making learning visible, touch-able, etc., breaks open students' understanding.

The 8-in-1 strategy is also great for review or for the culmination of a unit of study. You may use an 8-in-1 lesson to revisit key concepts and to integrate various concepts learned during the unit.

And, last but not least, this strategy can very quickly change the energy level in your classroom whenever students (or you!) find themselves bored with the learning at hand.

MAKING TIME FOR 8-IN-1 LESSONS

Frequently, when teachers first encounter the 8-in-1 strategy, they fear it will take more time to teach this way and that they will not be able to cover the curriculum. The truth is that this method takes no more time—and, in fact, it may save time! In 8-in-1 lessons, it is more likely that students will understand the material the first time, so the teacher will not need to teach the material over and over and over again.

Initially, it takes more time to plan 8-in-1 lessons. However, after you use the 8-in-1 method a few times and become more familiar with the Multiple Intelligences Toolbox (fig, I.1), you will become more efficient at planning lessons. The better you know the tools, the quicker and easier the planning will be. Be sure to "force" yourself to test all of the tools listed for each intelligence—even those you don't like or don't understand. Discover the possibilities and limits of each tool.

When I first started working with multiple intelligences, I used two forms of self-discipline to increase my fluency with the tools. First, I required myself to plan to use all eight intelligences in every lesson I taught for a month. (When I actually taught these lessons, I did not always use all eight intelligences, but I knew I *could* use them.) Second, each time I planned an 8-in-1 lesson that month, I placed a checkmark beside each tool I used from the toolbox and then I did not allow myself to reuse that tool until I used all the other tools in the list for that intelligence. This prevented me from overusing certain tools and also forced me to test the potential of all of the tools in the toolbox. After one month of these self-disciplines, I was thinking about planning and teaching lessons in a totally different way! I discovered that never again do I need to bore myself or my students during a lesson. If what I am doing is not working, I simply put together a new set of tools and I suddenly have a brand new lesson.

In one of my workshops in the Chicago area, a high school math teacher wondered how many possible combinations of tools can be made from the toolbox. She figured out the toolbox probably comprised at least ten million possible combinations! (And this happened before Gardner added the naturalist intelligence to the mix.) Never use the same tool combination twice!

A popular saying of teachers who participate in my multiple intelligences workshops through the Ministry of Education in Singapore is: To use the 8-in-1 strategy, sometimes you have to waste time to save time. What they mean is that it may take slightly longer to initially teach a concept using the 8-in 1 strategy. However, in the course of the year, the 8-in-1 strategy saves an immense amount of time, because teachers do not need to re-teach, and re-re-teach, and re-re-re-teach. Students understand the concept the first time. The 8-in-1 lesson holds this promise and possibility for all of us.

Following are three sample 8-in-1 lessons—one each for elementary, middle, and secondary school.

**AN EXAMPLE LESSON
FOR ELEMENTARY SCHOOL**

The Journey of Metamorphosis

LESSON SYNOPSIS

Begin by showing a video that illustrates the journey of the frog's metamorphosis from egg to mature frog. After the video, review vocabulary words for each stage, including words related to the frog's anatomy. Debrief students on what they remember from the video about each stage. Ask them to use the new words to describe each stage.

An alternative to the video is to ask students to surf the Internet to discover what they can find about the frog's metamorphosis.

Divide students in expert groups (2–3 students per group). Assign each group one stage in the metamorphosis process. Tell each group to draw pictures illustrating what happens to the developing frog during their stage.

Provide illustrations from books, the Internet, etc., to guide students in making their own drawings.

Ask groups to use their pictures as group banners. Tell the groups to form a line, placing themselves in the correct order for the metamorphosis process. Groups must be able to explain, via their drawings, what happens during their assigned stage of the process.

Arrange the drawings on a wall in the proper order. Explain to the class that they will soon act out the whole process, but first they must create an audiocassette tape of the background music and sounds that match each stage. Tell students that they will play the tape during the dramatic enactment.

Use this brainstorming time to reinforce students' understanding of the metamorphosis process. Question why certain music or sounds seem like a good match for specific stages in the process.

Students will most likely need more assistance from you on this part of the lesson than on any of the other parts.

Attach a piece of blank paper to each drawing. As a class, brainstorm ideas about what kind of music, sounds, rhythms, beats, etc., can be used to form a "sound illustration" for the events in each stage. For example, you might ask: What kind of music would you play for the frog eggs in the water? What sounds would you hear? As students offer ideas, write them on the blank sheets for each stage.

After the class has brainstormed a list of sounds for each stage, ask expert groups to reconvene and record a tape with the appropriate sounds for their stages.

As you have throughout the lesson, use this activity to deepen students' understanding of the process.

Ask the whole class to move to an open space. Tell students that they will now plan the dramatic enactment of the journey of metamorphosis. Discuss appropriate movements for each stage. Encourage students to get down on the floor and practice the movements. Talk to students about each stage as they practice; ask them to feel in their own bodies what happens to the developing frog at each stage. After students have mastered the movements, tell them to turn to a partner and say what they think the frog is feeling in this stage.

Now put it all together. Play the audiotapes the groups created as students act out each stage.

After the performance, explain that metamorphosis does not just happen to frogs. It also happens to butterflies, plants, and chickens. See if students can point out the stages for these other things. Explain that although humans don't go through metamorphosis, our bodies change dramatically from infancy to adulthood. Ask how their journey as humans is similar to and different from the frog's journey of metamorphosis.

Set up an aquarium and place some frog eggs in it. Allow students to experience the journey of metamorphosis firsthand. Ask students to record changes in their journals. Encourage students to build on the understanding that they gained by drawing pictures of, choosing sounds for, and acting out the metamorphosis process.

The Journey of Metamorphosis

VOCABULARY
Watch a video and learn the correct names for each stage of the metamorphosis process.

SEQUENCING PATTERNS
Put the stages in the proper order and explain why each stage occurs.

DRAWING
Draw pictures that illustrate what happens to the developing frog at each stage of the process. Show the changes.

ROLE PLAY/MIME
Act out the stages of the metamorphosis process. Incorporate appropriate movements for each stage that demonstrate what is happening.

MUSIC PERFORMANCE
Create a soundtrack of music, sounds, rhythms, beats, etc., that form an appropriate background for each stage of the process.

EMPATHY PRACTICES
Talk with a partner about what you think the developing frog is feeling at each stage of the process.

KNOW THYSELF PROCEDURES
Reflect on your own growth and changes from infancy to the present. Note similarities and differences between your journey and the frog's metamorphosis.

HANDS-ON LABS
Get some frog eggs and watch them grow. Keep a journal of your observations.

SUBJECT AREA: Elementary General Science

LESSON OBJECTIVE: Students will understand the distinct stages of a frog's metamorphosis from egg to mature frog, what occurs during each stage, and how each stage contributes to the frog's development.

SUPPLIES/MATERIALS:
- video showing the metamorphosis journey
- poster paper and colored marking pens
- audiocassette tape recorder and CD player
- variety of tapes and/or CDs with a variety of types of music, sounds, etc.
- tank and appropriate nutriments for observing the metamorphosis of frog eggs
- student journals

ROOM ARRANGEMENT:
- open space for movement activities
- art area for making posters
- music area for recording the soundtrack
- conversation area for discussing with partners

COMMENTARY AND REFLECTIONS

1. The underlying assumption of this lesson is that metamorphosis is a major concept and, therefore, it is appropriate to give metamorphosis this level of attention. The lesson could be completed in a couple of intense days, except for the naturalist experience. (Setting up the aquarium and watching the eggs grow will take longer.) Or the lesson could span a period of time, focusing on different sets of intelligences on different days. If metamorphosis is not a major concept in your curriculum, choose another concept that is important and adapt the learning activities. Or, better yet, choose different tools from the toolbox. My goal in presenting this lesson was to illustrate the 8-in-1 strategy with typical elementary content.

2. Another underlying assumption is that this lesson would be used to introduce students to metamorphosis. Therefore, it provides a certain amount of input via direct instruction and student investigation. However, the lesson could be used as a review of all students have learned in a unit on metamorphosis.

3. The more you work with students on improving their representations of the stages, the deeper their learning will become. For example, ask students to explain how their drawings represent the various stages. Point out aspects that they have overlooked and ask what they could add to their drawing to include these ideas. Taking time to work on each learning activity ensures that the lesson remains focused on the objectives and outcomes.

Shading must be contiguous.

Fraction and Decimal Equivalents

LESSON SYNOPSIS

Begin the lesson by allowing students to play with 10 x 10 charts. Hand out four charts to each student. Divide the class into two large groups. Ask one group to shade in 50% of the boxes. Ask the other group to shade in $\frac{1}{2}$ of the boxes. Boxes may appear as follows:

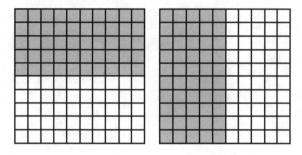

Ask students to show their completed charts to one another. Discuss the different ways to represent the shading in decimals and fractions (e.g., $\frac{1}{2}$, 50%, .50, $\frac{50}{100}$, etc.). The goal here is to help students see the fraction and decimal equivalents!

Repeat the process with three more examples for each group. Ask students in group one to shade in three charts to represent these amounts: 25%, .43, and .07. (See examples below.)

Fraction and Decimal Equivalents

IMPROMPTU SPEAKING
Students draw a fraction or decimal from a hat and must explain the conversion process.

CALCULATION
Learn the process for converting fractions to decimals and vice versa and know when to use which process.

PATTERNS/DESIGNS
Shade in the appropriate boxes on a 10 × 10 chart that corresponds to various fractional and decimal equivalents.

BODY SCULPTURE/TABLEAU
Groups perform various tasks based on decimal and fractional equivalents that they draw from a hat.

SINGING/HUMMING
Make up a song or rap that explains the decimal/fraction conversion process. Play with the song by performing certain fractional or decimal portions of the song.

GROUP PROJECTS
Play the fraction and decimal conversion game. (Students are given information and must arrange themselves as a decimal equivalent.)

INDEPENDENT STUDIES/PROJECTS
Complete problems on a worksheet to test your own understanding of fraction and decimal conversions.

NATURE ENCOUNTERS/FIELD TRIPS
Go outside and experience the fractional and decimal equivalents of a natural place.

SUBJECT AREA: Middle School Mathematics

LESSON OBJECTIVE: Students will understand the process for performing decimal and fraction conversions and will be able to demonstrate their understanding through a series of problem-solving scenarios and games.

SUPPLIES/MATERIALS:
• 10 x 10 box charts (four per student)
• colored marking pens

• props for the fraction/decimal conversion game (see description on page 27)
• practice worksheets for doing conversions
• appropriate pages from textbook dealing with fraction/decimal conversions

ROOM ARRANGEMENT:
• open space for movement activities
• music area for singing/humming
• outdoor area for brief field trip

Ask students in group two to shade in three charts to represent these amounts: $^1/_{10}$, 57%, and .3. (See examples below.)

Tell students in both groups to write all the ways they can represent their shadings in both decimals and fractions.

Choose representatives from each group to explain their box charts to the whole class. Ask for questions and check for understanding.

Tell the class they are now going to play a couple of games to test their understanding of fraction and decimal equivalents. Ask them to move to an area where they can move around freely.

Break the two large groups into teams of three. Choose a team to go first. Ask one person in this team to draw a card out of a hat. On the card, the team will find a task that relates to understanding fraction and decimal equivalents. Some example tasks follow:

- Arrange the class so that $^2/_3$ are sitting on the floor. Show the decimal equivalent of those still standing.

- Ask .50 of the class to take off their right shoe and $^3/_4$ to take off their left shoe. What percentage of the group has both shoes off?

- Divide the class into four groups according to birthday months: January–March, April–June, July–September, and October–December. Tell the fraction and decimal equivalents of the numbers in each group.

- Tell $^3/_4$ of the class to form a circle around 25% of the group. Ask .33 of the 25% in the middle to sit down on the floor. Show the fraction and decimal equivalents of all who are standing.

The team is to instruct the rest of the class on how to do the task. Give the team time to figure out how to accomplish the task before it instructs the class. When the team is ready, ask them to do the task with the whole class.

In turn, ask each team to draw a card, practice their task, and present the task to the whole class. As students play this game, check for understanding, make corrections, and give further explanation as needed. Refer to the experience of shading in the 10 x 10 charts as necessary.

Create enough tasks so that each threesome gets a shot a arranging the class and coming up with the fraction and decimal equivalents to explain the arrangements.

After teams have completed the game, they are ready to move on to the final part of the lesson: understanding decimal numbers and how to place decimal points.

Tell each threesome to join another threesome to form groups of six. Ask groups to write the following five numbers in large print on an 8½" x 11" piece of paper: 2, 4, 5, 3, and 6. Ask students to write a decimal point on a separate piece of paper.

Ask each person in every group to take one of the pieces of paper. Tell those who have the decimal papers to approach you. Give these students examples of how to arrange their teams:

- 436¼
- five hundred forty-three dollars and twenty-six cents
- the answer for 24536 divided by 100
- 3264½
- the answer for 2.4536 x 100

Explain that the contest is to see which team can create their decimal number and place the decimal point correctly first.

Briefly explain the conversion process to students:

- The numbers to the right of the decimal can be read as 100s. For example, .27 can be written as this fraction: $^{27}/_{100}$. (27 boxes out of 100 would be shaded.) The decimal number 4.13 can be written as $4^{13}/_{100}$.
- Every fraction represents a decimal equivalent; that is, every fraction represents a part of 100. For example, the fraction $^3/_4$ is the same as .75 ($^{75}/_{100}$, or 75 out of 100 boxes shaded). To find the decimal from a fraction, divide the numerator by the denominator and you'll get the decimal equivalent.

Create a song or rap to explain the conversion process. Here's an example rap I created to teach the conversion process to a group of seventh graders:

Decimals, decimals we're here to say,
"We do fractions the decimal way!"
When you put a decimal in and look to the right
All you'll see are hundreds throughout the night.

When you've got a fraction there's a bottom and a top
If you want a decimal then you've got to stop!
You take the topside number, and divide by the bottom
And the decimal will appear, without a problem.

Ask students to work with a partner and practice the conversion process. Tell pairs to choose various decimals and fractions out of a hat and explain to each other how to make the conversion of a fraction to decimal and decimal to fraction. Work with the pairs as necessary to help them understand.

COMMENTARY AND REFLECTIONS

Be sure to include easy and hard conversions in the hat.

1. This lesson is easily doable within a 45–50 minute period, but I suggest you spend more time on it. If you are teaching in a block scheduled period, you may complete the lesson in one block if you leave out the naturalist intelligence. Use the naturalist intelligence to provide a review on the second day. Take students on a fractions and decimal trip into nature. On the field trip ask students to think about nature in terms of fractions and decimals and see what they find. For example, you might ask students: What would it look like if only 33% of the trees were here? What would happen if you increased the annual rainfall by $1/2$?

2. This lesson, with some adjustments, could be used to introduce the fraction/decimal conversion process or to review the related concepts that students have likely been exposed to in earlier grades. If you are introducing the concepts, you may need to expand the activities in the lesson and spread the activities over several days.

3. This lesson assumes that the more ways students play with the concepts of decimals and fractions and their relationships, the more they will really understand them. Therefore, the lesson requires students to work on decimals and fractions via shading 10 x 10 charts, verbally describing the concepts, acting out the process, singing about conversions, playing a game, etc. The only weakness in this lesson is that it fails to make real-world applications. You may bring in application by asking students to work on problems on a worksheet. Craft the problems to illustrate the importance of decimals and fractions for everyday living. For example, a problem might read: Imagine that you are out with five of your friends for pizza. What percentage of the total pizza will everyone receive if the pizza is divided equally?

AN EXAMPLE LESSON
FOR SECONDARY SCHOOL

Literature Genre

LESSON SYNOPSIS

Be sure to assign appropriate roles, so that each person in every group has a job to do. Following are some suggested roles for this jigsaw activity: organizer, timekeeper, checker (checking for understanding), and encourager.

Begin by forming students into cooperative groups of three or four. Give each group a set of definitions for various genres of literature. (Or give students a list of genres and ask them to look up the definitions in the dictionary.) Tell members in each team to divide the definitions among themselves so that each team member has the same number of genres or definitions. Ask each team member to study their definitions and rewrite them in their own words. After individual study and rewriting, tell each person to teach their definitions to their team. Remind the checkers to make sure that all team members understand the definition of each genre.

Students use tools from four intelligences—verbal/linguistic, visual/spatial, bodily/kinesthetic, and musical/rhythmic—to create their presentations.

Now divide the class into expert groups. Assign each group one genre. Explain that the expert groups will make a dramatic presentation of their assigned genre to the rest of the class. Tell students that they will perform a television talk show where the genres are the guests. Students will complete four tasks to get ready for the show.

First, ask each team to write a two- or three-verse limerick for their genre. The limerick should include some of the distinguishing characteristics of the genre. Following is an example limerick about poetry:

> *There's a genre of literature called poetry,*
> *Through meter and rhyme tells a sto-or-ry.*
> *When written on paper*
> *Or recited to a neighbor*
> *Its verses and rhymes speak life's glo-or-y.*
>
> *Now each poem that you find has a meter*
> *The meter is each poem's heart beater*
> *Sometimes it is quick*
> *Other times it may stick*
> *But the meter is the greeter of the reader.*

Second, tell teams to create appropriate costumes for their genre's appearance on the television show. Explain that the costume must illustrate the distinguishing characteristics of the genre. Tell students that the costume must include the whole team—each individual must be dressed to show a different characteristic of the genre or all the individuals on the team may wear a similar costume that demonstrates the key aspects of the genre.

Work with students as necessary so they can explain why they chose certain body language and physical movements to represent their genre.

Third, ask teams to plan what actions they will perform on the television show. Explain that the team is to "become" the genre, as if the genre could become a person. Tell students to be sure their movements communicate the characteristics of the genre (e.g., How would the genre act? What facial expressions would it make?

Literature Genre

POETRY
Create limericks that illustrate the different literature genres.

GRAPHIC/COGNITIVE ORGANIZERS
Create a classification matrix for analyzing pieces of literature that have been studied in the past or will be studied in the future.

GRAPHIC REPRESENTATION
Create costumes that each genre of literature would wear if they were to appear on a television talk show. (Costumes must relate to the distinguishing characteristics of each genre.)

BODY LANGUAGE/PHYSICAL GESTURES
Make up physical movements, postures, gestures, and facial expressions that "embody" the essence of each genre of literature (i.e., how each genre would act if it were personified!).

INSTRUMENTAL SOUNDS
Record a series of sounds and tones that might be used to introduce each genre of literature if they were characters appearing on a television program.

JIGSAW
Individuals study definitions for several genre, then teach assigned pieces to their whole teams.

SILENT REFLECTION METHODS
In a journal, reflect on how you could use each genre to tell the story of your life.

SENSORY STIMULATION EXERCISES
Create a list of the sensory impact of each genre of literature. (What is the impact of each genre on the five senses?)

SUBJECT AREA: High School English Literature

LESSON OBJECTIVE: Students will understand the distinguishing characteristics of the various literature genres, how to recognize genres when they are reading, and how to reproduce genres in their own creative writing

SUPPLIES/MATERIALS:
- construction paper, crepe paper, and other objects for making costumes
- scissors and glue
- colored marking pens, paints, and colored pencils
- audiocassette tape recorders
- dictionaries for looking up genre definitions or definitions from a textbook
- student journals

ROOM ARRANGEMENT:
- open space for movement activities
- art area for making montages
- music area for recording the sounds and tones
- conversation area for discussing with partners

How would it walk, stand, sit, etc.?). Explain that teams may include their limericks in the presentation, if they choose.

Fourth, ask teams to create an instrumental introduction for the genre's television appearance. Tell teams that they may record the introductions or perform them live. Explain that the goal is to communicate some distinguishing characteristics of the genre through sound. For example, the sounds for a narrative might be single tones progressing up a scale, the sounds for poetry might be lyrical and flowing, and the sounds for a fable or folk tale may be whimsical. Teams may use traditional musical instruments or instruments that they create for the occasion.

After students complete the four tasks, allow time for their presentations. Do not lose sight of the objective of the lesson during the presentations. Students can learn quite a bit as they make their presentations and watch others' presentations. You may choose to play the role of the talk show host, ensuring that presentations don't lag and that students remain focused on learning about the genre. Ask questions: Who are you? What is your role in literature? Why is your role important? What do you think about the other genres?

After all groups have made their presentations, lead the class in a reflection on their experience of learning about genre. Ask questions: What do you remember most from the presentations? What surprised you? What was exciting? What new things did you learn about the genre from the presentations? What genre is your favorite?

With the whole class, create a master wall chart that gives examples for each genre. Examples might include literature pieces that they have studied during the year (or in previous years), pieces that they will study in the future, and literature from their childhood, television dramas, or movies.

Finally, allow students time to write in their journals. Ask them to imagine that they must use each genre to tell the story of their life to the present moment. Assign them to start writing in each genre. (Approximately four or five lines for each genre is sufficient.) Give them a few examples from your own life to jumpstart their thinking. For instance, you might give these examples:

> **Myth:** Once upon a time, in a land far away, known as the land of the big sky (Wyoming in my case), a magical child was born. His parents were king and queen (managers) of a wondrous realm where the animals roamed free (a cattle ranch).

> **Narrative:** On March 6, 1987, Charles and Mary Lou Snodgrass gave birth to a baby girl named Amanda. She was a big one, weighing in at 9 lbs., 4 oz. Her mother, also a big one, survived the birth.

Poetry
The winter wind blew cold.
Snow flurries were in the air.
But warmth filled the hospital room
As the smell of baking bread permeates a house.
A child was about to be born.

If appropriate, ask students to share some of their reflections, either with a partner or with the whole class. Or tell students to turn in their writing so that you may check to see if they understand the genre and know how to apply it to their own creative writing.

COMMENTARY AND REFLECTIONS

1. This lesson will likely require two periods in a block schedule or one week of 45- or 50-minute periods. Students must become familiar with the genre characteristics at the beginning of the lesson. This lesson asks students to acquire this knowledge in cooperative groups. One of the things I like about this approach is that it takes students beyond simply learning definitions for the genre (or whatever concept you are teaching) by asking students to do something with the information. Students must not only grasp the information intellectually, they must also be able to use the information!

2. To create 8-in-1 lessons, you do not have to use eight different learning activities. Some activities can happen simultaneously or may be integrated into a larger presentation. This lesson is a perfect example. Although all eight intelligences are involved, students will likely only notice three activities: studying definitions, creating and presenting the television show, and writing about their lives. Not all 8-in-1 lessons will be like this, but most will involve several tools in a single learning experience.

3. The more you work with students on improving their representations of the various genres, the deeper their learning will be and the more fully you will realize the objective of the lesson. This is especially true with the work they do to prepare for their television presentations. To deepen their learning, you may question groups about their costumes, asking them to explain why and how the costume is appropriate for the genre. You may also help students choose appropriate body language by helping them brainstorm ideas about how the genre would act if it were human. Students will likely need the most help choosing appropriate instrumental sounds, but once they get started, they just may have the most fun with this part of the lesson.

4. In some ways, the heart of the lesson happens when students write in their journals. Writing encourages students to actually apply the information they studied. If some students' writing skills are not quite "up to snuff," you may allow them to record their ideas or use visual/spatial techniques, such as drawings, along with their writing. Remember, the objective of the lesson is that students recognize the genres and understand how they are used.

SECTION

II

The Intelligence-Focused Lesson Planning Strategy

The Intelligence-Focused Lesson Planning Strategy

In his original research on multiple intelligences (*Frames of Mind*, 1983), Gardner observes:

 Multiple intelligences theory posits a small set of human intellectual potentials . . . of which all individuals are capable by virtue of their membership in the human species . . . [E]very normal individual should develop each intelligence to some extent, given but modest opportunity to do so.

The intelligence-focused lesson planning strategy is based on this insight; namely, that in each student some intelligences are more fully developed than others. Some intelligences will be favorites. Some will feel more comfortable. Nevertheless, every student has all eight intelligences, because the intelligences are part of our physiology and neurology as human beings. We all have at least eight intelligences—at least eight ways of knowing, understanding, processing information, and acquiring knowledge—and all of the intelligences can be further developed, enhanced, even taught! The intelligence-focused lesson strategy recognizes the fact that each student has dominant, comfortable, and favorite intelligences. But the strategy also assumes that students be stretched beyond their comfort zones and beyond their more developed intelligences.

When the intelligence-focused strategy is used on a regular and ongoing basis, each student has opportunities to work in their comfort zones using their more developed intelligences, but they are also given frequent opportunities to stretch their less developed intelligences. I believe that this stretch is very important to prepare students for success in their future lives beyond the classroom. Most successful individuals in our society are multi-modal; that is, they use several intelligences simultaneously. People who can use several intelligences simultaneously are flexible in their approaches to solving problems and meeting the challenges of everyday life. These people also have a great deal of creativity and insight, simply because they can process information in a wide variety of ways.

Each chapter in this section features a full-blown lesson that focuses on one of the eight intelligences. However, I must confess that from a neurological perspective, it is impossible to use only one intelligence in a lesson. The human brain is simply not wired to work this way. In almost any task we perform, all of the intelligences are involved in one form or another (although certain tasks trigger one or two intelligences more than the other intelligences). The intelligence-focused strategy takes into account how the brain uses multiple intelligences, yet suggests that it is possible to focus on one intelligence in the teaching/learning process. Focusing on one intelligence at a time helps students discover each of the eight ways of knowing and facilitates students' deeper understanding of the lesson content.

Following is an explanation of the various lesson planning tools that are employed in the chapters.

Lesson Design Palette

Using the palette as a metaphor for lesson planning is a technique I have found very helpful to remind myself that, as teachers, we are artists who are creating curriculum eventfulness for students. As in the 8-in-1 strategy, the role of the palette is to help you choose tools for the target intelligence. (For a list of tools for every intelligence see the Multiple Intelligences Toolbox [fig. II.1]. For a detailed explanation and technology tips for each tool, see appendix A, pp. 172–180.) Choosing tools for the intelligence-focused strategy is different from choosing tools for the 8-in-1 strategy. In the 8-in-1 strategy, you chose tools for all eight intelligences. In the intelligence-focused strategy, you only choose tools for the focus intelligence.

When planning your own lessons, begin by choosing the tools you will use and write them on the palette. (See appendix A, p. 181, for a blank palette.) Then write a brief description of how you will use each tool to achieve the objective of the lesson. Next, note other intelligences that may have a secondary emphasis in the lesson. Place a checkmark next to these intelligences and make notes to help you remember the connections you are seeing. Finally, fill in the bottom of the palette, listing the subject area, intelligence emphasis, lesson objective, supplies/materials, and room arrangement. Using the palette "forces" you to see the big picture of the lesson—helping you recognize all that will happen during the lesson.

Each chapter includes a palette that lists the ten tools for the target intelligence. On each of these palettes I have checkmarked the specific tools used in the lesson as well as the other intelligences that are involved.

Logical/Mathematical
- Abstract Symbols/Formulas
- Calculation
- Deciphering Codes
- Forcing Relationships
- Graphic/Cognitive Organizers
- Logic/Pattern Games
- Number Sequences/Patterns
- Outlining
- Problem Solving
- Syllogisms

Verbal/Linguistic
- Creative Writing
- Formal Speaking
- Humor/Jokes
- Impromptu Speaking
- Journal/Diary Keeping
- Poetry
- Reading
- Storytelling/Story Creation
- Verbal Debate
- Vocabulary

Visual/Spatial
- Active Imagination
- Color/Texture Schemes
- Drawing
- Guided Imagery/Visualizing
- Mind Mapping
- Montage/Collage
- Painting
- Patterns/Designs
- Pretending/Fantasy
- Sculpting

MULTIPLE INTELLIGENCES TOOLBOX

Musical/Rhythmic
- Environmental Sounds
- Instrumental Sounds
- Music Composition/Creation
- Music Performance
- Percussion Vibrations
- Rapping
- Rhythmic Patterns
- Singing/Humming
- Tonal Patterns
- Vocal Sounds/Tones

Bodily/Kinesthetic
- Body Language/Physical Gestures
- Body Sculpture/Tableaus
- Dramatic Enactment
- Folk/Creative Dance
- Gymnastic Routines
- Human Graph
- Inventing
- Physical Exercise/Martial Arts
- Role Playing/Mime
- Sports Games

Interpersonal
- Collaborative Skills Teaching
- Cooperative Learning Strategies
- Empathy Practices
- Giving Feedback
- Group Projects
- Intuiting Others' Feelings
- Jigsaw
- Person-to-Person Communication
- Receiving Feedback
- Sensing Others' Motives

Intrapersonal
- Altered States of Consciousness Practices
- Emotional Processing
- Focusing/Concentration Skills
- Higher-Order Reasoning
- Independent Studies/Projects
- Know Thyself Procedures
- Metacognition Techniques
- Mindfulness Practices
- Silent Reflection Methods
- Thinking Strategies

Naturalist
- Archetypal Pattern Recognition
- Caring for Plants/Animals
- Conservation Practices
- Environment Feedback
- Hands-On Labs
- Nature Encounters/Field Trips
- Nature Observation
- Natural World Simulations
- Species Classification (organic/inorganic)
- Sensory Stimulation Exercises

(Note: For a detailed explanation and technology tips for each tool, see appendix A, pp. 172–180.)

Figure II.1

SkyLight Professional Development

The Lesson at a Glance

Each chapter includes two staging models entitled The Lesson at a Glance. The staging models allow you to set up the lesson dynamics so that they are compatible with the neurological processes activated by the focus intelligence. (For more information on these processes, see *Eight Ways of Knowing* [Lazear 1998a].) Each model includes four distinct stages that a teacher must employ to tap into the full potential of the target intelligence. The stages are awakening, amplifying, teaching, and transferring (see fig. II.2).

Stage I: Awaken. First, we must become aware that we possess multiple ways of knowing and learning. Then we must learn various techniques and methodologies for triggering an intelligence within the brain-mind-body system.

Stage II: Amplify. We must learn how particular intelligences (ways of knowing) work: what capacities and/or skills are necessary, how to access these capacities and skills, and how to use and understand different intelligence modalities. This involves both practice in strengthening intelligence capacities as well as learning how to interpret and work with the different kinds of information we receive from each intelligence. We must learn to understand the unique language of each intelligence; that is, how each expresses itself. For example, the language of bodily/kinesthetic intelligence is physical movement, not words, sentences, writing, and speech.

Stage III: Teach. We must learn how to teach content-based lessons that apply different ways of knowing to the specific content of a given lesson. My first presupposition is that we can teach all students to be more intelligent in more ways and on more levels than they (or we) ever dreamed. My second presupposition is that anything can be taught and learned through all of the intelligences. This means that we as teachers must learn how to use the intelligences in the teaching and learning process. About ninety-five percent of the material we have to teach comes prepackaged in a verbal/linguistic or logical/mathematical form. However, in planning lessons that teach this material, we need not be bound by this packaging. My goal in writing this book is to help you learn to design and implement lessons that emphasize all intelligences.

Stage IV: Transfer. We must teach our students how to use all of the intelligences to improve their effectiveness in dealing with the issues, challenges, and problems they face in the task of daily living. This is primarily a matter of approaching these challenges on multiple levels, with a variety of problem-solving methods that use different intelligences.

The model in figure II.2 is the one I used as the basic structure for the chapters in *Eight Ways of Knowing* (Lazear 1998a). In this book, I use it to demonstrate the fundamental dynamics that I

What Does It Take to Teach Intelligence?

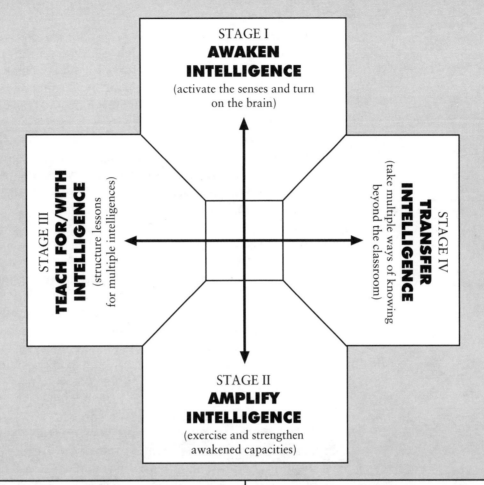

STAGE I **AWAKEN INTELLIGENCE**	STAGE II **AMPLIFY INTELLIGENCE**
Each of the intelligences is related to the five senses. In general, a particular intelligence can be activated or triggered through exercises and activities that use the sensory bases—sight, sound, taste, touch, smell, speech, and communication with others—as well as inner senses—intuition, metacognition, and spiritual insight.	This involves practices for expanding, deepening, and nurturing an awakened or activated intelligence. As with any skill, intelligence skills cannot only be awakened, but can also be improved and strengthened if used on a regular basis. And, like any skill, they will also go back to sleep if not used.
STAGE III **TEACH FOR/WITH INTELLIGENCE**	STAGE IV **TRANSFER INTELLIGENCE**
This stage involves learning how to use, trust, and interpret a given intelligence through knowing, learning, and understanding tasks. In this book, teaching *with* intelligence is approached from the perspective of classroom lessons that emphasize and use different intelligences in the teaching/learning process.	This stage includes the integration of an intelligence into daily living and its appropriate application to solving problems and meeting the challenges faced in the so-called real world. The goal of this stage is for the intelligence to become a regular part of one's cognitive, affective, and sensory life.

Figure II.2

believe need to be present in lessons that are designed to emphasize different ways of knowing and learning when teaching content-based information.

As you create your own intelligence-focused lessons, be sure to include all four stages in the model. (See appendix A, p. 182, for a blank staging model you can use on your own.) Think about the staging model as having two axes: the awakening and amplifying axis is the intelligence axis and the teaching and transfer axis is the curriculum axis.

Your main concern when planning the intelligence axis is first to awaken, stimulate, trigger, or otherwise activate the target intelligence. Don't worry about the content you will be teaching; worry about awakening the intelligence. Second, take time to amplify the intelligence by providing opportunities for students to practice using the tools of the target intelligence. Strive to increase students' comfort level for working in the focus intelligence. Again, don't worry about the content. Practice using the tools in fun and easy-to-connect-with ways before you use the tools with content. For example, if you are going to have students create a mind map of curricular concepts during the teaching stage, encourage them to practice the mind mapping process in the amplifying stage. Ask students to practice by creating a mind map about a hobby or caring for a pet. Once they are comfortable with using the tool—in this case, the mind map—move to the teaching stage where they will use the same tool with the lesson content.

In the intelligence-focused lesson, most of the instructional time will be spent on the curriculum axis. Once you have awakened and amplified the target intelligence (which will generally take no more than 8–10 minutes), you can then use the intelligence to teach and help students learn the material at hand.

The transfer should be viewed as the metacognitive part of the lesson. It is an opportunity for students to reflect on the lesson—both the content and the focus intelligence. This is the time for students to make personal connections, to process the lesson, and to informally assess their own learning—they should recognize what they feel about the lesson and what they got out of the lesson.

Two staging moels are included in each chapter and are entitled The Lesson at a Glance. The staging model on the left-hand page describes the theory for awakening, amplifying, teaching, and transferring the focus intelligence. The staging model on the right-hand page shows how the theory was applied to create the lesson featured in the chapter. This model explains how the lesson specifically seeks to awaken, amplify, teach, and transfer the target intelligence.

Lesson Procedures

Each chapter presents a set of step-by-step procedures for its respective lesson. The procedures are intended to help you visualize the lesson. The procedures should also serve as a model designing your own lessons. (You will not need to use as much detail in writing your own lessons!) The procedures include the four stages—awakening, amplifying, teaching, and transferring.

Probably the most important part of these procedures are my marginal notes. These notes feature my metacognitive processing of the lessons. They explain what is going on in the lesson from the perspective of multiple intelligences research and also refer to brain functions associated with the intelligences (see fig. 0.1, p. 3).

Spiral Adaptations of the Lesson

Because each lesson only focuses on one level—elementary, middle, or secondary school—I have included suggestions for "spiraling" each lesson for different levels. If the lesson is geared toward the elementary level, the suggestions spiral the lesson up so that it is appropriate for middle and secondary school levels. If the lesson is geared toward the secondary school level, the suggestions spiral the lesson down to elementary and middle school levels.

Spiral adaptations are based on Jerome Bruner's (Bruner, Goodnow, and Austin 1956) theories about spiral curriculum. He explained that you, as a teacher, can teach anything, to anyone, at any age, if you adopt the student's worldview and speak in language that is meaningful to the student in his or her developmental stage.

Assessment Tips

Each chapter presents two sets of tips for assessing students' learning in the lesson. In this book I have exclusively used two assessment techniques: portfolios (see fig. II.3) and journals (also known as learning logs or diaries; see appendix A, pp. 183–186, for models). I use these two techniques not because they are the only assessment models available nor because I believe they are the best. I use them because I believe they are the easiest methods for getting started with assessing multiple intelligences lessons. Portfolios and

A Model for Creating Student Portfolios

Q. What should be included to really show what they know?

A. Ask the students. Let them help decide.

Anything they want for whatever reason

Evidence of self-reflection and self-knowledge

Evidence of progress toward year's goal

Items that tell the story of the journey of the year

Items that indicate transfer of learning (beyond the classroom into life)

Things that convey learning activities (explicit and implicit artifacts from lessons)

Items that demonstrate students' best work to date

Things that show growth and change (skills, interests, extracurricular activities, attitudes)

Figure II.3

journals allow teachers to develop new views of the assessment process. (For more assessment techniques and instruments, please refer to my books *Multiple Intelligence Approaches to Assessment: Solving the Assessment Conundrum* [1994] and *The Rubrics Way: Using MI to Assess Understanding* [1998b].)

Technology Tips

New to this fourth edition is a set of technology tips for each chapter. The tips include ideas for including technology in the lesson. As you create your own lessons, be sure to include appropriate technology to enhance the learning experience.

Look to the Past and Look to the Future

I have included two blank palettes to help you reflect on how a past and future lesson could be restructured to incorporate the intelligence being emphasized in the lesson. As you dialogue with each lesson presented in the book, one of the best ways to transfer your insights is to instantly apply them. Use the Past palette to quickly rethink a lesson you have done in the past. How could you teach that lesson using the intelligence presented in the chapter? For example, you might not teach geometric formulas (chapter 4), but you might be able to adapt some of the ideas for using bodily/ kinesthetic intelligence from the lesson. Use the Future palette to think about an upcoming lesson (preferably within the next 2–3 weeks) in which you could experiment using some of the ideas from the sample lesson. Quickly outline your ideas on the palette. For example, you may not teach an elementary history lesson (chapter 5), but you may be able to incorporate some of the ideas for using musical/rhythmic intelligence into your future lesson.

I have also included the Eight Ways of Teaching Weekly Checklist in appendix A (p. 188). Use this chart to help you become more aware of the intelligence strategies you are using day by day in your teaching. The goal of the chart is to move more and more toward a balanced approach to instruction where all intelligences have more or less equal "air time," so to speak.

Lesson Planning Ideas Chart

The final page of each chapter—the Lesson Planning Ideas chart—has been many teachers' favorite page. This chart includes ideas for teaching with the targeted intelligence in traditional curricular areas. These ideas are not full-blown lessons; they are "lesson seedlings," some of which may grow into fully developed intelligence-focused lessons. The ideas are provided to help you jumpstart your thinking on how to incorporate a given intelligence into the teaching/learning process of your classroom.

I hope you have fun with these lessons and that they spark many new ideas for you and your students. I believe that the next stages of the research on multiple intelligences will happen in the laboratory of the normal school classroom. It will be based on what you discover as you conduct various experiments with eight ways of teaching, helping kids activate and use their eight ways of knowing.

TEACHING WITH

Verbal/Linguistic
Intelligence

EXPLORING NATURAL
OBJECTS

A General Science Lesson

ELEMENTARY SCHOOL LEVEL

The Lesson Palette

Verbal/ Linguistic
Emphasis

VERBAL/LINGUISTIC STRATEGIES

☑ Creative Writing

☐ Formal Speaking

☑ Humor/Jokes

☑ Impromptu Speaking

☐ Journal/Diary Keeping

☐ Poetry

☑ Reading

☐ Storytelling/Story Creation

☐ Verbal Debate

☐ Vocabulary

SUBJECT AREA: General Science

INTELLIGENCE EMPHASIS: Verbal/Linguistic

LESSON OBJECTIVE: To explore and understand the attributes of various objects from nature and how they differ from each other.

SUPPLIES/MATERIALS:
- one natural object (animate or inanimate) per team in a shoebox
- one large file folder per team
- 6 Ss worksheets (see blackline, p. 190)
- See/Feel T-Chart (see blackline, p. 191)

ROOM ARRANGEMENT: Desks in clusters of three with plenty of space between teams

THE LESSON . . .

STAGE I
AWAKEN

Awaken verbal/linguistic intelligence by using the spoken word, reading someone else's ideas or poetry, writing one's own ideas or poetry, telling stories, listening to stories, and using all kinds of humor including riddles, jokes, puns, and twists of the language.

VERBAL/LINGUISTIC

INTELLIGENCE

Teach for and with verbal/linguistic intelligence by using the specific tools of this intelligence and applying them to help learn the content, acquire specific knowledge, and achieve the lesson's goals and/or objectives.

STAGE III
TEACH

Transfer verbal/linguistic intelligence to life by discussing the intelligence tools used, finding applications beyond the lesson to other curriculum areas, and finally integrating it into the task of living in the world outside the classroom.

STAGE IV
TRANSFER

Amplify verbal/linguistic intelligence through practice in writing and reading, learning word meanings, formal speech (including debate and impromptu speaking), storytelling, poetry, and having fun with language, through humor, for example.

AMPLIFY
STAGE II

The Model

. . . AT A GLANCE

STAGE I
AWAKEN

- Lesson Introduction: Learn types of observation and description in scientific investigation.
- Teacher leads students through a series of Can You Guess What I Am? riddles.
- Students make up and share riddles of their own.

VERBAL/LINGUISTIC

INTELLIGENCE

STAGE III
TEACH

- Gather information about natural objects.
- Write descriptions of observations made.
- Play Can You Guess What I Am? game.

STAGE IV
TRANSFER

- Reflect on the observation and descriptive writing process.
- Reflect on scientific observation and what is involved.

- Teach students objective description using the 6 Ss.
- Teach students to observe personal data using the See/Feel T-Chart.

AMPLIFY
STAGE II

The Model *Applied*

Exploring Natural Objects

A *Science Lesson with*

Verbal/Linguistic Intelligence

Lesson Procedures

Verbal/linguistic intelligence is primarily located in the area of the left hemisphere of the brain known as Broca's area (see fig. 0.1, p. 3). The particular mental functions that are active when verbal/ linguistic intelligence has been turned on involve an acute sensitivity to the sound, rhythm, inflection, and meter of words; a sensitivity to the order among words and the various meanings and shades of meaning of words; and an interest in the different practical uses of language. Please refer to the Multiple Intelligences Capacities Wheel (fig. 0.3, p. 8) to see capacities that are active when working with verbal/linguistic intelligence.

INTRODUCTION

The world is full of interesting and surprising things that can be discovered if we learn to pay attention. In this science lesson students will observe natural objects with their senses (objective observation) and their own feelings or responses about what they are observing (subjective observation). They will then use this information to play the game Can You Guess What I Am? Tell the students that the lesson will emphasize verbal/linguistic intelligence, so they should pay attention to this during the lesson.

Although the main emphasis of this lesson is teaching with verbal/ linguistic intelligence, four other intelligences are consciously employed as well: interpersonal intelligence through cooperative group interactions, logical/mathematical intelligence through the use of cognitive organizers, intrapersonal intelligence through individual writing (especially about feelings), and naturalist intelligence through observing a natural object through the senses.

STAGE I

Here riddles are used as the trigger. When the brain is presented with a riddle, verbal/linguistic intelligence immediately kicks into gear to try to figure it out. It begins searching for clues within the linguistic structure of the riddle and tries to make connections between the riddle and prior knowledge. It starts looking for word associations. When

Awaken

1. Begin with a series of riddles. Have students see if they can guess the answers:
   - Of all the things in the world, I am the shortest and the longest, the fastest and the slowest. I am the thing people waste the most. Yet they need me more than anything else. What am I? *(Answer: time)*

students are asked to think of their own riddles to stump the class, the language center of the brain is stimulated even more, for you are asking them to be creative and have fun with their language.

Both the groans and the laughter, as well as the Of course, why didn't I figure that out? at the end of a riddle, are indications that verbal/linguistic intelligence has been awakened and that it is now ready for action.

- Everyone needs my help. I dig out tiny caves and put gold and silver in them. I also build bridges of silver and make crowns of gold. Sooner or later everyone needs my help. Yet many people are afraid to let me help them. Who am I? *(Answer: a dentist)*

- I have eyes but I see nothing. I have ears but hear nothing. I have a mouth but I cannot speak. I always will look the way I look now. If I am young I will stay young. If I am old I will stay old. What am I? *(Answer: a person in a painting or photograph)*

2. Ask students if they know any riddles they think could stump the class.

STAGE II   Amplify

Practice using the awakened intelligence will improve it. In addition to the intelligence itself getting stronger, we become more familiar with it, and understand more about how it works. We learn how to interpret information we get from it, how to use it most effectively, and in what situations it can most enhance our learning.

Teaching about the 6 Ss introduces the students to a specific intellectual tool you want them to use later in the content part of the lesson itself. It is crucial that you give them guidelines for using the tool and demonstrate how to use it. Your demonstration should be as close as possible to what you are going to ask them to do with the content of the lesson. Cognitive research has shown that any thinking skill we want our students to have must be explicitly taught and, furthermore, students must have an opportunity to practice it. I believe that the same is true of all of the intellectual capacities. We were born with them, but we must be taught how to use them and then be given opportunities to practice if we are to become masters of our intellectual capacities. Working with the 6 Ss also accesses logical/mathematical intelligence as students learn new patterns for thinking.

1. Pass out the 6 Ss worksheet to the students (see blackline, p. 190). Explain that in order for students to describe something they must learn to recognize its attributes. The 6 Ss worksheet can help students with this job. Explain the worksheet as follows:

6 Ss = Sight — the color, image, or look of something
Sound — the noise, tone, and voice of something
Smell — the odor, aroma, and scent of something
Sense (tactile) — the taste or touch of something
Size — the height, weight, width, and depth of something
Speciality — the use of something or what it's good for

Explain that the 6 Ss worksheet allows students to use their senses to determine what an object is and how it differs from another object. Scientists also use the 6 Ss when they are studying something.

2. Now practice using the 6 Ss as a class. Draw the 6 Ss chart on the board or overhead. Choose an object in the classroom that all students can see and write the name of the object at the top of the chart.

3. Have students number off by sixes to form six groups. Assign each group one of the 6 Ss. Now ask students to give you attributes that describe the object according to their assigned part of the 6 Ss.

4. Reflect with the class for a few minutes:
- How did the 6 Ss help?
- Which S was most difficult? easiest?
- What questions do you have about using the 6 Ss?

STAGE III

Teach

By placing students in cooperative groups you bring in interpersonal intelligence skills as well.

The very fact that you are using objects from nature will stimulate the naturalist intelligence.

Students use the intellectual skill you teach in this part of the lesson to gain information and explore the meaning of the lesson content. The key assumption of the previous two parts of the lesson is that the more aware students become of their own intelligence and how it works, the more they will know how to use that intelligence to access the necessary information and knowledge from a lesson. Now they have a chance to do just that. Writing the sentences helps them pull together the team's brainstorm for themselves and to enhance their own understanding.

The See/Feel T-Chart again draws on logical/mathematical intelligence. You teach a thinking skill and then provide students with a chance to practice and use it on their own.

After brainstorming information on the worksheet with their cooperative group, students are asked to translate their observations and feelings into writing. The creative writing exercise allows students to assimilate the team's brainstorm into sentences that are meaningful to them as individuals. Here you are likewise accessing intrapersonal intelligence as students look within at their own feelings and responses.

1. Group students in teams of three and assign a role to each student: lab assistant (gathers materials for the team), organizer (keeps team on task and makes sure all parts of the assignment are completed), and encourager (gives group support and keeps them motivated).

2. Have the lab assistants come to the lab table and get a box for their team. In each box you have placed an object from nature such as an interesting rock, a large pine cone, a twisted, gnarly twig, a flower, a lump of earth, etc. Tell students not to let other teams see their objects. They should sit so the other teams cannot see the objects and use their file folders as screens to hide the objects.

3. **ACTIVITY 1.** Lead students through the following steps:

   a. Have each student write the name of the object on their 6 Ss worksheet.

   b. Prompt teams to use the 6 Ss to describe the object that is in their box.

   c. Instruct each individual to write three sentences in the space provided on the 6 Ss worksheet that tell things about the object the team has been analyzing.

   d. Tell each student to quietly read their sentences to the rest of the team so the team can check for the writer's understanding.

4. Now pass out the See/Feel T-Chart (see blackline, p. 191) to the teams. Choose an object in the classroom that all students can see, and model for them how to use the See/Feel T-Chart:

   a. As you look at the object, find shapes, designs, and patterns that are interesting to you. Write these on the T-chart under What I See.

   b. Also try to find the shapes of animals, human faces, etc. in the design of the object and point these out to the students. Write them on the T-chart.

   c. Now spend a couple of minutes thinking out loud for the class, describing your own feelings about the object you have been describing. Record these feelings on the T-chart under How I Feel.

5. **ACTIVITY 2.** Lead students through the following steps:

   a. Instruct the students to write the name of their objects on the second worksheet.

   b. Tell them to do what you just did but with their own object—look for interesting shapes, patterns, designs, and pictures in their object. Ask them to record these things in the column labeled What I See.

(Note: Encourage maximum creativity in looking at and describing the object. Remember there are no right answers! Whatever they see or find in their object is real for them.)

 c. Have the teams talk quietly about how they feel about the object (e.g., interested, bored, excited, etc.).

 d. In the space provided on the worksheet, have each individual write two sentences: one about what the team saw or found in the object and one sentence about how they feel about it.

 e. Have each student quietly read their sentences to the rest of the team so the team can check for the writer's understanding.

6. Have the lab assistant put the objects back in the box and return them to the lab table.

7. Tell the class that they are now going to play a game called Can You Guess What I Am? that will let them practice describing things to others.

 a. Have students form new groups. Tell them to keep the identity of their original group's object a secret because their new group is going to try to guess what the object is.

 b. The new group will try to guess the object by asking questions that can be answered yes or no.

 c. When the group thinks they know the mystery object, they may make a guess. Then move on to another person until all have had a turn.

The Can You Guess What I Am? game further engages verbal/linguistic skills by asking students to speak extemporaneously about their object in response to questions from others. This requires a synthesis and deeper understanding of their earlier work of describing the objects.

STAGE IV   Transfer

The goal of the transfer section of the lesson is to help students make the lesson relevant to their lives outside the classroom. Here we want to go beyond the lesson itself, into other curriculum areas, and finally beyond the formal classroom setting.

 Students discuss the two observation exercises with the 6 Ss and the See/Feel T-Chart, their reactions to them, and other situations where they could be used. Then in finishing the sentences, they have an opportunity to make conscious the learnings that happened in the lesson. This also helps them distill the essential parts of the lesson for themselves.

1. Start at the beginning of the lesson asking some or all of the following questions of the whole class:

 • What part was easy in this lesson? What was hard? What was fun?

 • What did you like about the 6 Ss? About the See/Feel T-Chart?

 • What did you not like about these charts?

 • When could we use the 6 Ss and the See/Feel T-Chart in other subjects?

2. Now spend a few minutes having students talk in their game groups about what they learned in the lesson. Have each person in the game group write and then read their answers to the following sentences:

 One new thing I learned about natural objects is_____.

 One new thing I learned about working on a team is_____.

SPIRAL ADAPTATIONS OF THE LESSON

Middle School Level

1. Focus the lesson on learning the scientific method for accurate observation and the ability to accurately record observations.

2. Teach about and have students practice two thinking patterns involved in scientific experiments:
   - looking at and analyzing an object (objective)
   - looking at yourself and your response to the object being observed (subjective)

3. Have students write detailed descriptive paragraphs that report on their factual observations about the objects, and their personal responses and reactions to the object.

Secondary School Level

1. Focus the lesson on three thinking/observation patterns at work in science: empirical observation (the facts, the senses), subjective responses (feelings, emotions, etc. about what is being observed), and creative interpretation (trying to fit observations into existing paradigms).

2. Practice each type of thinking/observation in conducting science lab experiments. For each type, have students keep a log in which they record what they have learned using each of the three methods of observation. Ask them to report on what they have observed to other students.

3. Have students write the steps for a scientific observation project that uses all three types of observation.

TECHNOLOGY TIPS

1. Ask students to make up a story about their objects and then create an audio book to tell the story.

2. Tell students to create a report (using a computer) to share what they've learned about their objects with their parents.

3. Lead students in conducting an Internet search to find more information about their objects.

ASSESSMENT TIPS

PORTFOLIOS

1. Have students include their notes from the 6 Ss worksheet from the team discussion and their individual sentences describing the object.

2. Ask students to include notes from the See/Feel T-Chart from the team discussion and their individual sentences.

JOURNALS

1. Have students draw the object their team studied earlier.

2. Ask students to transpose the sentences they wrote into their journals with their drawings.

3. Prompt students to write their answers to the closing sentences in their journals after reading them to their teams.

Look to the Past . . .

Rethink a lesson you have completed recently. How would you restructure it to teach *for* and *with* verbal/linguistic intelligence?

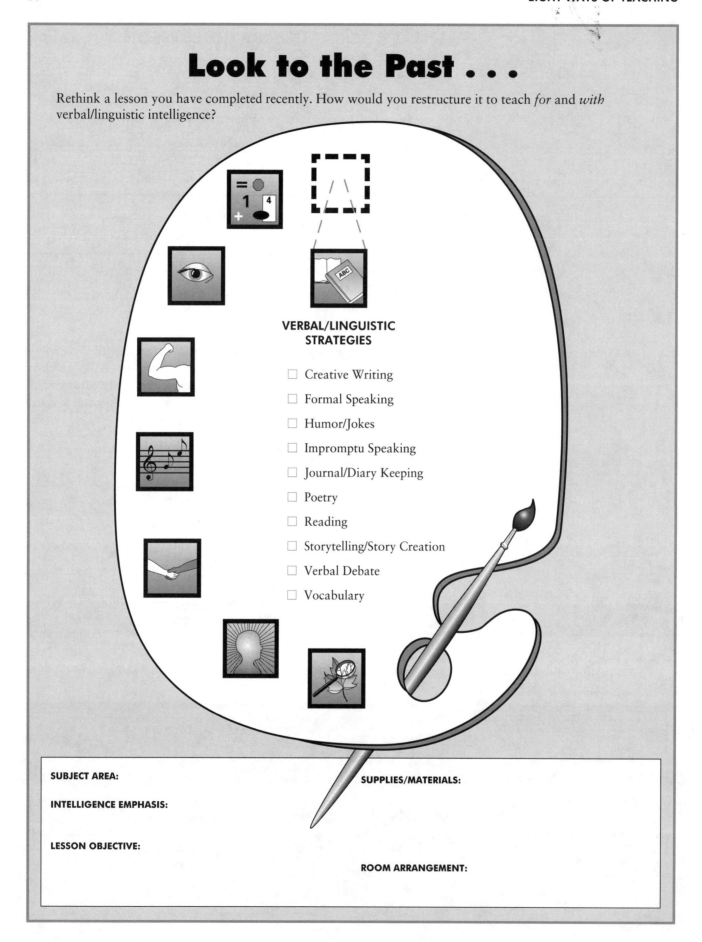

VERBAL/LINGUISTIC STRATEGIES

☐ Creative Writing

☐ Formal Speaking

☐ Humor/Jokes

☐ Impromptu Speaking

☐ Journal/Diary Keeping

☐ Poetry

☐ Reading

☐ Storytelling/Story Creation

☐ Verbal Debate

☐ Vocabulary

SUBJECT AREA:

INTELLIGENCE EMPHASIS:

LESSON OBJECTIVE:

SUPPLIES/MATERIALS:

ROOM ARRANGEMENT:

Look to the Future . . .

Think about a lesson you have coming up in the near future. How would you structure it to teach *for* and *with* verbal/linguistic intelligence?

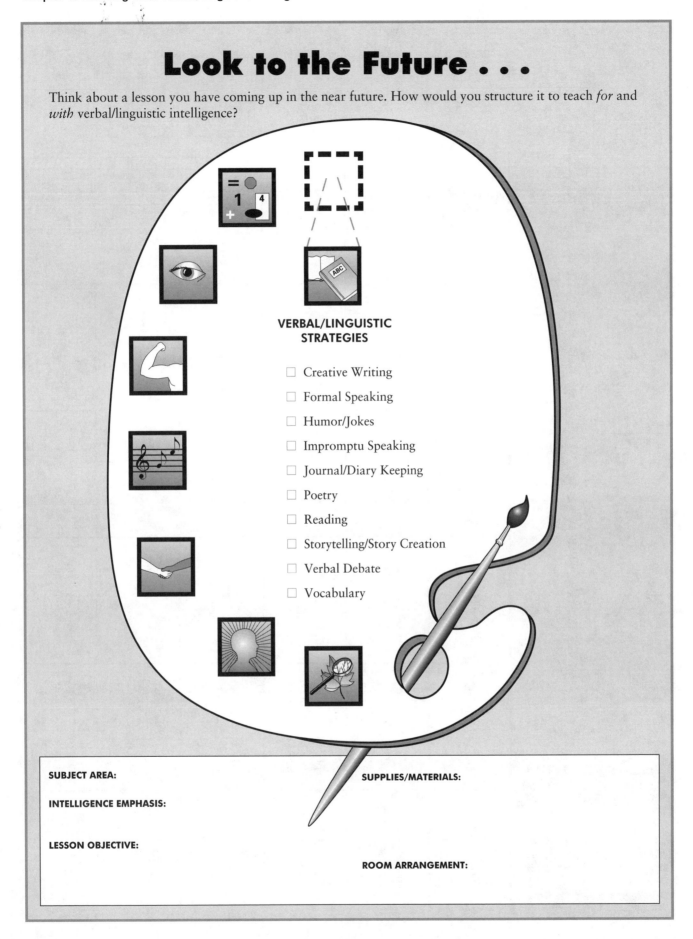

VERBAL/LINGUISTIC STRATEGIES

☐ Creative Writing

☐ Formal Speaking

☐ Humor/Jokes

☐ Impromptu Speaking

☐ Journal/Diary Keeping

☐ Poetry

☐ Reading

☐ Storytelling/Story Creation

☐ Verbal Debate

☐ Vocabulary

SUBJECT AREA:

INTELLIGENCE EMPHASIS:

LESSON OBJECTIVE:

SUPPLIES/MATERIALS:

ROOM ARRANGEMENT:

LESSON PLANNING IDEAS
Verbal/Linguistic

HISTORY	MATHEMATICS	LANGUAGE ARTS	SCIENCE & HEALTH	GLOBAL STUDIES & GEOGRAPHY	FAMILY/CONSUMER SCIENCES, INDUSTRIAL TECHNOLOGY, & PE	FINE ARTS
Play What's My Line? with figures from history	Write a series of story problems for others to solve	Teach concept mapping* to help remember content	Write a humorous story using science vocabulary or formulas	Read stories, myths, and poetry from other cultures	Give verbal explanation of gymnastic routines	Listen to a piece of music and make up a story about it
Debate important issues and decisions from the past	Explain how to work a problem to others while they follow	Write a sequel or next episode to a story or play	Create a diary on The Life of a Red Blood Cell	Hold Countries of the World spelling and pronunciation bee	Write instructions for use and care of shop machines	Verbally describe an object while a partner draws it
Create limericks about key historical events	Make up puns using math vocabulary or terms	Create crossword puzzles or word jumbles for vocabulary words	Write steps used in an experiment so someone else can do it	Keep an Insights from Other Cultures for Us log	Tell another how to run a word processing program—then do it	Tell a partner the steps to a dance while they perform it
Study poetry from different periods of history	Solve problems with a partner—one solves and one explains process	Play New Word for the Day** game	Make up an imaginary conversation between parts of the body	Study a road map and give verbal instructions to get someplace	Pretend you are a radio sportscaster describing a game in progress	Turn a Greek or Shakespearean tragedy into a situation comedy
Compile a notebook of history jokes	Create poems telling when to use different math operations	Practice impromptu speaking and writing	Give a speech on Ten Steps to Healthful Living	Learn basic conversation in several foreign languages	Play Recipe Jeopardy—make questions for answers given	Describe an emotion or mood and play music it suggests

* See Glossary and appendix C
** See Glossary

2

TEACHING WITH

Logical/Mathematical Intelligence

UNDERSTANDING OTHER CULTURES

A Social Studies Lesson

MIDDLE SCHOOL LEVEL

The Lesson Palette

Logical/ Mathematical Emphasis

LOGICAL/MATHEMATICAL STRATEGIES

- ☐ Abstract Symbols/Formulas
- ☐ Calculation
- ☐ Deciphering Codes
- ☑ Forcing Relationships
- ☑ Graphic/Cognitive Organizers
- ☑ Logic/Pattern Games
- ☐ Number Sequences/Patterns
- ☐ Outlining
- ☐ Problem Solving
- ☐ Syllogisms

SUBJECT AREA: Social Studies

INTELLIGENCE EMPHASIS: Logical/Mathematical

LESSON OBJECTIVE: To recognize the basic economic, political, social, and symbolic dynamics of another culture and to be able to communicate these to others in a positive manner.

SUPPLIES/MATERIALS:
- article about a culture
- graphic organizer sheet (see blackline, p. 192)
- colored marking pens
- newsprint

ROOM ARRANGEMENT: Desks moved so students can work together in groups of three

THE LESSON . . .

STAGE I
AWAKEN

Awaken logical/mathematical intelligence in situations requiring problem solving or meeting a new challenge, as well as in situations requiring pattern discernment and recognition (numbers, geometric designs, word patterns, or patterns in nature).

LOGICAL/MATHEMATICAL

INTELLIGENCE

STAGE III
TEACH

Teach for and with logical/mathematical intelligence by using the specific tools of this intelligence and applying them to help learn the content, acquire specific knowledge, and achieve the lesson's goals and/or objectives.

STAGE IV
TRANSFER

Transfer logical/mathematical intelligence to life by discussing the intelligence tools used, finding applications beyond the lesson to other curriculum areas, and, finally, integrating it into the task of living in the world outside the classroom.

Amplify logical/mathematical intelligence by practicing rational thinking, working with numbers, solving problems, using logical thought processes, communicating with abstract symbols or language, finding patterns, and creating unusual connections between things.

AMPLIFY
STAGE II

The Model

. . . AT A GLANCE

STAGE I
AWAKEN

- Lesson Introduction: Learn analytical tools for understanding the key social dynamics of a culture.
- Initiate guessing games:
  Guess My Attributes
  Guess My Classification Scheme
  Guess My Rank Ordering Rationale

LOGICAL/MATHEMATICAL

INTELLIGENCE

STAGE III
TEACH

- Web—classify and rank order—key features of a culture.
- Create brochure to sell or market the culture to tourists.

STAGE IV
TRANSFER

- Reflect on the use of the graphic organizers.
- Reflect on when to use attributing, classifying, or rank ordering.
- Reflect on learnings about this culture.

- Learn and practice the skill of naming attributes.
- Learn and practice the skill of classifying.
- Learn and practice the skill of rank ordering.

AMPLIFY
STAGE II

The Model *Applied*

Understanding Other
Cultures

A Social Studies Lesson with

Logical/Mathematical Intelligence

Lesson Procedures

INTRODUCTION

Logical/mathematical intelligence represents an intriguing mix of left- and right-brain operations. The ability to read and produce mathematical signs and symbols is a left-brain processing operation not unlike what happens when we learn language. On the other hand, the ability to understand numerical relationships, to discern abstract patterns, and to comprehend logical/mathematical concepts is a right-brain operation. When presented with a problem that needs to be solved or a challenge that must be met, the brain operates like a high-tech computer working to find an answer or solution to the problem or challenge.

The ability to look at another culture or nation and appreciate its gifts and contributions to the world is critical to our global future. In this social studies lesson, students will learn how to analyze another culture. First, they will brainstorm different things they know about a culture using a web (see glossary, p. 218, and blackline, p. 212). Second, they will classify their brainstorm list into economic, political, and social dynamics. Third, they will rank order each classified list according to which factors are the most important for the culture. Tell students that the lesson uses logical/ mathematical intelligence and ask them to be aware of using this way of knowing as they work.

The intelligence emphasis of this lesson is logical/mathematical. However, verbal/linguistic intelligence is also used, especially in the initiating guessing games, the writing activities, and creating the television script. Visual/spatial intelligence is employed in the creation of the brochure or flyer for the culture. Interpersonal intelligence is incorporated in and through the cooperative group structure and interaction.

STAGE I

Awaken

In general, logical/mathematical intelligence is awakened in situations that require problem solving or meeting a new challenge, as well as situations where pattern discernment is needed, such as number patterns, geometric designs, and word patterns.

Begin with a series of thinking patterns games:

1. **Can You Guess My Attributes?** Have three students, from different ethnic backgrounds, who have at least three similar attributes

The attributes, classification, and rank order games trigger logical/mathematical intelligence. When the brain is presented with a hidden pattern or rationale, as in these initiating games, its natural love of problem solving automatically engages. It relentlessly tries to find the pattern, the rationale, or the schema to make sense out of the situation. This is the heart of logical/mathematical intelligence.

Once you have told the students that there is a hidden organizing pattern or principle behind what you are doing, watch them struggle, argue, and guess, trying to outfox you in the games. When you see this happening, this is an indication that logical/mathematical intelligence has indeed been awakened and that it is now ready for action.

(e.g., wearing glasses or tennis shoes, curly hair, same height, etc.) come to the front of the room.

Ask the class to guess why you selected this group. Do not be surprised if they find many more common attributes than your original ones!

2. **Can You Guess My Classification Scheme?** Gather a group of ten items from a culture you have been studying. Classify the items into three groups (e.g., by color, shape, texture, size, etc.) and ask students to guess why you put certain items together in the same group.

   Again, they will probably come up with more classification categories than you originally had in mind.

3. **Can You Guess My Rank Ordering Rationale?** Show a list of key persons from a culture you have been studying. Rank order the names three different ways (e.g., by dates of death, by best known to least known, etc.). See if students can figure out why you have placed each list in the given order.

STAGE II

Amplify

Almost anything we do well takes practice. The same is true of working with our intelligence capacities—we must practice using the awakened intelligence and, just like any skill, it will improve. Part of the task here is to train ourselves to understand how the intelligence itself works.

Students need to be introduced to the specific intelligence tools they will be using in the lesson and have an opportunity to practice using them. As you introduce these tools, try to make the practice session activities mirror what you want them to do with the content of the lesson.

The attribute web helps strengthen inductive thinking patterns. By having students talk about their school you have hopefully hooked them with a topic of interest to them. You are likewise accessing verbal/linguistic intelligence through their dialogue about the school and their writing on the web, and interpersonal intelligence by placing them into cooperative groups. During the webbing they brainstorm the basic data on the school.

1. Introduce attribute webbing to the students. Explain that the web is a diagram that can help students describe the attributes of something. Ask the class to pretend the school is a culture. Draw a web on the board or overhead and ask students to brainstorm attributes of your school (see blackline, p. 192).

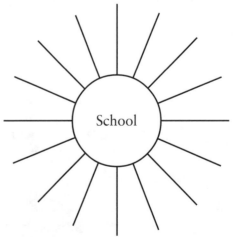

Keep brainstorming until you have at least twenty-five items on the web. Remind students that the key in brainstorming is to accept all ideas. There are no wrong answers as long as they are a response to the brainstorm question.

The classification chart enhances deductive thinking patterns. It asks students to sort their particular brainstorm information from the web into general pre-established categories (in the same way they will do later on with data from another culture) and to make judgments about the data and prioritize it.

2. Introduce classifying to students (see blackline, p. 192). Explain that classifying similar things, or grouping like things together, helps students better understand them. In groups of three, have students briefly classify the brainstorm list of school attributes into four categories—economic, political, social, and symbolic.

CLASSIFICATION CHART

ECONOMIC ATTRIBUTES	POLITICAL ATTRIBUTES	SOCIAL ATTRIBUTES	SYMBOLIC ATTRIBUTES

Have one team share their classification chart. Note similarities and differences with the other teams.

The rank ordering helps students learn and improve their priority thinking skills. To do this they must make judgments about their data and arrive at a consensus. This further activates and uses interpersonal intelligence capacities.

3. Introduce rank ordering to students. Tell students that when they rank order things they will put them in an order according to how important they think each item is. For each category on their classification charts have the teams decide which item is most important for the school and mark that #1, which is second most important and mark that #2, and which is third most important and mark that item #3. Use the ranking ladders (see blackline, p. 192).

RANKING LADDERS

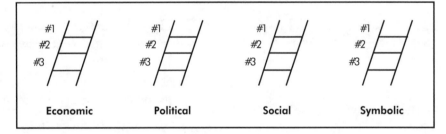

Economic   Political   Social   Symbolic

Have several groups share what they picked as #1 for each category.

4. Tell students that they have been practicing some logical thought processes that are now going to be applied to a social studies lesson. Reflect on the three processes (attribute webbing, classifying, and rank ordering) by asking students these questions:

• Which of the three was easiest? most difficult?

• How did they help your thinking?

• What questions do you have about using these organizers?

Teach

Students apply the logical/mathematical skills you taught in the amplifying part of the lesson to gain knowledge and explore the meaning of the lesson content.

They begin by studying a section from the textbook that describes a particular culture. Each of the cognitive organizers is then applied in turn to that content, and students are asked to organize and reorganize the basic information into different patterns—attributes that describe a culture, attributes organized under predetermined categories, and attributes ranked in terms of their importance to the culture.

1. Using the same groups as before, begin by assigning students the roles of organizer/timekeeper, recorder/materials gatherer, and encourager/motivator within each group. The lesson has two parts: analyzing another culture and using what they have learned to appreciate the culture.

2. **ASSIGNMENT PART I.** Tell students they will be using the same basic process just used on the school to analyze another culture. Have the students turn to the appropriate page(s) in their text-books. Put the following instructions on the board or overhead:

Analyzing Another Culture

As a group, complete these tasks:

1. Read the appropriate section(s) of the text.

2. Brainstorm and list the attributes of this culture using the web.

3. Classify the attributes using the economic, political, social, symbolic classification chart.

4. Rank order the first, second, and third most important factor of economic, political, social, and symbolic life for each column on the chart.

---

a. Ask students if they have any questions about the assignment. Have the materials person gather supplies for the group— newsprint, marking pens, and the graphic organizers worksheet (see blackline, p. 192).

b. When the teams have finished Part I, have them post their graphic organizers where all can easily see them.

3. **ASSIGNMENT PART II.** Tell students they are now going to play a game with the analysis they have been doing of this culture. Post the following on the board or overhead:

The final stage of the lesson is a creative thinking process in which students must synthesize what they have learned about the culture and communicate it to others. Two additional intelligences get into the act at this point: verbal/linguistic through the creative writing involved in making up the advertisement and visual/spatial through the creation of the brochure or flyer. Make sure you have plenty of colored marking pens (or paint) for them to use at this point.

Appreciating Another Culture

As a team, pretend that you are a travel agency that is trying to convince tourists to vacation in this culture. Using the items on your newsprint, your team is to create two items:

• A brochure or flyer advertising the features of the culture

• A script for a television advertisement for the culture

When the teams have completed their work, have them make their presentations to the rest of the class as if they were salespersons from the travel agency.

STAGE IV

Transfer

The goal of the transfer section is to help students find the relevance of the lesson for their own lives. Here we want the lesson to extend beyond the lesson, into other curriculum areas, and finally into students' lives beyond the classroom.

The reflection on using cognitive organizers makes students aware of the patterns for thinking that were used in the lesson and that these same patterns can be employed elsewhere. Sharing what they learned with a partner brings to consciousness the key points of knowledge gained in the lesson. The reflective journal/log helps them make personal connections to and associations with the lesson.

1. Reflect on the lesson with the whole class, beginning with the use of the cognitive organizers.
   - Which of the three graphic organizers did you like most? Why?
   - Which did you like the least? Why?
   - What ideas do you have about other ways you could use these organizers in school (in this subject or another)?
2. Have students conclude the lesson by turning to a partner and discussing the following questions:
   - What new things did you learn about this culture?
   - What was exciting? surprising? distressing?
   - What would you say is this culture's greatest gift to our world today?
3. Finally have students write a reflection log entry that begins:

   I [would/would not] like to visit this culture someday because . . .
4. Ask volunteers to share what they wrote with the rest of the class.

SPIRAL ADAPTATIONS OF THE LESSON

Elementary School Level

1. Focus the lesson on understanding and appreciating the ethnic diversity represented in the class, or invite several persons from other cultures to visit the class.
2. Teach students how to use a simple matrix with the various cultures down the side of the matrix and the food, language, and family customs across the top.

MATRIX

	Food	Language	Customs
Mexican			
Korean			
German			
South African			

3. Have students fill in the boxes of the matrix with pictures from magazines and/or pictures they draw and color themselves.

Secondary School Level

1. Focus the lesson on comparing and contrasting key similarities and differences in the values, customs, and beliefs of three different cultures.

2. Use the attribute web and classification chart (see blackline, p. 192), then introduce a three-way Venn diagram organizer for comparing and contrasting the cultures.

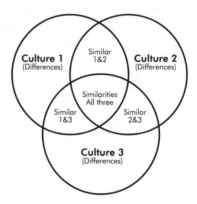

3. Role-play a debate on a contemporary issue with students assuming the values, beliefs, and customs of the different cultures in the discussion. For example, discuss the conflicts between technology and the environment, how to achieve world peace, or the pros and cons of having a large family.

TECHNOLOGY TIPS

1. Ask students to use a computer graphing program to display statistics (e.g., income groups, employment distribution, etc.) from the culture they are studying.

2. Help students use a concept mapping program to record, organize, and analyze information about a culture.

3. Instruct students to conduct online research about different aspects of the culture (e.g., economy, political process, social structures, religion, etc.).

ASSESSMENT TIPS

PORTFOLIOS

1. Have students include the graphic organizer worksheet with their notes on the team's discussion and analysis.

2. Lead students to decide some way to reproduce the advertising brochure or flyer the team created, including the script.

JOURNALS

1. After students discuss the lesson with a partner (#2 of transfer stage), ask them to make a list of the most important things for them from the lesson.

2. Ask students to write the following log entry in their journals: I [would/would not] like to visit this culture someday because . . .

Look to the Past . . .

Rethink a lesson you have completed recently. How would you restructure it to teach *for* and *with* logical/mathematical intelligence?

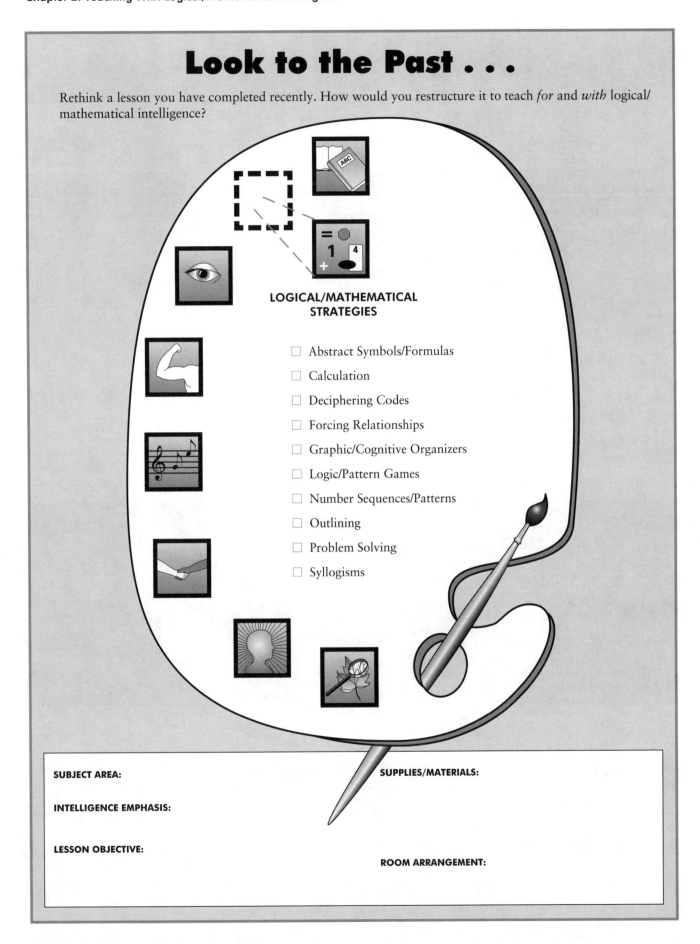

LOGICAL/MATHEMATICAL STRATEGIES

- ☐ Abstract Symbols/Formulas
- ☐ Calculation
- ☐ Deciphering Codes
- ☐ Forcing Relationships
- ☐ Graphic/Cognitive Organizers
- ☐ Logic/Pattern Games
- ☐ Number Sequences/Patterns
- ☐ Outlining
- ☐ Problem Solving
- ☐ Syllogisms

SUBJECT AREA:

INTELLIGENCE EMPHASIS:

LESSON OBJECTIVE:

SUPPLIES/MATERIALS:

ROOM ARRANGEMENT:

Look to the Future . . .

Think about a lesson you have coming up in the near future. How would you structure it to teach *for* and *with* logical/mathematical intelligence?

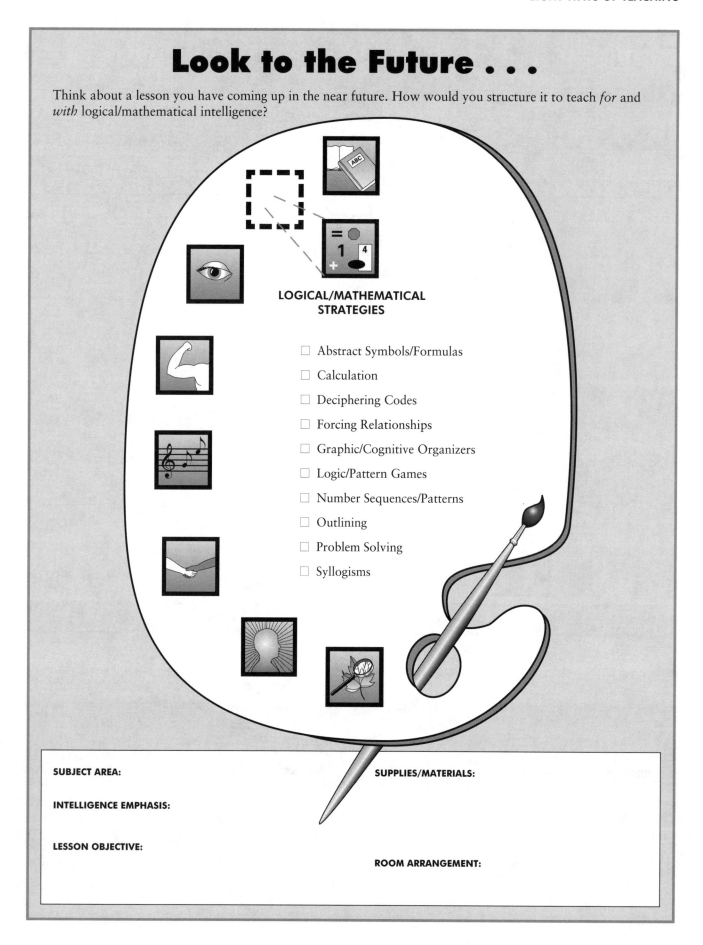

LOGICAL/MATHEMATICAL STRATEGIES

- ☐ Abstract Symbols/Formulas
- ☐ Calculation
- ☐ Deciphering Codes
- ☐ Forcing Relationships
- ☐ Graphic/Cognitive Organizers
- ☐ Logic/Pattern Games
- ☐ Number Sequences/Patterns
- ☐ Outlining
- ☐ Problem Solving
- ☐ Syllogisms

SUBJECT AREA:

INTELLIGENCE EMPHASIS:

LESSON OBJECTIVE:

SUPPLIES/MATERIALS:

ROOM ARRANGEMENT:

LESSON PLANNING IDEAS

Logical/Mathematical

HISTORY	MATHEMATICS	LANGUAGE ARTS	SCIENCE & HEALTH	GLOBAL STUDIES & GEOGRAPHY	FAMILY/CONSUMER SCIENCES, INDUSTRIAL TECHNOLOGY, & PE	FINE ARTS
Find examples when history repeated itself	Find unknown quantities or entities in a problem	Predict what will happen next in a story or play	Use the symbols of the Periodic Table of Elements in a story	Play Follow the Legend map-reading games and exercises	Follow a recipe to make bread from scratch	Learn patterns of ten different dance steps
Compare and contrast different periods of history	Teach someone else how to use a calculator for problem solving	Create a 4 x 4 x 4 outline* on a favorite hobby	Find five different ways to classify a collection of leaves	Play Guess the Culture based on artifacts in a time capsule	Find the relation of keyboard actions and computer performance	Compose a piece of music from a matrix*
Ask fat and skinny questions* about key historical decisions	Create number sequences and have a partner find the pattern	Learn to read, write, and decipher code language	Do a KWL goal-setting chart* for a study of AIDS	Rank order key socioeconomic factors that shaped a culture	Design a physical exercise routine using a matrix*	Use a Venn diagram* to analyze characters in a play
Create time sequence charts with titles for major eras of history	Mind-map** proofs for geometry theorems	Analyze similarities and differences of various pieces of literature	Learn the pattern of successful and reliable scientific experiments	Predict what will happen in several current event stories	Create problem-solving scenarios for shop machines	Create a paint-by-numbers picture for another person to paint
Predict what the next decade will be like based on patterns of the past	Design classification charts for math formulas and operations	Use a story grid* for creative writing activities	Practice webbing* attributes of various systems of the body	Learn cause and effect relations of geography and geological events	Make a matrix* on meanings of computer symbols	Analyze plays using the dramatic structure model**

*See Glossary and appendix C
**See Glossary

TEACHING WITH

Visual/Spatial Intelligence

THE INCREDIBLE JOURNEY OF PHOTOSYNTHESIS

A Biology Lesson

SECONDARY SCHOOL LEVEL

The Lesson Palette

Visual/ Spatial Emphasis

VISUAL/SPATIAL STRATEGIES

- ✔ Active Imagination
- ☐ Color/Texture Schemes
- ✔ Drawing
- ✔ Guided Imagery/Visualizing
- ☐ Mind Mapping
- ☐ Montage/Collage
- ☐ Painting
- ☐ Patterns/Designs
- ✔ Pretending/Fantasy
- ☐ Sculpting

SUBJECT AREA: Biology

INTELLIGENCE EMPHASIS: Visual/Spatial

LESSON OBJECTIVE: To understand what occurs in the process of photosynthesis in a plant and to be able to communicate this to others through diagrams and/or pictures.

SUPPLIES/MATERIALS:
- article about photosynthesis (see blackline, p. 193)
- colored marking pens or pencils
- art paper for drawing
- discussion questions (see blackline, p. 194)

ROOM ARRANGEMENT: Desks moved so students can work in groups of three

THE LESSON . . .

STAGE I
AWAKEN

Awaken visual/spatial intelligence by presenting the mind with and/or creating unusual, delightful, and colorful designs, patterns, shapes, and pictures. Engage in active imagination through such things as guided imagery and pretending exercises.

VISUAL/SPATIAL

INTELLIGENCE

STAGE III
TEACH

Teach for and with visual/spatial intelligence by using the specific tools of this intelligence and applying them to help learn the content, acquire specific knowledge, and achieve the lesson's goals and/or objectives.

STAGE IV
TRANSFER

Transfer visual/spatial intelligence to life by discussing the intelligence tools used, finding applications beyond the lesson to other curriculum areas, and finally integrating it into the task of living in the world outside of the classroom.

Amplify visual/spatial intelligence using active imagination to picture things that are outrageous or fantastic, using visual media such as paint, colored marking pens, or clay. Use mind-mapping skills and draw patterns or designs.

AMPLIFY
STAGE II

The Model

... AT A GLANCE

STAGE I
AWAKEN

- Lesson Introduction: Understand the process of photosynthesis from the inside out—from the perspective of a plant.
- Teacher leads students in inner seeing exercises with a partner.
- Students lead each other in inner seeing exercises with a partner.

VISUAL/SPATIAL

INTELLIGENCE

STAGE III TEACH

- Students discuss photosynthesis.
- Teacher leads an imagination exercise about photosynthesis.
- Students draw, paint, and write stories about what they saw.

STAGE IV TRANSFER

- Reflect on the imagination exercise.
- Reflect on the drawing or painting.
- Reflect on key things learned about photosynthesis.

- Practice imagination exercises about a familiar spot, a space scene, and a fantasy scene.
- Students try to draw or sketch what they saw in the imagination exercises.

AMPLIFY
STAGE II

The Model *Applied*

80

The Incredible Journey
of Photosynthesis

A Biology Lesson with

Visual/Spatial Intelligence

Lesson Procedures

INTRODUCTION

The natural world is an awesome miracle if we but open our eyes and see. In this lesson, students have an opportunity to explore and understand the process of photosynthesis in a unique way—from the inside out; that is, from the perspective of the plant! The lesson is modeled after the movie *The Incredible Journey,* where human beings became microscopic and traveled through the body in the bloodstream. In this lesson, students imagine that they can journey into a plant and participate in the amazing photosynthesis process. They will be using their visual/spatial intelligence in the lesson so ask them to be aware of this and notice what happens.

In addition to visual/spatial intelligence, this lesson employs verbal/linguistic, interpersonal, and naturalist intelligence. The verbal/linguistic emphasis can be seen in the writing students do in the transfer section of the lesson. The interpersonal emphasis is in the cooperative group work students do throughout the lesson. The naturalist intelligence is used when the students visualize a plant.

The realm of visual/spatial intelligence is the realm of images, patterns, colors, designs, textures, pictures, and the like. The process of seeing something with the external eyes (mostly from the stimulation of the retina) activates the visual area of the brain. In the case of visual/spatial intelligence, we are mostly dealing with a right-brain hemispheric operation—an area known as the parietal lobes (see fig. 0.1, p. 3). When sets of neural pathways fire, we experience an image. Researchers have found that the firing of these neural pathways can also be caused by internal stimulation. Many of the same physical operations present in normal, external eye perception are likewise present in mental imagery, when one is seeing with the mind's eye. Often the mere creation of a strong mental image will cause us to react as if the imagined thing is real.

STAGE I

Awaken

Visual/spatial intelligence is awakened by presenting the mind with unusual, delightful, and colorful designs, patterns, shapes, and pictures, and engaging in active imagination through such things as imagination and pretending exercises.

When you engage in this kind of image association, the visual part of the brain

1. Tell students you are going to ask them to see various things with the mind's eye, and that you are going to help them access and turn on the parts of the brain that will help them do this. Ask students to find a partner, put their heads together, and close their eyes. Tell students that you are going to suggest a series of images to them and they are to tell their partner what they see

immediately creates pictures, memories, emotions, and other sensations that it connects with the image suggested. Not only do the students see their own associations, but they also receive further image input as their partners describe their respective associations. When you have completed the image associations, just listen to the buzz in the room!

with the mind's eye. (Note: This is like a word association test but with images instead.) Suggest these images:

- an animal
- a machine
- a park
- a storm
- an elderly person
- a trip
- a food
- a relative
- swimming
- a party
- yourself as a baby
- shopping

2. Have students discuss the process of inner seeing with each other. Prompt them to ask each other What happened? and What was this like?

3. Ask several partners to share some of their observations with the whole class.

STAGE II

Amplify

One of the key findings of researchers is that, although one or two of our intellectual capacities tends to be more developed than the others, they can all be strengthened and improved. This is especially true of our visual/spatial potentials. When we were much younger our visual/spatial capacities were generally very strong and often second nature to us in daydreaming, pretending, and role playing. However, as we get older, we are told that this world of active imagination is only for children, so we tend to use these capacities less and less. Nevertheless, contemporary research has documented that the capacity for imagination is inherent in the nervous system, and thus can be relearned and improved.

1. Tell students that in their biology lesson today they will be participating in an imagination exercise and that they will sketch what they have seen using the mind's eye. But first lead them in a few practice imagination exercises so they have an understanding of the basic process.

2. Pass out blank paper and colored pencils or marking pens to students. Students are to work individually this time. Instruct them to try to imagine as vividly as possible the things you are going to suggest to them.

3. Begin by having them close their eyes, take several deep breaths, and relax as much as they can. After a couple of minutes, give these instructions:

   a. Now I'd like you to imagine that you are in your bedroom at home. Look around and try to see as much as you can with your mind's eye. (pause)

   b. Notice whether or not the bed is made. (pause)

   c. Are any clothes lying out? How light is it? Notice any other special things in the room. (pause)

   d. Now on a sheet of blank paper, briefly draw or sketch what you are seeing in your mind's eye.

Here students imagine a familiar scene and then sketch on paper what they have seen inside their heads. Remember, this is not an art lesson! It is therefore important to emphasize that whatever they are seeing is fine and however they represent on their papers what they are seeing is perfectly acceptable.

4. Have students share their drawings and talk about the imagination exercise with their partners.

5. Tell students that you want them to practice this once again, but this time they will have to use their imagination even more, because you will be taking them on a journey to an unfamiliar place. Again ask them to close their eyes and relax, breathing

The purpose of the second imagination exercise is to help students practice using their imagination more fully by imagining an unfamiliar scene. Granted, they are likely to draw pictures they have seen of outer space, but their active imagination must fill in the gaps and this is point of the exercise. This practice is important for it is more akin to the photosynthesis journey on which you take them later in the lesson.

It is important to recognize that there are no wrong answers in an imagination exercise. Whatever happens, whatever they experience is right! Make sure students are aware of this.

deeply from the abdomen. After a couple of minutes suggest the following images to the students:

a. Imagine that you are lying down in a favorite outdoor place of yours. Take a couple of moments to think of that place and then, as vividly as you can, imagine that you are there. (pause)

b. Imagine that you are lying there, completely relaxed, and enjoying yourself, and that you are able to slowly float upwards into the clouds. Let yourself do that now. Try to notice everything you can about what this is like. (pause)

c. Now imagine that you can continue to float higher and higher until you leave the atmosphere of the earth and you find yourself in space. Spend a few minutes looking around and getting a sense of what space is like. (pause)

d. When you feel ready, allow yourself to float back into the earth's atmosphere, into the clouds, and back to the favorite spot where you began. (pause)

e. Now open your eyes and quickly sketch what you saw and experienced on your trip to space on a piece of blank paper.

6. Once again have students briefly share their drawings and their experience of the imagination exercise with their partners.

Teach

STAGE III

The traditional academic content part of the lesson can either be a review of previously studied material, or it could be an introduction to a more in-depth study of photosynthesis.

Whether you use the article provided or another from your own biology textbook is not important. (If you do use a different article, you will need to make alterations in the guided imagery instructions so they match the article the students have studied.) The purpose of reading the article is for students to have the basic stages of the photosynthesis process in a fairly concise form, for it is these stages that will be the stages of the guided imagery journey on which you take them after their initial study. At this point you are also accessing both verbal/linguistic intelligence through the reading and discussion and interpersonal intelligence in and through the cooperative group structure.

For many students, especially those who have a more fully developed naturalist intelligence, the visualization may stimulate and trigger this intelligence within them. What you are attempting to do, in any event, is create a virtual experience of nature by asking students to vividly and actively imagine a plant.

1. Have students get into cooperative groups of three. Assign the roles of organizer, encourager, and checker. Have the organizer gather supplies for the team: colored marking pens or pencils, blank paper, and a copy of the article on photosynthesis (see blackline, p. 193).

2. Instruct students to read the article as a team and answer the discussion questions (see blackline, p. 194). Tell them that they are to help each other understand the process; that is, what happens during photosynthesis.

3. Now tell the class that they are going to have a chance to experience the process of photosynthesis. Ask if any of the students have seen the movie *The Incredible Journey*. If so, have them tell the story to the rest of the class. If not, tell it yourself (see lesson introduction). Explain that students are going to take an incredible journey into a plant and experience the process of photosynthesis firsthand.

4. Introduce the process by telling the students that you are going to lead them in an imagination exercise as you did earlier.

a. Ask them to think about some of the things that are in a factory, such as machines, an energy supply, workers, a water supply, etc. Tell them they are to imagine that the leaf is a

It is very important that you find ways to help students get into the imagination exercise. We all imagine things in our mind's eye, but not in the same way. Some students will see in their minds with the same clarity that they see television. Others will only have a vague impression of what you are suggesting. Still others may see nothing at all in the traditional sense of seeing, but may have an inner feeling for what you are suggesting. In any guided imagery, success is whatever works for the individual. There is no right way! If the images suggested are not working, give students permission to cheat! Have them pretend it is working, or even better, tell them they can change the images for themselves so they do work. With practice, inner seeing can be improved.

Doing the exercise with eyes closed generally helps the active imagination work better. It also helps students stay focused on the journey and not get distracted. However, if any are uncomfortable with closing their eyes, make sure they know they can keep them open. But ask them to experiment with closed eyes if they want.

small photosynthesis factory. Tell them that you will be taking them on a tour of this factory so they can see and experience the stages of photosynthesis they have just been reading about.

b. Tell them you will pause after each stage of the tour and give them a chance to briefly sketch what they are seeing in their mind's eye on a piece of paper.

c. Explain that at the end of the tour the team will look at the different pictures individuals have drawn and incorporate different individual pictures into a single picture of the photosynthesis process. Encourage students to let their minds run wild and see how much they can get into this journey.

5. Now begin the process by asking students to close their eyes. Instruct them to breathe deeply and relax as much as possible for a few minutes. When you sense they are ready, lead them in the process outlined below. Read the following instructions to the class:

a. Imagine that you are in the middle of a beautiful, green woods. It is a gorgeous spring day and the warm sun is shining brightly above. (pause)

b. Pretend that you have the power to make yourself much, much smaller than you are now. Maybe you do this as the characters did in *The Incredible Journey* movie by drinking some special drink, or maybe there is a special seed you eat, or you may have some other way to do this. But now I'd like you to make yourself very, very tiny. In fact, I'd like you to make yourself so small that you become microscopic. I'll now give you a few minutes to do this by whatever means you choose. (pause)

c. You have now become so small that you are able to walk through a pore in the leaf of a nearby plant. As you enter the plant you suddenly find yourself surrounded by hundreds of thousands of cells. As you look more closely at one of the cells you notice that it is like a little factory. There is a supply of water flowing through it from the veins of the plant. There is an acceptor module (like a special chamber in the factory) that is gathering carbon dioxide as it enters the plant through the pores in the leaf.

d. Now, open your eyes and briefly sketch a cell as if it were a factory. Include the water supply, the carbon dioxide acceptor chamber (molecule), and anything else you are seeing or sensing. What does it look like? (pause)

e. Close your eyes again. As you continue walking around this cell, you notice a football-shaped, green plate that seems to be seeking out and turning in the direction of the sunlight that is striking the surface of the leaf. You remember from your reading that this is the chloroplast. It is the light radar system of the plant and it can move to take best advantage of the light.

f. Pause for a moment again and add the chloroplast light radar system to your picture. What does this look like in your mind's eye? (pause)

g. As you look more closely at the cell you notice that there are many chloroplast light radar stations stacked on top of each other. In between the chloroplasts is a green, sponge-like substance that you suddenly know is the chlorophyll molecules—the plant's light absorbing unit. You notice the chlorophyll molecules soaking up the sunlight. Again, pause for a moment and draw what you are seeing. (pause)

h. Now close your eyes again. You hear the sound of water and notice that it is flowing into the cell from the veins of the leaf. Pause and add this to your picture. (pause)

i. Close your eyes again. Focus again on the chlorophyll. You suddenly become aware that the chlorophyll molecules are much more than sun-sucking sponges. They are like little reactors in and of themselves. As they get more and more charged with energy from the sun, they begin to split the water molecules flowing through the cell into hydrogen and oxygen. The oxygen is expelled back into the atmosphere through the pores of the leaf and the hydrogen atoms are seized by a special escort module and held in a special place for later in the process. Open your eyes and draw what you are seeing—the chlorophyll splitting the water molecule, the oxygen being expelled, and the hydrogen being held by the escort module. (pause)

j. Close your eyes again. Once the chlorophyll has split the water molecules, it gives off more energy as it returns to its normal state. This energy, however, turns on a new molecule, the ATP. ATP is like an electric generator that empowers the escort module that is holding on to the hydrogen atom. Pause now and sketch this image. (pause)

k. The escort module now leads the hydrogen to the carbon dioxide acceptor module and they combine to form PGA molecules. These PGA molecules combine with each other to form sugar, and the sugar is placed in storage areas in the plant to be used later for food. For the last time now, pause and draw what this part of the process looks like to you in your mind's eye. (pause)

l. The process is now complete. Pause for a moment and allow yourself to appreciate what you have just experienced. Reflect on the amazing process of photosynthesis in this microscopic factory that makes food from sunlight. (pause)

m. Now, as you are ready, find your way back to the pore in the leaf of the plant where you originally entered and exit to the place where you began. Slowly allow yourself to become your normal size again, by whatever means you choose. (pause)

n. As you are ready, bring yourself back to this room, and to this time and space. Open your eyes and stretch, looking at your picture of the photosynthesis factory, remembering the journey in which you have been participating.

6. Now give time for each student to share his or her picture with the other members of the team.

7. Pass out poster paper and colored markers to each team and have them create a single picture of a photosynthesis factory based on the ideas from the different pictures the individual members of the team have drawn. Make sure they know that they are to include ideas from each member of the team and that you want the individual pictures attached to the final product so you can check to make sure each person has contributed to the final drawing.

8. Have three teams get together and share their final pictures with each other. Note similarities and differences in the pictures of the factories.

Every idea of each individual does not need to to be included in the final picture, but you want some of the ideas from each member of the team to be included in the final product.

STAGE IV

Transfer

The goal of the transfer part of the lesson is to help students take what they have learned in the lesson and apply it in other areas of their schoolwork and in their everyday lives outside of school.

Reflecting on the process serves two metacognitive functions: it helps students be more aware of their own visual/spatial intelligence capacities and helps them think about how these capacities can be improved. The reflective log/journal writing allows students to distill the key points of the lesson for themselves in language and terminology that makes sense to them.

If you like, use the Discussion Questions blackline (p. 194) to process the lesson with the entire class.

1. Reflect on the imagination exercise with the students using the following questions:

   • What happened in the imagination exercise? What was it like for you?

   • What surprised you? What was exciting? What was difficult?

   • How was this imaginary journey different from just reading about photosynthesis?

   • What new things did it add to your understanding?

2. Reflect on the learnings from the content part of the lesson.

   a. Ask students to write a reflection in their logs describing their journey into the cell factory of the plant. The log is to be titled A Day in the Life of a Plant Cell.

   b. Ask for volunteers to share something from their log entry.

SPIRAL ADAPTATIONS OF THE LESSON

Elementary School Level

1. Focus the lesson on understanding the different parts of a plant and the function each part performs (e.g., the roots absorb water and nutrients from the earth, the leaves soak up sunshine from which the plant makes its food, etc.).

2. Have students draw pictures of plants showing all of the different parts discussed above. Then let them paint their pictures with watercolors. You could also have them make a plant from clay.

3. Ask students to pretend they can talk to their plant and ask it questions about what it is like to be a plant. Pretend that the plant can answer. Let the plant ask the students questions about what it is like to be human.

Middle School Level

1. Focus the lesson on learning about the life of a plant that is beyond what the naked eye can see (e.g., pores in a leaf, the different kinds of cells that make up a plant, the tiny veins, etc.).

2. Have students observe differents parts of plants under a microscope and draw what they are seeing on paper using colored marking pens and/or pencils.

3. Place students in cooperative groups and have them paint a large mural that shows the inner aspects of the life of a plant and incorporates the different things they have seen under the microscope. The murals are to tell the story of the life of a plant from the inside out.

TECHNOLOGY TIPS

1. Ask students to design a Web page for younger children entitled The Incredible Journey of Photosynthesis.

2. Tell students to create an electronic poster that demonstrates the photosynthesis process. Encourage them to use animated GIFs, 3-D modeling, morphing, etc.

3. Help students create a video, digital pictures, or an iMovie that illustrates the various stages of photosynthesis.

ASSESSMENT TIPS

PORTFOLIOS

1. Have students include the pictures they drew on their own during the *Incredible Journey* imagination exercise.

2. Ask students to decide on a way to reproduce the team's composite drawing for each individual's portfolio.

JOURNALS

1. Encourage students to include their log reflection, A Day in the Life of a Plant Cell, in their journals.

2. Prompt students to write about what happened in the lesson affectively and cognitively and/or about their learnings on visual/spatial intelligence.

Look to the Past . . .

Rethink a lesson you have completed recently. How would you restructure it to teach *for* and *with* visual/spatial intelligence?

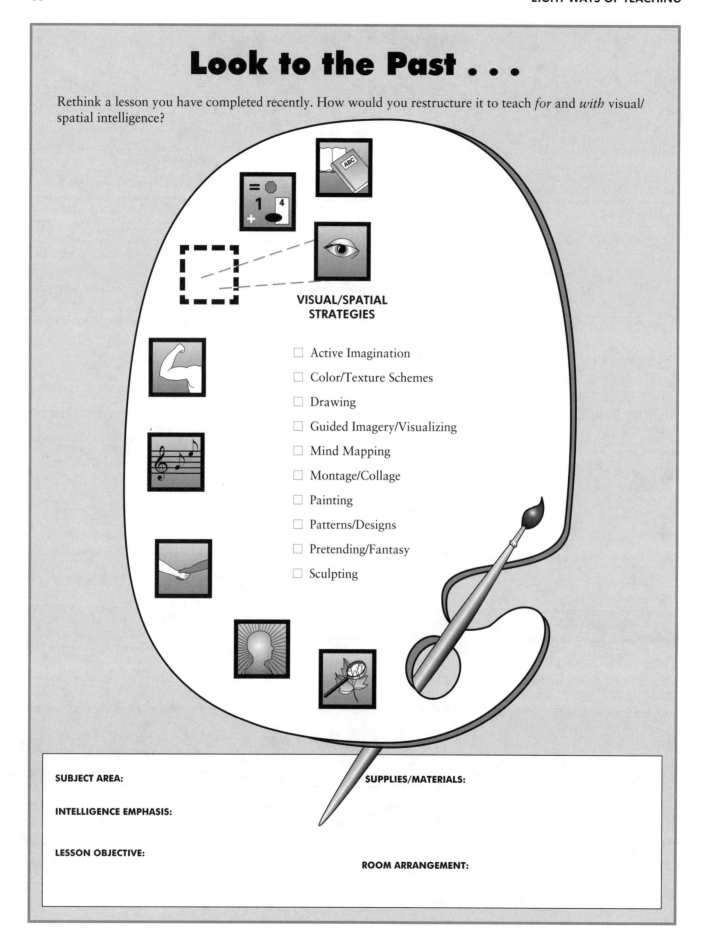

**VISUAL/SPATIAL
STRATEGIES**

- ☐ Active Imagination
- ☐ Color/Texture Schemes
- ☐ Drawing
- ☐ Guided Imagery/Visualizing
- ☐ Mind Mapping
- ☐ Montage/Collage
- ☐ Painting
- ☐ Patterns/Designs
- ☐ Pretending/Fantasy
- ☐ Sculpting

SUBJECT AREA:

SUPPLIES/MATERIALS:

INTELLIGENCE EMPHASIS:

LESSON OBJECTIVE:

ROOM ARRANGEMENT:

Look to the Future . . .

Think about a lesson you have coming up in the near future. How would you structure it to teach *for* and *with* visual/spatial intelligence?

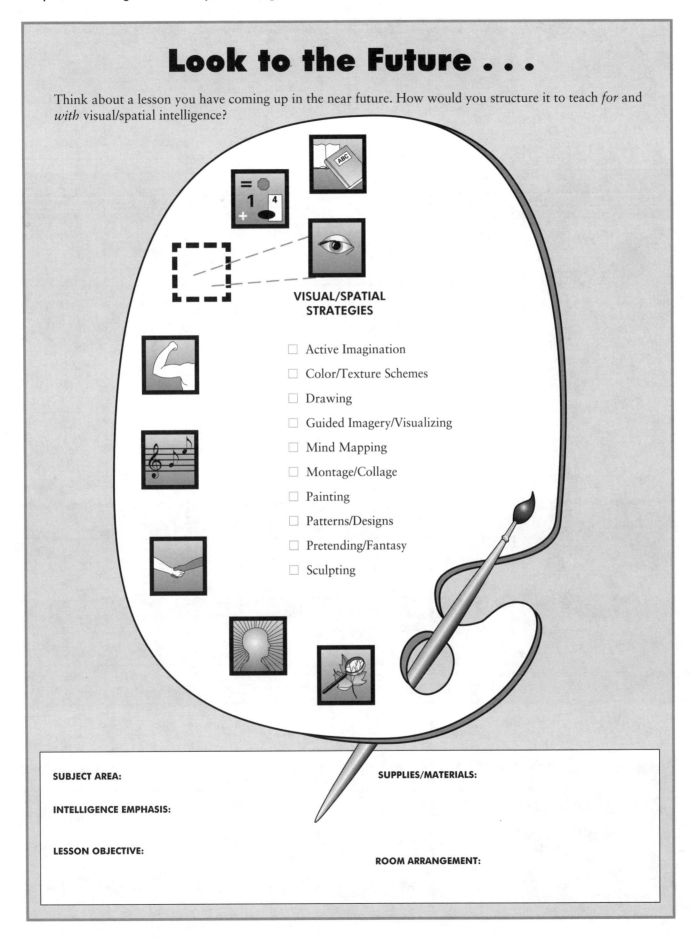

VISUAL/SPATIAL STRATEGIES

- ☐ Active Imagination
- ☐ Color/Texture Schemes
- ☐ Drawing
- ☐ Guided Imagery/Visualizing
- ☐ Mind Mapping
- ☐ Montage/Collage
- ☐ Painting
- ☐ Patterns/Designs
- ☐ Pretending/Fantasy
- ☐ Sculpting

SUBJECT AREA:

INTELLIGENCE EMPHASIS:

LESSON OBJECTIVE:

SUPPLIES/MATERIALS:

ROOM ARRANGEMENT:

LESSON PLANNING IDEAS

Visual/Spatial

HISTORY	MATHEMATICS	LANGUAGE ARTS	SCIENCE & HEALTH	GLOBAL STUDIES & GEOGRAPHY	FAMILY/CONSUMER SCIENCES, INDUSTRIAL TECHNOLOGY, & PE	FINE ARTS
Have imaginary talks or interviews with people from the past	Do a survey of students' likes and dislikes, then graph the results	Play Pictionary with vocabulary words	Draw pictures of things seen under a microscope	Draw maps of the world from your visual memory	Draw pictures of how to perform certain physical feats	Watch dancers on video and imagine yourself in their shoes
Make visual diagrams and flowcharts of historical facts	Estimate measurements by sight and by touch	Use mind mapping* as a notetaking process	Create posters or flyers showing healthy eating practices	Study a culture through its visual art—painting and sculpture	Create visual diagrams of how to use shop machines	Pretend you can enter a painting—imagine what it is like
Imagine going back in time—see what it was like back then	Add, subtract, multiply, and divide using various manipulatives	Draw pictures of the different stages of a story you are reading	Create montages or collages on science topics (e.g., mammals)	Make maps out of clay and show geographical features	Practice drawing objects from different angles (drafting)	Listen to music with eyes closed and create a sculpture from clay
Paint a mural about a period of history	Imagine using a math process successfully, then really do it	Learn to read, write, and decipher code language	Draw visual patterns that appear in the natural world	Make decor for the classroom on a culture you are studying	Learn a series of spatial games (e.g., horseshoes, ring toss)	Draw the sets for the various scenes of a play you are reading
Imagine and draw what you think the future will be like	Learn metric measurement through visual equivalents	Use highlighter pens to colorize parts of a story or poem	Pretend you are microscopic and can travel in the bloodstream	Use a map to get around an unfamiliar place or location	Imagine your computer is human—draw how it works	Draw the visual and color pattern of a dance

*See Glossary

CHAPTER

4

TEACHING WITH

Bodily/Kinesthetic Intelligence

How Does It Feel to Be a Circle?

A Geometry Lesson

MIDDLE SCHOOL LEVEL

The Lesson Palette

**Bodily/
Kinesthetic**
Emphasis

BODILY/KINESTHETIC STRATEGIES

☑ Body Language/Physical Gestures

☐ Body Sculpture/Tableaus

☑ Dramatic Enactment

☐ Folk/Creative Dance

☐ Gymnastic Routines

☐ Human Graph

☐ Inventing

☑ Physical Exercise/Martial Arts

☐ Role Playing/Mime

☐ Sports Games

SUBJECT AREA: Geometry

INTELLIGENCE EMPHASIS: Bodily/Kinesthetic

LESSON OBJECTIVE: To learn how to find the circumference of a circle and the area of a rectangle, and how to use and understand the formulas for performing these tasks.

SUPPLIES/MATERIALS:
- physical movement formulas (see blackline, p. 195)
- notebook paper
- pens or pencils

ROOM ARRANGEMENT: Desks against the wall so there is plenty of space for moving around

THE LESSON . . .

STAGE I
AWAKEN

Awaken bodily/kinesthetic intelligence through physical movement such as sports games and all forms of self-expression that use the physical body (e.g., body language, drama, and creative or interpretive dance).

BODILY/KINESTHETIC

INTELLIGENCE

STAGE III
TEACH

Teach for and with bodily/kinesthetic intelligence using the specific tools of this intelligence and applying them to help learn the content, acquire specific knowledge, and achieve the lesson's goals and/or objectives.

STAGE IV
TRANSFER

Transfer bodily/ kinesthetic intelligence to life by discussing the intelligence tools used, finding applications beyond the lesson to other curriculum areas, and finally integrating it into the task of living in the world outside of the classroom.

Amplify bodily/kinesthetic intelligence through physical gestures and body movement, role-playing, drama, mime and charade games, kinesthetic skills (e.g., sports, exercise, dance), or inventing something with the hands.

AMPLIFY
STAGE II

The Model

...AT A GLANCE

STAGE I
AWAKEN

- Lesson Introduction: Learn geometric formulas through physical movement.
- Teacher demonstrates playing charades using the title of a movie and a song.
- Students play charades, acting out names of television shows.

BODILY/KINESTHETIC

STAGE III
TEACH

- Class forms itself into geometric shapes.
- Students embody geometric formulas to find area and circumference.
- Create original formulas and relate them to classical ones.

STAGE IV
TRANSFER

- Reflect on using the body in learning.
- Reflect on discoveries about the formulas.
- Reflect on use of the formulas outside school.

INTELLIGENCE

- Teacher performs simple physical movements and turns them into symbolic formulas.
- Students repeat the process with a partner, turning a physical movement into a symbolic formula.

AMPLIFY
STAGE II

The Model Applied

How Does It Feel to
Be a Circle?

A Geometry Lesson with

Bodily/Kinesthetic Intelligence

Lesson Procedures

INTRODUCTION

In this lesson students will learn two different geometric formulas by physically "embodying" them. They will learn the formulas with their bodies, create their own formulas to describe the physical movements they have made, and finally transfer this learning to the classical geometric formulas. Tell the students that this lesson will emphasize bodily/kinesthetic intelligence as the primary way of knowing. Ask them to be aware of this as they work.

Two other intelligences are also used in this lesson. Logical/mathematical intelligence is involved when students recognize patterns, in this case physical movement patterns, and convert these patterns into abstract symbolic formulas. Interpersonal intelligence is involved as students work with a partner to create their formulas.

Bodily/kinesthetic capacities involve a set of highly complex brain, mind, and body operations. We know that the right side of the brain controls the motor functions of the left side of the body, and the left side of the brain controls the right side of the body. The cerebral cortex of the brain (see fig. 0.1, p. 3) is like a radar system that continually monitors and interprets the meaning of various data all over the body. This information is fed to the cerebral cortex through the spinal cord. Once the cerebral cortex has this information and has processed and interpreted it, the motor cortex kicks into gear and produces the bodily movement needed to respond to what the cerebral cortex has discerned. All of this happens in a split second!

STAGE I

Awaken

The very act of physical movement creates an immense amount of activity in the brain. When you add to this the necessity to communicate in and through that movement, the fullness of the body as a vehicle of expression and/or knowing is activated.

For centuries people have understood that there are things that can be known and expressed physically that cannot be known or expressed in any other way—consider the world's rich traditions of drama, creative dance, mime, various cultural festivals, and religious pageantry. When you ask

Begin by playing charades with the class:

1. Think of a movie that most students have seen and the name of a popular song they know. Act out clues to the various words in the movie title while students guess. After they have succeeded in guessing the movie title, act out the song title.

2. Now break the class into teams of three. Have the teams play charades with each other by drawing the names of current television shows from a hat and acting out their titles for each other.

students to act out something, you call all of this potency to the foreground so that you can use it in the rest of the lesson.

Allow three rounds so that each student gets a chance to act out a title.

STAGE II

 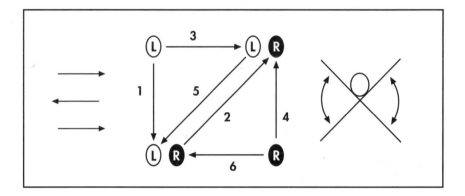

Amplify

It is often easier to understand the need to practice body movement skills than it is to understand the need to practice some of the other intelligences. This is most likely because our culture is very much aware of the training athletes go through to compete in sports events. We know that through careful and regular practice we can improve such things as our serve in tennis, our skill in ice skating, and the ability to parallel park. There are many things that our bodies know that are not necessarily clear to the mind, such as how to ride a bike, how to type without looking at the keyboard, how to ski, and how to walk without toppling over.

1. Introduce the intelligence skill by putting the following formulas on the board or overhead and see if students can guess what the formulas represent (see blackline, p. 195).

After they have had a few minutes to guess, tell them they are formulas that symbolize different kinds of physical movement. Perform the three different movements (#1—walking back and forth across the room, #2—the box step, #3—a jumping jack) and see if they can guess which movement goes with which formula. Help them see the relationship between the various parts of the formula and the movement it represents.

The teacher first models the skill that the students later employ in the lesson. It is important that the modeling be as close as possible to what you are actually going to have them do in the lesson. However, the more content-free the demonstration is, the more students will be able to focus on learning the skill itself without being distracted by

2. Working in the same groups of three in which they played charades, have students draw an item out of a hat. This time they will get a physical movement they are to perform as a team and then turn it into a symbolic formula as you have demonstrated above. Remind them that they are learning how to do this in order to use this skill later in the lesson. (Note: Items in the hat might include doing five push-ups, moving from your desk to sharpen your pencil and back to your desk, throwing a piece of paper into the trash can, etc.)

Students need a chance to experience what it is like to learn and know things with the body, especially in the classroom where they are generally asked to leave their bodies outside! Here they are given an opportunity to practice creating physical movement formulas of their own as you modeled earlier.

STAGE III

This is a process of translating physical movements into symbolic formulas of students' own creation, this time to learn geometry concepts. It gives students an opportunity to experience the relationship between their movements and an abstract formula that symbolizes the movement.

Teach

1. The first task is to find the area of a rectangle. Have ten students volunteer to form a rectangle having the width of four students and the length of six students. Give them a rope to stretch around the inside of the rectangle they have formed.

2. Ask the class to guess how many students it will take to fill in the rectangle. Record these estimates on the board or overhead.

3. Now have the students one by one enter the rectangle and fill it in by rows until it looks like this:

4. Count the number of students inside of the rope boundary and compare this with the estimates made earlier.

5. Have students now return to their seats and with a partner create a symbolic formula that describes what they have just experienced: how many people it takes to fill in a rectangle that is four students wide by six students long.

Once they have learned a movement with their bodies and have created a symbolic formula for that movement, often the formula alone can trigger the body knowing of the movement and, in turn, the meaning of the formula. This happens because the pattern has been encoded in the brain through the physical activity. An example of this can be seen when Olympic athletes use imagination exercises to improve the performance of their sport or when children learn social roles through creative play.

6. Now have the entire class form itself into a circle. Have the class guess how many steps it will take to get around the outside of the circle.

7. Choose five different students to walk the circumference of the circle, one at a time, counting the number of steps they take. Record their numbers on the board or overhead.

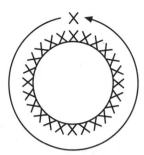

8. Ask the students if they have any ideas on other ways to figure out how many steps it takes to get around the circle. Now have the same students walk the diameter of the circle, counting the number of steps they take. Again record the numbers.

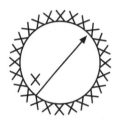

9. Now ask the class to notice the relationship between the number of steps it takes to get around the circle compared to the number to get across it. What do you notice? Approximately how many times across would equal one time around?

10. Again have students return to their seats with a partner. Together they are to create a symbolic formula to explain what they have just experienced.

11. Now write the classical formulas for finding the area of a rectangle and for finding the circumference of a circle on the board and explain the formulas to the students: A = l x w and C = πd

This comparison helps students bridge the formulas from the textbook into their own experience, for they have actually "embodied" the formulas!

12. Have student pairs compare the formula they wrote to the formula on the board. Listen carefully as they talk and help them understand the relationship between their formula and experience and the classical geometric formula for these things.

STAGE IV

Transfer

The goal of the transfer part of the lesson is to help students take what they have learned in the lesson and apply it in other areas of their schoolwork and in their everyday lives outside of school. The reflection on using the body to help learn information increases students' awareness of their own bodily/kinesthetic intelligence and how to make it work better for them.

Reflect on the lesson with the students in the following manner:

1. Discuss what it was like to use the body to learn. Ask questions like the following:

   • Which of the two formulas was easier to understand with your body? Why?

   • Which was more difficult? Why?

- How did using your body help you understand the formulas?
- What ideas do you have about other ways you could use your body to help you with your learning (in both mathematics and other subjects)?

2. Create columns for the rectangle and for the circle.

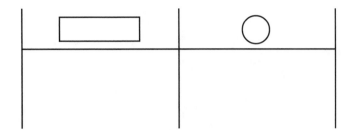

This reflection on the formulas helps students see that they have gained something they can use in their lives outside of the classroom situation. Education research clearly shows that if the payoff of a lesson is immediate, the motivation for learning will dramatically increase.

Now brainstorm with the class when in their everyday lives these formulas might come in handy. Following are some examples:

- Will a 14" diameter pizza feed the number of people at your table? (How many inches of pizza will each get?)
- How many 2" x 3" photos would fit on an $8\frac{1}{2}$" x 11" page?

SPIRAL ADAPTATIONS OF THE LESSON

Elementary School Level

1. Focus the lesson on learning to divide wholes into parts and on understanding the meaning of simple fractions.

2. Learn the meaning of one half, one third, and one fourth by tearing paper and then drawing pictures of the results; for example:

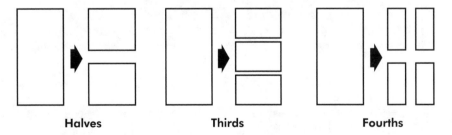

Halves **Thirds** **Fourths**

3. Have the students stand as a group, then divide themselves in half, into thirds, and then into fourths when you hold up signs with pictures like those above. Help them transfer these pictures to the fraction symbols that mean the same thing, namely:

$\dfrac{1}{2}$ $\dfrac{1}{3}$ $\dfrac{1}{4}$

Secondary School Level

1. Focus the lesson on learning the paper-and-pencil math process for finding unknown quantities in algebraic equations.

2. Practice "embodying" written math operations in physical movements. For example, physically demonstrate answers to various math problems such as:

$$10 \div 5 = ? \quad \text{or} \quad \frac{(3+1)}{2} \times 2 = ?$$

3. Have students physically become different equations and find the unknown quantities with their bodies; for example:

$$\frac{(2 + x)}{2} = 4$$

4. Have them relate their discoveries to math operations they know can produce the same results.

TECHNOLOGY TIPS

1. Ask students to create a robotics demonstration that shows what they have learned about area, perimeter, etc.

2. Watch a video or DVD of a professional dance troupe. Help students find examples of geometry in the dances. Ask them to draw the geometric shapes of the dance and figure out areas, perimeters, hypotenuses, etc.

3. Divide students into teams. Tell teams to create a computer game that applies geometric concepts and that requires players to use geometric concepts when they play the game.

ASSESSMENT TIPS

PORTFOLIOS

1. Have students include the symbolic formulas they created with their partner.

2. Ask students to write an explanation of their original formulas in light of the classical ones.

JOURNALS

1. Prompt students to do a PMI (see glossary, p. 218, and blackline, p. 208) on using the body in learning.

2. Have students include individual brainstorm notes on how the formulas can be useful in life outside the classroom.

Look to the Past . . .

Rethink a lesson you have completed recently. How would you restructure it to teach *for* and *with* bodily/kinesthetic intelligence?

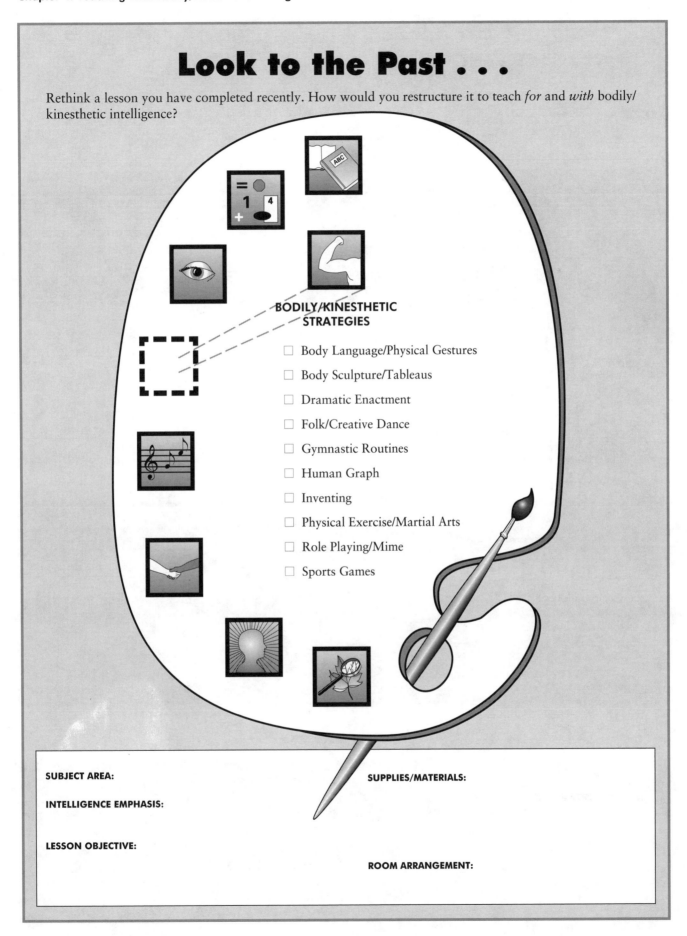

BODILY/KINESTHETIC STRATEGIES

- ☐ Body Language/Physical Gestures
- ☐ Body Sculpture/Tableaus
- ☐ Dramatic Enactment
- ☐ Folk/Creative Dance
- ☐ Gymnastic Routines
- ☐ Human Graph
- ☐ Inventing
- ☐ Physical Exercise/Martial Arts
- ☐ Role Playing/Mime
- ☐ Sports Games

SUBJECT AREA:

INTELLIGENCE EMPHASIS:

LESSON OBJECTIVE:

SUPPLIES/MATERIALS:

ROOM ARRANGEMENT:

Look to the Future . . .

Think about an upcoming lesson. How would you structure it to teach *for* and *with* bodily/kinesthetic intelligence?

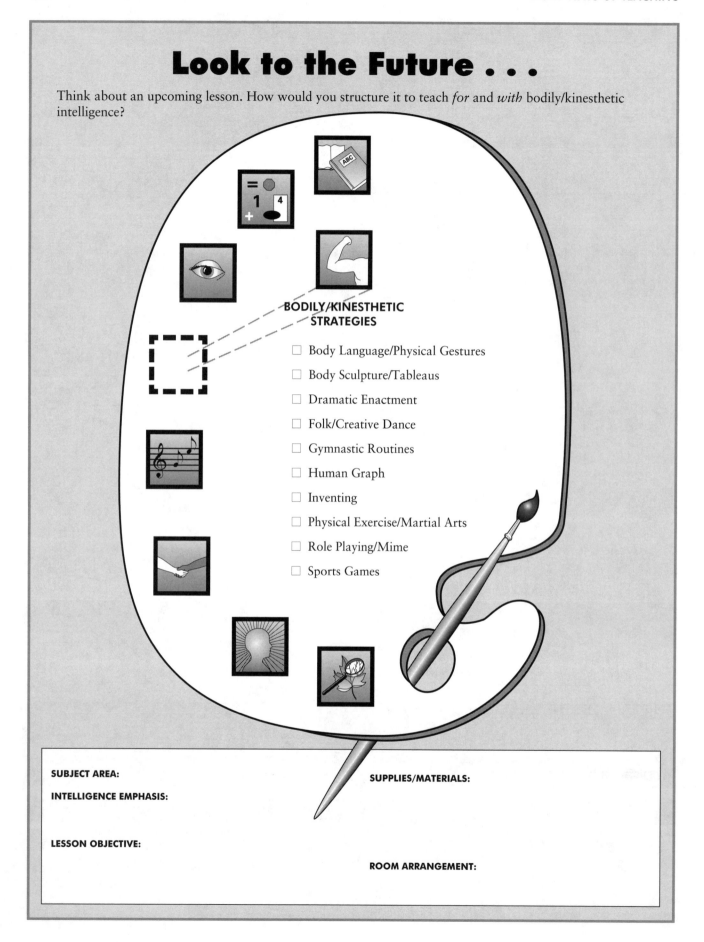

BODILY/KINESTHETIC STRATEGIES

- ☐ Body Language/Physical Gestures
- ☐ Body Sculpture/Tableaus
- ☐ Dramatic Enactment
- ☐ Folk/Creative Dance
- ☐ Gymnastic Routines
- ☐ Human Graph
- ☐ Inventing
- ☐ Physical Exercise/Martial Arts
- ☐ Role Playing/Mime
- ☐ Sports Games

SUBJECT AREA:

INTELLIGENCE EMPHASIS:

LESSON OBJECTIVE:

SUPPLIES/MATERIALS:

ROOM ARRANGEMENT:

LESSON PLANNING IDEAS
Bodily/Kinesthetic

HISTORY	MATHEMATICS	LANGUAGE ARTS	SCIENCE & HEALTH	GLOBAL STUDIES & GEOGRAPHY	FAMILY/CONSUMER SCIENCES, INDUSTRIAL TECHNOLOGY, & PE	FINE ARTS
Perform and/or create dramas from a period of history	Use different parts of the body to measure things	Play The Parts of a Sentence charades	Role-play the parts and dynamics of the life of a cell	Learn folk dances of a culture being studied	Learn and perfect various multitracking* routines	Create the dance equivalent for different inventions
Reenact great scenes or moments from history for today	Add and subtract members to and from a group to learn about fractions	"Embody" (act out) the meaning of vocabulary words	Create the rotation of planets with the class members acting as the solar system	Create gestures to represent the legend of a map	Invent something in shop class such as a new household tool	Create human sculpture tableau* to express an idea
Hold an historical period, costume, and food day	Design something that requires applying math concepts	Act out a story or play that you are studying	Become and act out the different states of matter	Play physical movement games from another culture	Practice physical movements in your mind then with your body	Make up gestures for parts of a musical score
Play Great Moments from the Past charades	Create and act out a play in which the characters are geometric shapes	Learn the alphabet by body movements and physical gestures	Conduct a series of hands-on scientific experiments	Simulate going shopping using currency from another country	Make up a new kind of snack food, prepare it, and eat it	Design a "live painting"* of a classical work
Learn dances from previous periods of history (e.g., minuet)	Make up a playground game that uses math concepts or operations	Make up a Parts of Speech folk dance	Study and try various biofeedback* techniques or methods	Study body language from different cultural situations	Create and perform a drama on how a computer operates	Practice doing impromptu dramatic mime activities

* See Glossary

TEACHING WITH

Musical/Rhythmic
Intelligence

THE PAST IS ALIVE WITH
THE SOUND OF MUSIC

A History Lesson

ELEMENTARY SCHOOL LEVEL

The Lesson Palette

Musical/ Rhythmic Emphasis

MUSICAL/RHYTHMIC STRATEGIES

- ☑ Environmental Sounds
- ☑ Instrumental Sounds
- ☑ Music Composition/Creation
- ☑ Music Performance
- ☐ Percussion Vibrations
- ☐ Rapping
- ☐ Rhythmic Patterns
- ☑ Singing/Humming
- ☐ Tonal Patterns
- ☑ Vocal Sounds/Tones

SUBJECT AREA: History

INTELLIGENCE EMPHASIS: Musical/Rhythmic

LESSON OBJECTIVE: To grasp an historical period as an unfolding, dramatic story that has a number of messages and much relevancy for our current world situation.

SUPPLIES/MATERIALS:
- written summary of key events of a period of history
- notebook paper
- pens or pencils
- a variety of instruments (drums, noise makers, etc.)
- Team Reflection Log (see blackline, p. 197)

ROOM ARRANGEMENT: Desks arranged in groups of five around the room with the center of the room as the stage (like theatre in the round)

THE LESSON . . .

STAGE I
AWAKEN

Awaken musical/rhythmic intelligence with the resonance or vibrational effect of music and rhythm on the brain. Use such things as the human voice, sounds from nature, musical instruments, and percussion instruments.

MUSICAL/RHYTHMIC

INTELLIGENCE

STAGE III
TEACH

Teach for and with musical/rhythmic intelligence using the specific tools of this intelligence and applying them to help learn content, acquire specific knowledge, and achieve the lesson's goal and/or objectives.

Transfer musical/rhythmic intelligence to life by discussing the intelligence tools used, finding applications beyond the lesson to other curriculum areas, and finally integrating it into the task of living in the world outside of the classroom.

STAGE IV
TRANSFER

Amplify musical/rhythmic intelligence by practicing listening to music and other sounds, expressing feelings through tones, beats, and vibrations, creating songs or jingles to communicate thoughts, and using music, humming, and rhythm to alter moods.

AMPLIFY
STAGE II

The Model

. . . AT A GLANCE

STAGE I
AWAKEN

- Lesson Introduction: Teacher demonstrates that history is a story about students' lives and that history has meaning for students today.
- Students view pictures and make up stories to go with each.
- Students think of songs that could go with each picture.

MUSICAL/RHYTHMIC

INTELLIGENCE

STAGE III
TEACH

- Read about and discuss historical events.
- Write scripts for radio shows.
- Add special effects and songs to scripts.
- Perform the radio shows.

STAGE IV
TRANSFER

- Reflect on our approach to history in this lesson.
- Reflect on connections between past and present.
- Reflect on ways to use music and rhythm in learning.

AMPLIFY
STAGE II

- Play audiotapes of old-time radio shows and listen for sound effects.
- Guess how the sound effects were produced.
- Discuss the music involved.

The Model Applied

The Past Is Alive with the
Sound of Music

A History Lesson with

Musical/Rhythmic Intelligence

Lesson Procedures

INTRODUCTION

History is a story about our lives—where we have come from and where we are going. In this lesson students will illustrate an event from the past with sound, music, and rhythmic patterns. First, they will learn about something that happened in American history, either by reading a short article or by hearing a teacher lecture. Then, in cooperative groups, they will create songs and sound effects for retelling the story as if it were an old-time radio show. Tell the students that this lesson will emphasize the musical/rhythmic way of knowing. Ask them to be aware of this as they work on the lesson.

In addition to the musical/rhythmic emphasis of this lesson, verbal/linguistic, visual/spatial, and interpersonal intelligences are involved. Verbal/linguistic intelligence tools are employed at several points: reading, answering questions, and writing about an historical event. Interpersonal intelligence is involved in working with a team. Visual/spatial intelligence is accessed through using pictures, both in the opening exercise and in the pictures of historical scenes.

In some ways the consciousness-altering effect of musical/rhythmic intelligence is greater than any of the other intelligences, precisely because of the impact of music on the state of the brain. Music, rhythm, and sound possess tremendous evocative power in our lives. Just think about how music and rhythm can calm you when you are stressed; stimulate you when you are bored; inspire your religious beliefs, national loyalty, or feelings for a beloved; and help you express experiences of great loss or intense joy. Also consider how effectively music is used in all forms of television and radio advertising! Both the left and right hemispheres of the brain are involved in musical/rhythmic intelligence. The left hemisphere is involved in the formal, systematic approach to music and rhythm. For example, we can learn to read notes, beat out a prescribed rhythm, and recognize different tones and/or instruments. The right hemisphere is the place of the sheer enjoyment of music for its own sake, whether or not we know anything about it as a formal system.

STAGE I

Awaken

Musical/rhythmic intelligence is activated by the resonance or vibrational effect of music, rhythm, and sound on the brain.

1. Begin by showing students a series of pictures from a magazine. Ask volunteers to tell what they think is happening in the pictures. (Note: Try for a variety of pictures, such as people relaxing

As students make music and other sounds as the accompaniment for various pictures and stories, the effect of these sounds activates the musical centers of the brain (both left and right) and, with it, an immensely creative way of knowing.

Remember that the more sounds you can get the students to make, the greater the effect on the brain, because the vibrational impact on the brain catalyzes this way of knowing. As students are given permission to express themselves and their feelings through sound (beyond the traditional speaking of words), many of them will be opened to realms of knowing and understanding that transcend verbal expression.

on a beach, people involved in an argument, a family eating dinner, etc.)

2. Ask the class to imagine that these scenes are on television but something is wrong and they cannot see the pictures. Ask them how they could figure out what was happening. Make a list on the board or overhead of such things as the dialogue, the music being played, sound effects, etc.

3. Now have them think of a kind of music that might be played for each picture that would help someone know what was happening. Prompt the class to hum or sing it.

4. Ask them to think of sounds and noises that would be necessary to help someone know what was happening if they couldn't see the picture. Encourage the class again to make some of the sounds.

STAGE II

 # Amplify

Enhancing musical/rhythmic intelligence has nothing to do with what is usually referred to as musical talent. It is rather knowing how to use music and rhythm to put ourselves into optimal states for dealing creatively with different situations. Likewise, we can learn to sense different moods, paces, themes, and ideas that are embedded in a piece of music or a rhythmic pattern which are inexpressible in words.

In the listening, you are trying to draw them into a new experience; namely, a world where there was no television. You help them catalyze their active imagination as they listen to the radio shows. By beginning with a short lecture you sensitize them to, and intrigue them with, the possibilities of communication by sound alone.

By having students try to figure out what was done to actually produce the various background sounds, you are preparing them to come up with creative ideas for augmenting their own radio shows with sound and music in the next part of the lesson.

1. Give a short lecture on the old days of radio, before television. Remind students that people only had radios, so when a radio story was being told the storytellers had to use special sounds, music, conversation between people, and different noises to help the listening audience understand the story. For example, they would often use wooden blocks to make it sound as if a horse were running, or they would rattle a bag of broken glass to make it sound as if a window had been broken.

2. Play several examples of different kinds of old radio shows so they get a sense of what this was like. (Note: You might try the *Lone Ranger, Fibber McGee and Molly, The Shadow*, or some other suspense or detective show. Make sure the segments you play illustrate the importance of sound and music in these productions.)

3. Ask the students the following:

   • How do you think the radio programs produced the different sounds?

   • How did the music help the story?

STAGE III

Teach

1. Divide the students into cooperative groups with four members in each group. For a musical way to break into groups, have everyone pull a song out of a hat. Then have the students start humming their songs and find their groups by identifying the students who are humming their song. Assign the roles of reader, encourager, recorder, and group organizer.

2. Pass out pictures, one picture per team, that depict important events from the early days of American history (e.g., Columbus landing on the shores of the New World, the signing of the Declaration of Independence, Abraham Lincoln at Gettysburg, etc.). On the back of each picture have one or two paragraphs that explain what is happening in the picture along with two or three discussion questions (see p. 196 for an example).

3. Assign teams to look at their pictures while the reader reads the paragraph on the back. After reading the paragraph, the group organizer is to ask the discussion questions while the recorder writes down the team's answers.

4. Ask the students to recall the radio shows they listened to earlier. Tell them they are to create a radio show about their pictures and the stories they tell. Each team will perform its program for the class just like the old-time radio shows.

5. In order to get ready for the show, each team will do the following:

    a. Write a simple script that tells the story of the picture and involves all members of the team with a speaking part.

    b. Create a song about the event and/or find a piece of music to start off and end the show. They can either make up the music themselves or find recorded music to play, or a combination of both!

    c. Decide on at least five special sound effects to be used during the show to help the audience understand what is happening.

    (Note: You will have to monitor the groups very closely to make sure they do not get stuck. You may have to become more actively involved with some groups than others. Also, this project could extend over several days with teams working on one part of the assignment each day.)

6. When they are ready, have the teams perform their show from another room using an amplification system to transmit the program to the main classroom (if possible). If you cannot do this, have them perform their shows from behind a screen so they are hidden from view and must rely only on sound to communicate their story. If you can, tape-record each show so they can listen to it later.

The discussion questions help the teams rehearse the basic information in the paragraphs about the pictures. By asking them to record their team's answers to the questions you are promoting discussion and whole-team understanding of the picture and paragraph. At the same time this accesses verbal/linguistic intelligence capacities.

The script-writing assignment is also a comprehension exercise and further utilizes verbal/linguistic intelligence capacities. When students move into the task of creating a song and/or finding a musical piece that will set up and conclude the radio show and illustrating their script with sound, they have moved to the heart of musical/rhythmic intelligence. In these tasks you are helping them to move beyond mere head knowledge of their event to a gut-level emotional understanding of what is going on.

As students perform their radio shows for each other, they help their fellow students know and learn using musical/rhythmic intelligence. The fact that the performing team cannot be seen by their classmates further activates and calls to the fore the fullness of musical/rhythmic intelligence, both in the performing team and in the listening class!

You may have to do some re-teaching and/or clarifying at this point. Have the team that presented the program help you with any teaching that is needed so the whole class understands the event.

7. After each team has completed its show, thank them for their work and ask the class some questions to check their understanding of the event that was portrayed.

STAGE IV

Transfer

The goal of the transfer part of the lesson is to help students take what they have learned in the lesson and apply it in other areas of their schoolwork and in their everyday lives outside of school.

1. Ask the whole class to reflect on the radio programs:

  • What do you remember from these different radio programs?

  • What sounds are still ringing in your ears?

  • What lines of dialogue do you remember?

  • What music stands out for you?

2. Pass out the Team Reflection Log to each individual (see blackline, p. 197). Post the names of the different shows on the board or overhead and have the teams write them in the appropriate columns.

3. For each show have the teams discuss the following questions and have each individual write down thoughts from the team:

You are asking them to synthesize the key learnings and implications from the lesson in terms of its relevance for today. This is a key element in building bridges between the past, the present, and the future. And, after all, this is what makes history worth studying in the first place.

  • What was the story being told? Can you remember its parts?

  • How did it make you feel?

  • What are your questions about this event?

  • Why is this story important for us today?

SPIRAL ADAPTATIONS OF THE LESSON

Middle School Level

1. Practice turning relatively simple information—parts of speech, multiplication tables, and states and capitals—into songs or raps.

2. Have students read material from their history textbook, then retell the story in their own words, illustrating it with songs or raps.

3. After creating several songs about history, turn them into a Broadway-style musical.

Secondary School Level

1. Focus the lesson on learning about the mood, feel, and temperament of a part of history through music, rhythm, and sound.

2. Learn to recognize patterns in music and rhythm that communicate such things as emotions, actions, and moods, as well as patterns that can evoke certain feelings in people.

3. Gather a series of examples of music from a period of history you have been studying (e.g., Gregorian chant, madrigal, minuet, waltz, cantata, etc.). Listen to the music and challenge students to describe what this period must have been like based on its music. Then discuss what today's music says about us! Compare students' impressions with textbook descriptions.

TECHNOLOGY TIPS

1. Ask students to write songs about their historical events. Tell students to share their songs by using a karaoke machine. Encourage the class to sing along.

2. Help students find and download sound clips or music files from the Internet that they can use to tell about their events.

3. Show students how to scan a picture of their historical event. Then help them create an interactive picture that includes sound. Explain that others should be able to click on different areas to hear an audio element or to trigger an animated GIF.

ASSESSMENT TIPS

PORTFOLIOS

1. Ask students to include a copy of the script their teams wrote for the radio show.

2. Have students include a copy of the team's answers to the questions about their picture.

JOURNALS

1. Prompt students to include the Team Reflection Log about the different radio shows.

2. Challenge students to write a brief log entry on what they liked or did not like about the lesson.

Look to the Past . . .

Rethink a lesson you have completed recently. How would you restructure it to teach *for* and *with* musical/rhythmic intelligence?

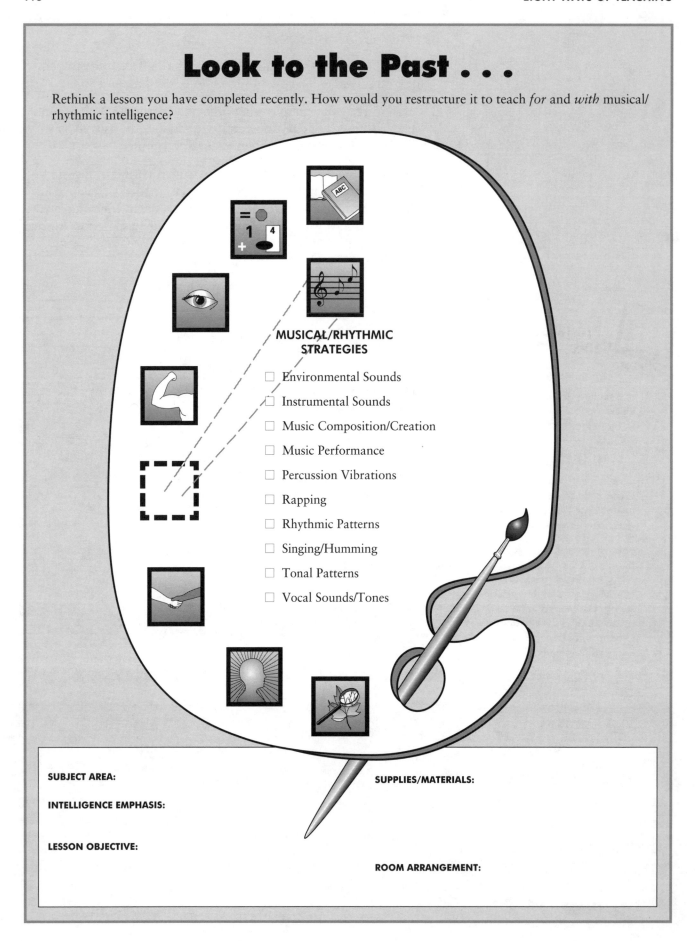

MUSICAL/RHYTHMIC STRATEGIES

☐ Environmental Sounds

☐ Instrumental Sounds

☐ Music Composition/Creation

☐ Music Performance

☐ Percussion Vibrations

☐ Rapping

☐ Rhythmic Patterns

☐ Singing/Humming

☐ Tonal Patterns

☐ Vocal Sounds/Tones

SUBJECT AREA:

INTELLIGENCE EMPHASIS:

LESSON OBJECTIVE:

SUPPLIES/MATERIALS:

ROOM ARRANGEMENT:

Look to the Future . . .

Think about a lesson you have coming up in the near future. How would you structure it to teach *for* and *with* musical/rhythmic intelligence?

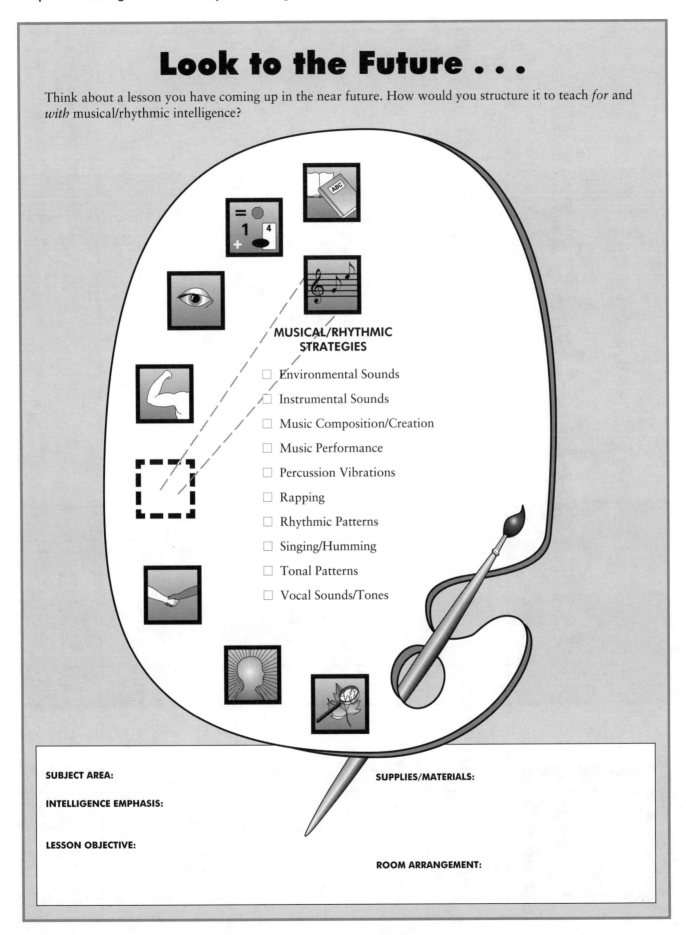

MUSICAL/RHYTHMIC STRATEGIES

- ☐ Environmental Sounds
- ☐ Instrumental Sounds
- ☐ Music Composition/Creation
- ☐ Music Performance
- ☐ Percussion Vibrations
- ☐ Rapping
- ☐ Rhythmic Patterns
- ☐ Singing/Humming
- ☐ Tonal Patterns
- ☐ Vocal Sounds/Tones

SUBJECT AREA:

INTELLIGENCE EMPHASIS:

LESSON OBJECTIVE:

SUPPLIES/MATERIALS:

ROOM ARRANGEMENT:

LESSON PLANNING IDEAS
Musical/Rhythmic

HISTORY	MATHEMATICS	LANGUAGE ARTS	SCIENCE & HEALTH	GLOBAL STUDIES & GEOGRAPHY	FAMILY/CONSUMER SCIENCES, INDUSTRIAL TECHNOLOGY, & PE	FINE ARTS
Analyze different historical periods through their music	Learn mathematical operations through songs and jingles	Learn Morse Code and practice communicating with it	Learn to use music to reduce stress	Listen to music from different cultures	Perform physical exercise routines in sync with music	Play Guess the Rhythm or Guess the Instrument with musical pieces
Create a series of key dates in history raps	Learn addition and subtraction through drum beats	Use different kinds of music for different kinds of writing	Listen to sounds of things in the natural world	Play musical instruments from around the world	Learn to recognize shop machines through their sounds	Draw or paint a piece of music as it plays
Make musical instruments from the past and compose a piece	Play a rhythm game* to learn multiplication tables	Learn and practice phonetic punctuation (a lá Victor Borge)	Experiment with the effect of vibration on sand in a metal plate	Create a sound- or tonal-based legend for a map	Record and recognize the varying sounds of a computer operating	Turn a nonmusical play into a musical play
Teach songs that were sung in previous eras (e.g., Gregorian chant)	Break a set of tones into various groups to learn division tables	Create songs or raps to teach grammar and syntax	Try various humming patterns to see how they change mood	Learn characteristic rhythm patterns of different cultures	Experiment with the effect of different kinds of music on how you eat	Practice impromptu music composition
Watch films about the past and focus on the sounds of history	Make up sounds for different math operations and processes	Illustrate a story or poem with appropriate sounds	Assign sounds to systems you are studying such as the nervous system or circulatory system	Sing songs from nations or countries being studied	Use music to help improve keyboarding skills and speed	Make up a creative or interpretive dance to a piece of music

* See Glossary

TEACHING WITH

Interpersonal Intelligence

FORMING A PERSONAL ADVISORY COUNCIL

A Literature Lesson

MIDDLE SCHOOL LEVEL

The Lesson Palette

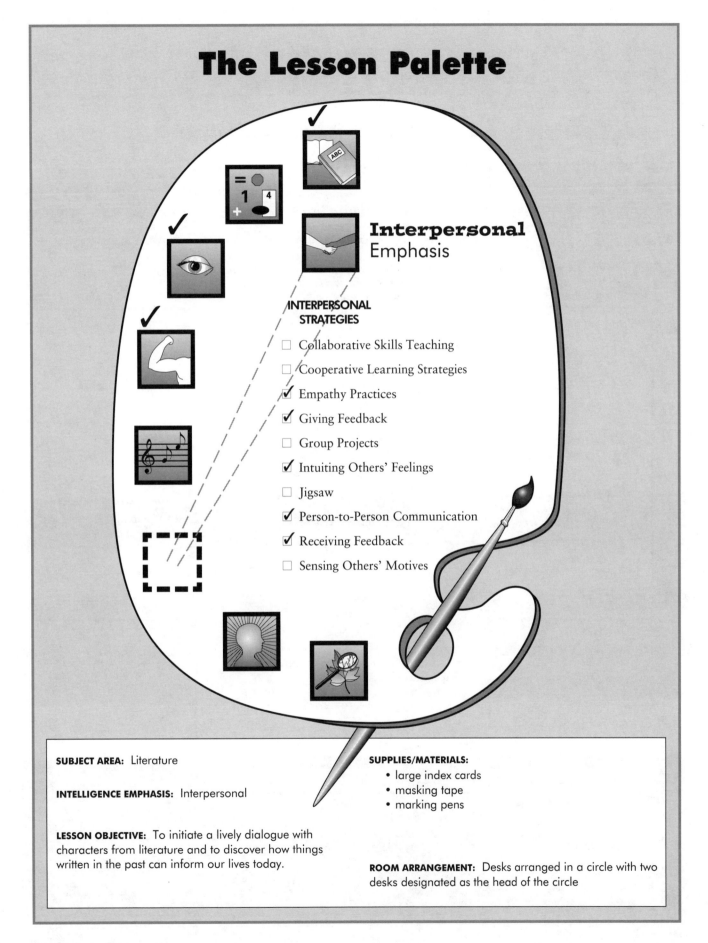

Interpersonal Emphasis

INTERPERSONAL STRATEGIES

- ☐ Collaborative Skills Teaching
- ☐ Cooperative Learning Strategies
- ☑ Empathy Practices
- ☑ Giving Feedback
- ☐ Group Projects
- ☑ Intuiting Others' Feelings
- ☐ Jigsaw
- ☑ Person-to-Person Communication
- ☑ Receiving Feedback
- ☐ Sensing Others' Motives

SUBJECT AREA: Literature

INTELLIGENCE EMPHASIS: Interpersonal

LESSON OBJECTIVE: To initiate a lively dialogue with characters from literature and to discover how things written in the past can inform our lives today.

SUPPLIES/MATERIALS:
- large index cards
- masking tape
- marking pens

ROOM ARRANGEMENT: Desks arranged in a circle with two desks designated as the head of the circle

THE LESSON . . .

STAGE I
AWAKEN

Awaken interpersonal intelligence by creating situations where people are working together with others for common goals, where they are having meaningful encounters with each other, and where being able to notice distinctions among persons is important and necessary.

INTERPERSONAL

INTELLIGENCE

STAGE III
TEACH

Teach for and with interpersonal intelligence using the specific tools of this intelligence and apply them to help learn the content, acquire specific knowledge, and achieve the lesson's goals and/or objectives.

Transfer interpersonal intelligence to life by discussing the intelligence tools used, finding applications beyond the lesson to other curriculum areas, and finally integrating it into the task of living in the world outside of the classroom.

STAGE IV
TRANSFER

Amplify interpersonal intelligence by practicing reflective listening, working as a member of a team, giving and receiving empathic feedback, being aware of others' feelings, motives, and opinions, and using effective person-to-person communication.

AMPLIFY
STAGE II

The Model

. . . AT A GLANCE

STAGE I
AWAKEN

- Lesson Introduction: The class sets up a personal advisory council made up of characters from literature.
- The teacher initiates the lesson with these communication games: Gossip, *How* I Say *What* I Say, and Lion Hunt.
- Students make a list of what is involved in effective communication.

INTERPERSONAL

INTELLIGENCE

STAGE III
TEACH

- Students choose characters from literature.
- Students introduce themselves in character.
- Students role-play the advisory council discussing a problem.

STAGE IV
TRANSFER

- Reflect on learnings about the characters.
- List characters for students' personal advisory councils.
- Discuss how and when to use the council.

- Brainstorm a list of contemporary figures that are familiar to the class.
- Name an issue that is facing the students at the present moment.
- Pick figures and role-play their advice on the named issue.

AMPLIFY
STAGE II

The Model *Applied*

Forming a Personal
Advisory Council

A Literature Lesson with

Interpersonal Intelligence

Lesson Procedures

INTRODUCTION

Interpersonal intelligence is the person-to-person way of knowing, and as such, it must rely on all the other intelligences in order to express itself. It therefore involves a great deal of neurological activity including both the right and left hemispheres of the brain, the limbic system (the seat of emotion), the cortex (the place of relating, loyalty, and trust), and the neo-cortex (the complex, eighth-inch thick covering of the brain that is responsible for higher-order thinking and reasoning processes). In addition, researchers have observed that the frontal lobes of the brain are active in interpersonal encounters, although not much beyond this is known about their function. (See fig. 0.1, p. 3.)

Literature is the study of other people's ideas and feelings about living. At the same time, to study literature is to study oneself— one's own ideas and feelings. In this lesson, students will enter into dialogue with various characters from a story or play. In the process they will discover how things written in the past can inform their lives today. They will learn how to seek advice on contemporary problems and issues by consulting wisdom from the past. Inform the students that they will be using their interpersonal intelligence in this lesson and ask them to pay attention to what this is like and what happens as they use this way of knowing.

At least three ways of knowing beyond the interpersonal are active in this lesson. Verbal/linguistic intelligence is involved when students spontaneously create dialogue for a character from literature. Visual/spatial and bodily/kinesthetic intelligences are involved as they role-play a chosen character.

STAGE I

The heartbeat of interpersonal intelligence is the sense of positive interdependence—we sink or swim together, two heads are better than one, and all of us can do more together than any one of us can do alone. It is awakened in situations that require the support, energy, and cooperation of other people to complete a given task. These communication games

Awaken

1. Begin by leading students in several communication/listening games. You might try such things as

   a. **The Gossip Game.** Whisper a message in one student's ear and have each in turn repeat the message by whispering it in their neighbor's ear until it has made its way around the class.

SkyLight Professional Development

127

are designed to trigger both the desire to relate to each other and the use of some of the capacities that are part of interpersonal intelligence, especially the ability to listen to each other.

When you ask students to list things that are involved in effective communication, you are creating an awareness that there are social skills that can be learned, and, like any skill, practiced and improved.

Students are often deeply fascinated with this whole area of interpersonal relationships and the possibility of improving them. This is especially true for middle school and secondary students whose own peer relationships may be their most important locus of self-identity, esteem, and security. Almost any initiating activity that asks students to relate to and rely on each other will work to awaken this very powerful way of knowing.

Have the last student repeat the message aloud and note how it has changed in the process.

b. *How* I Say *What* I Say. Choose a short love poem and read it to the class. Then read it as if you are very upset. Have several students practice reading it in different ways and notice what happens to the message of the poem when it is read in different ways. For example, read the poem as if it were a comedy script, as if you were speaking to an infant, or as if you were totally bored.

c. **Lion Hunt.** Begin by saying (and have the class say with you), "We're going on a lion hunt, through the deepest jungle, we're going on a lion hunt and I'm going to take a _____." Fill in the blank with some item you think will be needed on the lion hunt. Then begin the chant again, only this time when you get to the blank, ask the student sitting to your left to repeat what you said and add something of his or her own. The game proceeds around the circle with each student repeating all the previous items before adding their own.

2. On the board or overhead, have students brainstorm what is involved in effective communication and listening. Just what does it take?

3. Tell the class that in this lesson they are going to have a chance to communicate with and listen to characters from literature.

STAGE II

Amplify

This exercise requires the students to step outside of their own ideas, opinions, and feelings and to assume those of other people.

A certain degree of self-transcendence occurs here. As a result, students have an opportunity to unlearn some of the poor interpersonal habits they may have developed. Common among these habits are thinking there is only one right answer to a problem or issue, not being able to communicate effectively when there is disagreement, and getting so caught up in their own opinions, thoughts, and feelings that they completely miss what another person is trying to communicate.

1. Tell the class that you want them to experiment with what it is like to stand in someone else's shoes and become another person.

2. Model the following process for the students and then let them practice with each other:

a. Brainstorm a list of contemporary figures that are familiar to the class.

b. Have students list five issues that are of concern to them at the present moment.

c. Pick a figure and one of the issues from the list and pretend that you are that person giving your advice or opinion about the issue. Speak in character as fully as you can.

d. Ask students to think of other things the figure might say or do in relation to the issue.

3. Ask for several volunteers to choose a different figure from the brainstorm list and to role-play their figure's advice, response, and opinions about another issue on the list.

4. Explain to students that they will do the same thing with characters from literature in the lesson.

Teach

The advisory council game provides an opportunity for students to use a wide range of their interpersonal knowing capacities to learn more about literature and to discover some of the wisdom of the past that can help them with their lives today.

Students should choose a character with whom they are familiar and with whom they already have a certain degree of identification. If more than one student has chosen a particular character, you may want them to sit together as a group, or you may want them to choose certain times or periods of the character's life to represent. In the choosing process they begin to establish an interpersonal linkage with their character. They then present themselves to the rest of the class in character. This presentation adds two other intelligences—visual/spatial when students actively imagine themselves as their character and bodily/kinesthetic when students make gestures or physical movements like the character would.

By having to become another person and give advice they imagine this person would give, students gain both a deeper appreciation of their character and a sense of personal connection to the past.

By posing a modern-day problem to the advisory council you are helping students to integrate their knowledge about their character (and the story or play they represent) with their own lives. In this process, students experience the fact that there are usually multiple perspectives on a given problem. Try to encourage the council members to occasionally talk among themselves, challenging each other, disagreeing, and arguing. However, do not let them get off on tangents and lose the focus of the discussion.

1. Pass out a large index card and marking pen to each student. Individually, they are to think of a character they have studied in literature whom they feel they know fairly well and can identify with in some way. (Note: You may have to prime the pump by reminding them of some of the stories or plays you have studied and help them think of some of the characters they have encountered.)

2. When they have chosen their characters, have them write the character's name on the index card so that everyone else can see. Distribute tape and instruct them to tape the name of their character to their chest. (Or, have them fold their card so it stands up on the desk in front of them.)

3. Now give them a moment to figure out how to introduce themselves in character to the rest of the class (e.g., My name is Pip, and I am filled with many great expectations for the future.). When they are ready, proceed around the circle with each student introducing him- or herself in character.

4. Explain that students will play a game in which they pretend that this group of characters is an advisory council trying to help someone solve a problem. Ask for a volunteer to be the advisee in the game.

5. Have the advisee name a real problem or issue that he or she is facing now that he or she would be willing to share with the class. Have him or her briefly tell the class what the issue is.

6. Now have the advisee ask the advisory council questions that relate to the issue or problem on which they need counsel. The advisee addresses the character by the name on the card, and the student behind the card responds as if they were their chosen character. (Note: Play the role of the moderator in this discussion, making sure that the students take turns and that all have a chance to participate. Keep it lively, and encourage the characters of the council to talk or argue with each other about the advice they are giving. The key is to help students stay in character as they speak.)

7. Conclude by going around the circle again with each member of the council having a chance to say a final word to the advisee. Then have the advisee tell the council what advice was helpful. Have everyone shake hands with each other and say, "It was good to see you again," etc.

8. Bring the game to a close by having students take off the character cards, come out of character, and talk about the process.

Transfer

The goal of the transfer part of the lesson is to help students take what they have learned in the lesson and apply it to other areas of their schoolwork and their everyday lives outside of school.

There are two dynamics of transfer that occur at this point: (1) students speak about what they learned about their character and/or the story or play in which the character appears, thus appropriating the content of the lesson; and (2) they list characters from literature they think could help them gain fresh perspectives on their own lives. They think about the possibility for further experimentation with the advisory council, thus making connections between the lesson and life beyond the classroom.

1. Ask the class the following questions as a way to process the game:

   - What words of advice or comments do you remember?
   - What did you like about the exercise? dislike?
   - What was easy about the exercise? difficult?

2. Have students brainstorm a list of people they would like to have on their own personal advisory council and explain why they would choose them.

3. Ask students to individually write down situations in which they would use their council. What would be the most effective use of the council?

SPIRAL ADAPTATIONS OF THE LESSON

Elementary School Level

1. Focus the lesson on understanding characters from a story students have just read. What kind of characters are they? What do they like? How do they feel? Do you like them? Why or why not?

2. Practice role-playing conversations between different characters in the context of the story. Extend the story and see how characters relate and react in new situations.

3. Pretend the story characters are present in our world today. Role-play what it might be like if certain characters were the teacher of this class, what they would be like as a member of the family, and what it would be like if they were the student's best friend.

Secondary School Level

1. Focus the lesson on analyzing different characters and what they bring to the story or play. For example, they may represent certain motifs, different virtues (such as in a morality play), or various factors of the human condition (such as in a Shakespearean play).

2. Teach students how to create mind maps (see Glossary, p. 217) that show all the different aspects of a character that they can think of.

3. Create a mock UN Security Council meeting with students playing the council members as if they were one of the characters they mind-mapped. Discuss such things as how to improve the plight of Third World countries, how to deal with an aggressor nation that violates the sovereignty of another, or how to protect the world's natural resources.

TECHNOLOGY TIPS

1. Encourage students to conduct an Internet or e-mail survey to find out what types of literature are important in different parts of the world.

2. Help students set up an intranet or Internet chat room that focuses on themes from a favorite piece of literature and how these themes inform our lives today.

3. Create an instant messaging game. Ask students to assume the persona of a character from literature and use the persona in the game.

ASSESSMENT TIPS

PORTFOLIOS

1. Have students include the card that lists their character's name and their character's key traits.

2. Ask students to write a brief paragraph on what they learned from their character and the story in which the character appears.

JOURNALS

1. Prompt students to include the brainstorm list they made on the characters for their own advisory council.

2. Challenge students to add notes from the discussion on when and how to most effectively use their advisory council.

Look to the Past . . .

Rethink a lesson you have completed recently. How would you restructure it to teach *for* and *with* interpersonal intelligence?

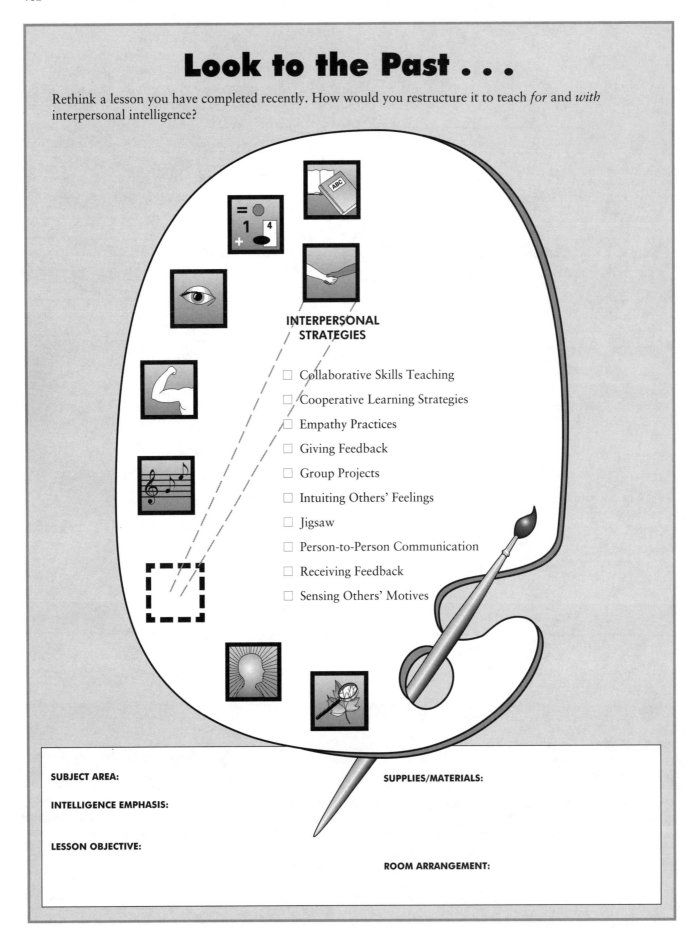

INTERPERSONAL STRATEGIES

- ☐ Collaborative Skills Teaching
- ☐ Cooperative Learning Strategies
- ☐ Empathy Practices
- ☐ Giving Feedback
- ☐ Group Projects
- ☐ Intuiting Others' Feelings
- ☐ Jigsaw
- ☐ Person-to-Person Communication
- ☐ Receiving Feedback
- ☐ Sensing Others' Motives

SUBJECT AREA:

INTELLIGENCE EMPHASIS:

LESSON OBJECTIVE:

SUPPLIES/MATERIALS:

ROOM ARRANGEMENT:

Look to the Future . . .

Think about a lesson you have coming up in the near future. How would you structure it to teach *for* and *with* interpersonal intelligence?

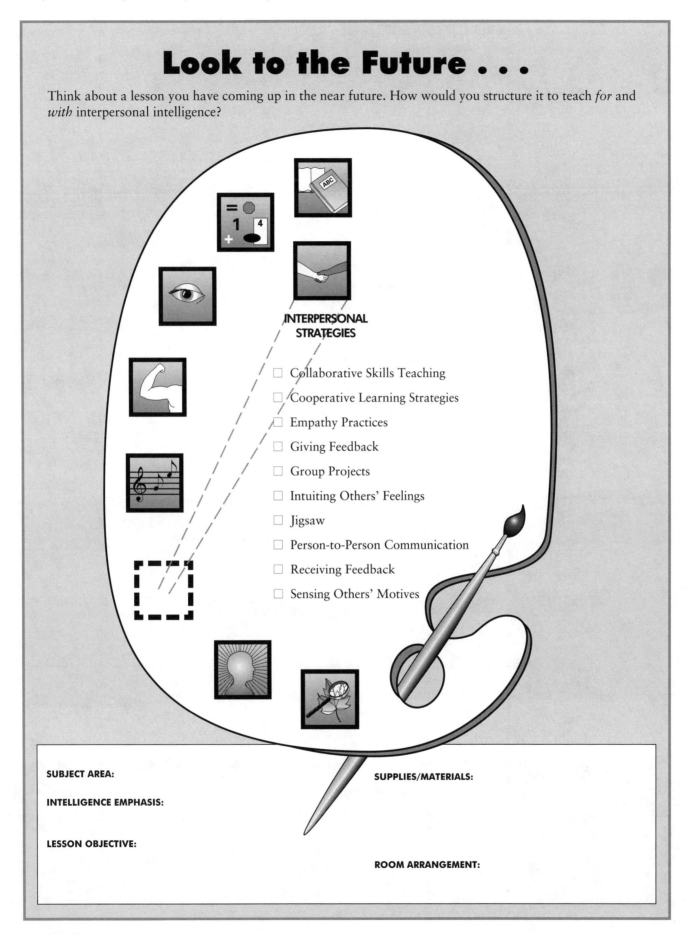

INTERPERSONAL STRATEGIES

☐ Collaborative Skills Teaching

☐ Cooperative Learning Strategies

☐ Empathy Practices

☐ Giving Feedback

☐ Group Projects

☐ Intuiting Others' Feelings

☐ Jigsaw

☐ Person-to-Person Communication

☐ Receiving Feedback

☐ Sensing Others' Motives

SUBJECT AREA:

INTELLIGENCE EMPHASIS:

LESSON OBJECTIVE:

SUPPLIES/MATERIALS:

ROOM ARRANGEMENT:

LESSON PLANNING IDEAS
Interpersonal

HISTORY	MATHEMATICS	LANGUAGE ARTS	SCIENCE & HEALTH	GLOBAL STUDIES & GEOGRAPHY	FAMILY/CONSUMER SCIENCES, INDUSTRIAL TECHNOLOGY, & PE	FINE ARTS
Do an historical period investigation jigsaw*	Solve complex story problems in a group	Experiment with joint story writing—one starts then passes it on	Discuss Saying No to Drugs and create Say No strategies	Assume the perspective of another culture and discuss a news item	Teach and play a series of noncompetitive games**	Learn a new dance and teach it to others
Role-play a conversation with an important historical figure	Do a statistical research project and calculate percentages	Analyze a story and describe its message—reach a consensus	Assign group research projects—groups design and implement plans	Find the relation of geography or climate to cultural values and customs	Assign teams to prepare and serve meals from foreign countries	Create a cooperative team sculpture from clay
Pass over** into the lives of historical people and describe their feelings or thoughts	Each One Teach One** new math processes or operations	Use a human graph** to see where a group stands on an issue	Use lab teams for science experiments and exercises	Create scenarios of culture shock and analyze it for its causes	Use peer coaching teams** for individual shop projects	Sketch your partner with different expressions
Make a case for different perspectives on the Revolutionary War	Describe *everything* you do to solve a problem with a partner	Read poetry from different perspectives and in different moods	Discuss controversial health topics and write team position papers	Brainstorm and prioritize ways to overcome "ugly Americanism"**	Have students work in pairs to learn and improve sports skills	Practice Stop the Action and Improvise** with a play
Discuss the impact of key historical decisions on today's world	Have teams construct problems linking many math operations, then solve them	Conduct language drill exercises with a partner	Describe the before and after of key scientific paradigm shifts	Learn to read different kinds of maps, then teach someone how to understand them	Create cooperative computing teams to learn computer skills	Learn to sing rounds and countermelody** songs

* See Glossary and appendix C

** See Glossary

TEACHING WITH

Intrapersonal Intelligence

How Am I Involved and What Can I Do?

A Current Events Lesson

SECONDARY SCHOOL LEVEL

The Lesson Palette

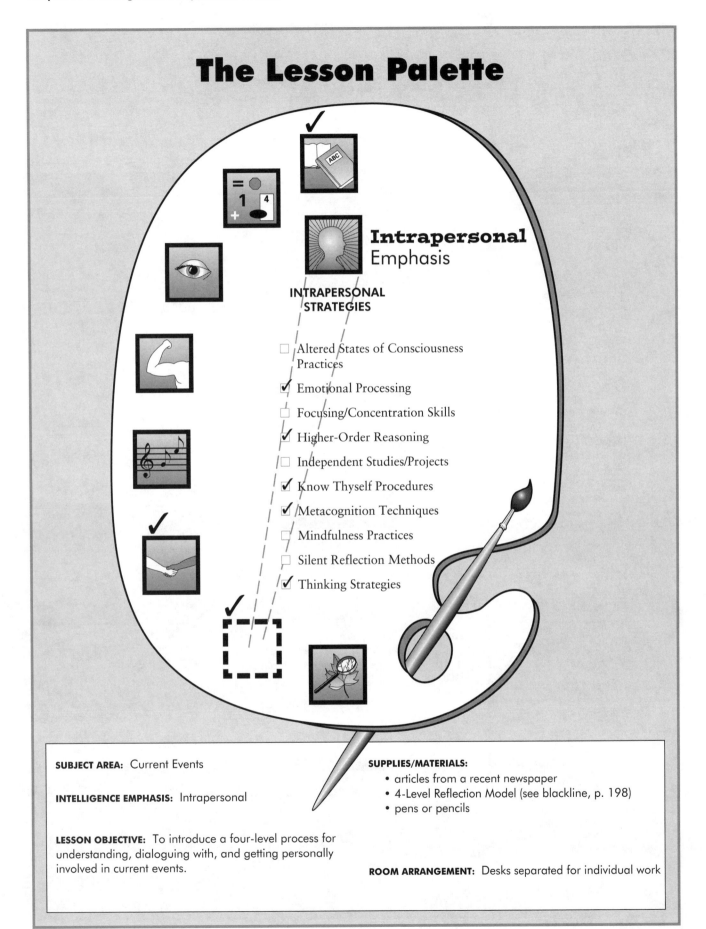

Intrapersonal Emphasis

INTRAPERSONAL STRATEGIES

- ☐ Altered States of Consciousness Practices
- ☑ Emotional Processing
- ☐ Focusing/Concentration Skills
- ☑ Higher-Order Reasoning
- ☐ Independent Studies/Projects
- ☑ Know Thyself Procedures
- ☑ Metacognition Techniques
- ☐ Mindfulness Practices
- ☐ Silent Reflection Methods
- ☑ Thinking Strategies

SUBJECT AREA: Current Events

INTELLIGENCE EMPHASIS: Intrapersonal

LESSON OBJECTIVE: To introduce a four-level process for understanding, dialoguing with, and getting personally involved in current events.

SUPPLIES/MATERIALS:
- articles from a recent newspaper
- 4-Level Reflection Model (see blackline, p. 198)
- pens or pencils

ROOM ARRANGEMENT: Desks separated for individual work

THE LESSON . . .

STAGE I
AWAKEN

Awaken intrapersonal intelligence by creating situations that cause introspection and require knowledge of internal aspects of the self, such as awareness of feelings, thinking processes, self-reflection, spirituality, or situations that simply raise the question Who am I?

INTRAPERSONAL

INTELLIGENCE

STAGE III
TEACH

Teach for and with intrapersonal intelligence by using the specific tools of this intelligence and applying them to help learn the content, acquire specific knowledge, and achieve the lesson's goals and/or objectives.

STAGE IV
TRANSFER

Transfer intrapersonal intelligence to life by discussing the intelligence tools used, finding applications beyond the lesson to other curriculum areas, and finally integrating it into the task of living in the world outside of the classroom.

Amplify intrapersonal intelligence and practice metacognition by using higher-order critical and creative thinking processes, the skills of focusing and centering the mind, mindfulness exercises, and self-conscious emotional or affective processing techniques.

AMPLIFY
STAGE II

The Model

...AT A GLANCE

STAGE I
AWAKEN

- Lesson Introduction: Learn about the self in dialogue with current events.
- Initiate the lesson with several Who Am I? games.
- Conduct a structured conversation on What is the most important thing in your life right now?

INTRAPERSONAL

INTELLIGENCE

STAGE III
TEACH

- Partners discuss news items.
- Students write about the news item (4-level worksheet).
- Students share thoughts with partners.

STAGE IV
TRANSFER

- Reflect on using the 4-level model.
- Share team insights about news items.
- Reflect on when the 4-level model would be helpful.

- Brainstorm a list of recent things that have happened to students.
- Introduce students to the 4-Level Reflection Model with a teacher example.
- Students turn to a neighbor and discuss an experience using the 4-level model.

AMPLIFY
STAGE II

The Model *Applied*

How Am I Involved
and What Can I Do?

Intrapersonal Intelligence

Lesson Procedures

INTRODUCTION

I like to call intrapersonal intelligence the introspective intelligence for it involves awareness about the self and feelings. Interpersonal intelligence looks outward and knows in and through relationships with others—it is the person-to-person way of knowing. Intrapersonal intelligence, on the other hand, looks inward and knows in and through investigating the self. As with interpersonal intelligence, intrapersonal intelligence needs all the other intelligences to express itself, and thus it is an integrator and synthesizer of the other ways of knowing.

There is an ancient saying that goes, No person is an island entire in itself; every person is a piece of the continent, a part of the main. The truth of this is very evident in our world today—what happens in even one small corner of the world affects us all. In this current events lesson, students will be dialoguing with current events from around the world. The process of the lesson will lead them to various levels of self-discovery as they begin to see their connection to, and involvement in, these events. Inform students that they will be using their intrapersonal intelligence in the lesson and ask them to observe what this is like and what happens.

This lesson uses verbal/linguistic and interpersonal intelligences in addition to intrapersonal intelligence. Verbal/linguistic intelligence tools are employed when students read and discuss the news article. The interpersonal intelligence includes participating in cooperative groups and students listening to each other and effectively communicating their own feelings and points of view.

STAGE I

Awaken

Intrapersonal intelligence is awakened when we are in a situation that requires knowledge of the internal aspects of the self, such as our emotional state, thinking patterns, intuitions, creativity processes, and spiritual values or beliefs.

1. Tell the students to pretend they can travel twenty years into the future and ask, "What are you doing with your life?" Go around half of the class, asking each student to answer the question.

These questions are designed to get students to look within themselves and begin to raise questions such as Who am I? and What am I about? In essence these questions help them reflect on a reflection about another reflection! When you see this happening and hear them reflecting deeply about their own lives, you know that intrapersonal intelligence has indeed been activated.

- Ask the class to reflect on what they heard. Prompt students to make up summary statements or observations about their answers to this question.

2. Now go around the other half of the class and ask, "What's the most important thing in your life right now?"

3. Once again ask the class to reflect on what they heard. Prompt students to make up summary statements or observations about their answers to the question.

STAGE II

Amplify

Working with intrapersonal intelligence is especially difficult in our culture given our attitudes about introspection. On the one hand, we are often like a bunch of Mad Hatters rushing about because we are "late, late for a very important date." Our lives are so full of things that must be done, we often feel there is no time to stop and go inside ourselves. Thus we do not learn the specific skills of self-reflection and self-awareness. Furthermore, we carry with us a certain fear of what we might find if we look too deeply within. Some of this probably stems from popular images of the subconscious parts of our personality. These ideas about the subconscious have been fed by our impressions that Freudian analysis opens deep, dark closets full of terrible secrets and repressed problems from our childhood. We relate to the subconscious as something that is better left alone for it can open a Pandora's box!

In spite of all this bad press, researchers today are discovering that far from something to be feared, the inner worlds of the self are a vast storehouse of untapped potentials that are available to us if we learn the methods and techniques of accessing their riches. And the good news is the methods and techniques do exist and you do not have to be a spiritual guru or a neurological sophisticate to learn them!

1. Tell the class that in this lesson they will have an opportunity to think about the daily news and how it affects their lives as well as how their lives affect the daily news.

2. Pass out two 4-Level Reflection Model worksheets to each student (see blackline, p. 198). Put the following questions from the model on the board or overhead and briefly explain the model to students:

How am I involved? Where and how does the issue or concern touch my life? How does it make me feel? What are my thoughts and opinions about it?

PMI (pluses, minuses, interesting; see Glossary). What are the pluses of the issue (positive things about it)? What are its minuses (negative aspects)? What do I find interesting about the issue?

My brainstorm of what could or should be done. If I was totally, completely, unconditionally in charge, what would I do? What do I think needs to happen in this situation? What action(s) should be taken?

What I can do now? What steps could I take now (even if they seem very small and inconsequential) to bring about a resolution to this issue? (For example, I can recycle to do my small part to save the environment.)

Explain that this model can help you think about an event on different levels.

3. Have each student write down three to five things they are struggling with in their life at the present moment. These items can be from school, family, church, friends, etc.

4. Explain that students will have a chance to talk about one of their issues with a partner using the 4-Level Reflection Model. Then, after they practice using the model, they will have an opportunity to apply it to current events in the world. Give them an example of an issue from your own life. (An example follows.)

When you, as the teacher, model how to do something for the students, try to simulate as closely as possible the operation or exercise they will be performing later in the content part of the lesson. However, in the practice itself, use familiar content so that students can give their attention to learning the skill you are teaching and not worry about getting some information they will need for a test later on.

EXAMPLE

Issue: Daughter's College Education

I. How am I involved?

- I want her to go to college.

- I think a year off between high school and college might be helpful to her.

- It is going to cost me a bundle.

- It makes me feel old. (It seems that just yesterday she was entering elementary school!)

II. PMI

Pluses (of college)

- Sets her up for a higher salary when she enters the workplace.

- It brings about a maturing and sense of responsibility for one's own life.

- Tight finances will force her to have a job to help pay.

Minuses (of college)

- She is not diligent with her high school studies and college is much more demanding.

- We have tight finances; therefore she may not be able to pick the school she wants most.

- Tight finances will force her to have a job to help pay.

Interesting

- If she took a year off between high school and college, she might be more ready for college.

- She is very interested in drama and other cultures.

III. What could or should be done?

- If I was in charge I'd put her in a school that uses cooperative learning extensively.

- I should be working more with her on her studies—helping her learn study methods for greater lesson success.

IV. What now?

- We can start gathering information about different schools and costs.

- We can explore work-study programs which provide time in the real world.

- We can brainstorm job possibilities that utilize drama and multicultural interests.

When the students are practicing using the 4-level reflection sheet with each other, it is important that you carefully monitor and observe their discussions to ensure that they are using the model and that they are staying on task. One way to do this is to have each person take notes as the other is speaking and then give those notes to his or her partner. This will also help students track and focus their reflections on the 4-level model.

Working with a partner activates interpersonal intelligence skills. The sharing and discussion between them calls forth verbal/linguistic capacities.

5. Now have students turn to a partner and each take one of their issues through the 4-level reflection process. Be sure to instruct them to listen to each other and ask that they not make wisecracks while the other is speaking.

6. After both partners have had a chance to share their issue using the 4-level process, stop and briefly reflect with the whole class using questions such as the following:

- What was this like for you? What happened?

- What did you you notice about the different levels? How did they make you feel?

- What happened to your issue as you discussed it using these four levels?

- What questions do you have about using this model?

Teach

STAGE III

Once students understand how to use the 4-Level Reflection Model, they can apply it to academic content.

This task again uses interpersonal intelligence skills to help students understand the item, necessary background information, and its relevance and importance. They also use interpersonal skills to discuss initial feelings and thoughts about the item.

In this time of sharing, students often learn a great deal from each other and about themselves. They begin to notice similarities and differences between themselves and their fellow students. They begin to develop a sense of security and/or confidence about their own thoughts, opinions, and ideas. As they share, also encourage them to steal any good ideas or thoughts from each other and add these to their own reflections. This can help them understand that our so-called self-identity is really a combination of what goes on inside and what we experience in the outside world.

It is important for them to write something for all four levels, even if they are not sure about what they are writing. Encourage them to trust their intuitions and record whatever pops into their head without evaluating it too much at this point. Some students may want to draw diagrams, pictures, or symbols to express their feelings. Others may want to write poetry or even turn their thoughts into a very short story. Anything they want to do is fine as long as they can demonstrate to you that they are in fact reflecting on all four levels of the model.

1. Tell students that they are now going to use the 4-level reflection process to have discussions with each other about the previous evening's news. Remind them that in thinking about and dialoguing with the news they can often gain a much deeper appreciation for what is going on in our world.

2. Now have students select a new partner, different from the person they talked with in the practice conversation. Pass around a hat with news articles from the previous day's paper in it. Each pair is to select one news article from the hat.

3. Give the pairs an opportunity to read and understand the article together. When they have completed the reading, ask them to discuss it using questions such as the following:

- What are the main points of the article? Who is involved?

- What do we know about the background or history of this article?

- What are the main issues or points of view?

- How do I feel about this? What are my thoughts and opinions?

4. When the partners have had time to discuss the article with each other, instruct them to turn to their second 4-level reflection worksheet and to work individually, writing answers to the questions on the sheet. They must have something for each level of the reflection to succeed in this lesson, so watch carefully and give assistance to any students who seem to be having trouble.

5. When you notice that most students have completed the assignment, have them turn to their partner again and each share answers to the questions on the 4-level reflection worksheet. If time permits, have one pair join another pair and share their reflections on their article.

STAGE IV

Transfer

The goal of the transfer part of the lesson is to help students take what they have learned in the lesson and apply it in other areas of their schoolwork and in their everyday lives outside of school.

Two things take place in these reflections. They, first of all, discuss the pros and cons of the 4-level model and think about how to use it beyond this lesson and the classroom environment. This is an important transfer or bridging of the learning strategy. Second, they discuss insights and thoughts that the study of the news provoked. This dimension of reflection helps students learn to become thinkers rather than simply digesters of information.

1. Reflect with the whole class on the use of the 4-level model to discuss the news. Ask questions like the following:

   • What did you find interesting about approaching the news in this way?

   • Which level was the easiest? hardest?

   • What do you like about this model? dislike?

2. Make a brainstorm list on the board or overhead of other times students think the 4-level process could be helpful to them.

3. Now have each pair share with the rest of the class an insight or thought they had about the news as they talked together about it in this manner.

SPIRAL ADAPTATIONS OF THE LESSON

Elementary School Level

1. Focus the lesson on learning to recognize pictures and names of key people in the news today and on being aware of how these people affect us.

2. Teach students to ask questions about what is happening in a story they already know, such as the "Three Little Pigs," "Goldilocks," etc. Have them make up questions they would ask the characters or a message they would give to the characters, if this were possible.

3. Show students pictures of key people in the news and tell a brief story about why they are in the news. Have students pretend they can ask the people questions or that they can give them a message—What would they say?

Middle School Level

1. Focus the lesson on listening to the evening news and understanding what is going on (including key people, places, and events).

2. Lead students to practice listening to a prerecorded curriculum event in the classroom from the previous day. Ask them to recognize who was speaking, remember what they said, and recall what was going on in the classroom. Have students tell about how they feel and what they think about the tape.

3. Show students a video segment of the evening news from the night before. Recall people, places, and events with the class. Then have students write a letter to one of the people telling their feelings about what was reported on the news.

TECHNOLOGY TIPS

1. Encourage students to gather information from Internet sources related to their topic. Ask them to create an electronic dialogue (e.g., via word processing) of their reflections on the information.

2. Tell students to use multimedia (e.g., digital camera, camcorder, presentation software, etc.) to create a report on how their news issue personally impacts them.

3. Ask students to use electronic brainstorming software to formulate as many solutions as they can for the problems or challenges they found in their news items.

ASSESSMENT TIPS

PORTFOLIOS

1. Ask students to include their written responses to the news on the 4-Level Reflection Model.

2. Prompt students to keep a copy of the news article and any notes they made as they discussed it with their partner.

JOURNALS

1. Have students do a PMI on using the 4-level model.

2. Ask students to choose three different situations from the brainstorm list (step #2 of the transfer section) where they think the 4-level model can help them. Have them write a few lines about how to adapt it for their own needs.

Look to the Past . . .

Rethink a lesson you have completed recently. How would you restructure it to teach *for* and *with* intrapersonal intelligence?

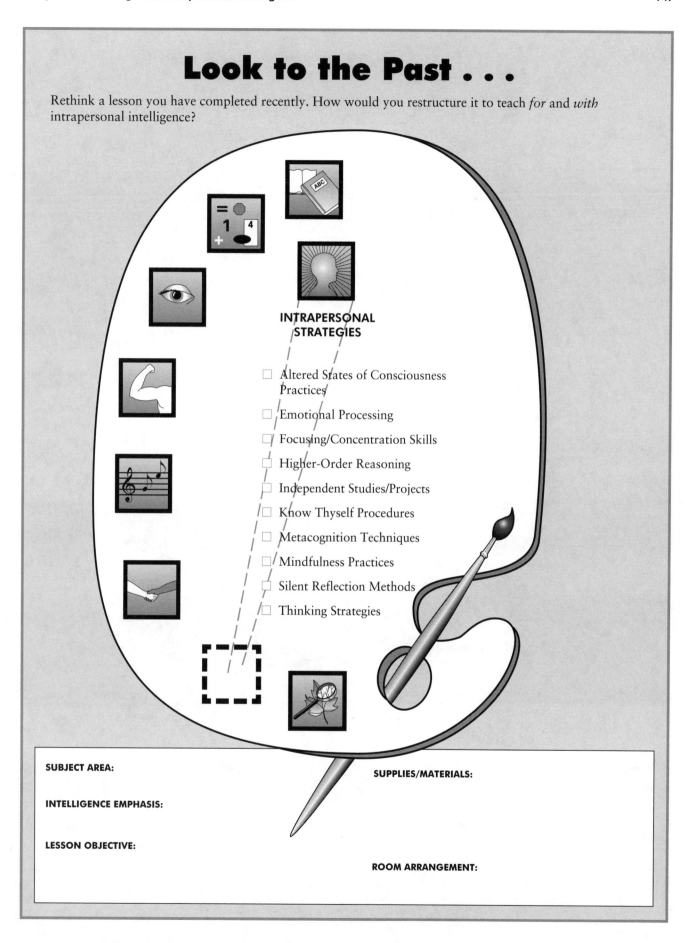

INTRAPERSONAL STRATEGIES

- ☐ Altered States of Consciousness Practices
- ☐ Emotional Processing
- ☐ Focusing/Concentration Skills
- ☐ Higher-Order Reasoning
- ☐ Independent Studies/Projects
- ☐ Know Thyself Procedures
- ☐ Metacognition Techniques
- ☐ Mindfulness Practices
- ☐ Silent Reflection Methods
- ☐ Thinking Strategies

SUBJECT AREA:

INTELLIGENCE EMPHASIS:

LESSON OBJECTIVE:

SUPPLIES/MATERIALS:

ROOM ARRANGEMENT:

Look to the Future . . .

Think about a lesson you have coming up in the near future. How would you structure it to teach *for* and *with* intrapersonal intelligence?

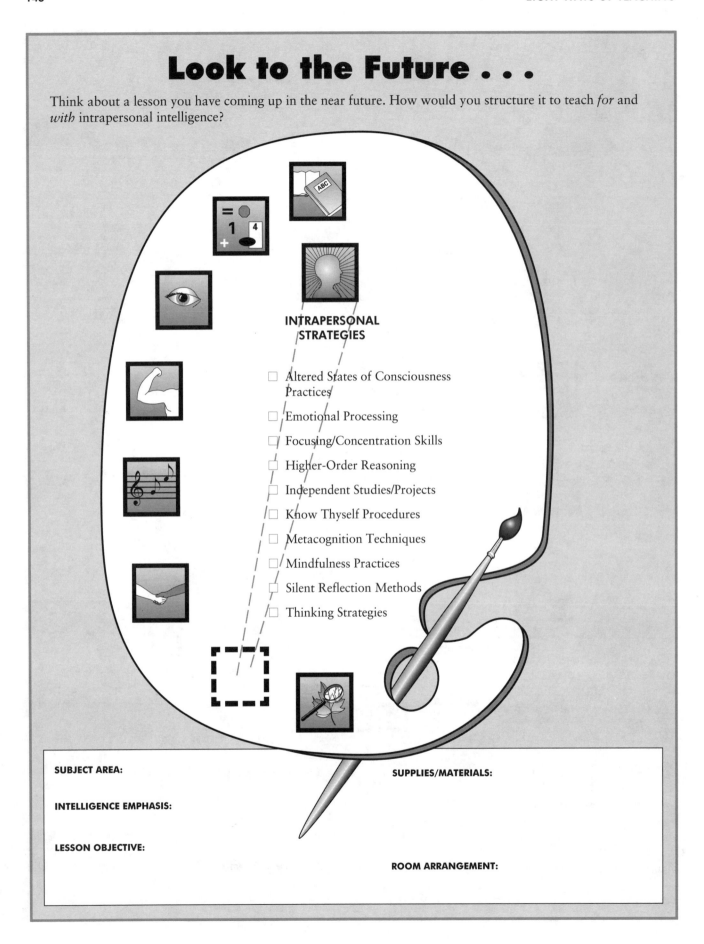

INTRAPERSONAL STRATEGIES

- ☐ Altered States of Consciousness Practices
- ☐ Emotional Processing
- ☐ Focusing/Concentration Skills
- ☐ Higher-Order Reasoning
- ☐ Independent Studies/Projects
- ☐ Know Thyself Procedures
- ☐ Metacognition Techniques
- ☐ Mindfulness Practices
- ☐ Silent Reflection Methods
- ☐ Thinking Strategies

SUBJECT AREA:

INTELLIGENCE EMPHASIS:

LESSON OBJECTIVE:

SUPPLIES/MATERIALS:

ROOM ARRANGEMENT:

LESSON PLANNING IDEAS
Intrapersonal

HISTORY	MATHEMATICS	LANGUAGE ARTS	SCIENCE & HEALTH	GLOBAL STUDIES & GEOGRAPHY	FAMILY/CONSUMER SCIENCES, INDUSTRIAL TECHNOLOGY, & PE	FINE ARTS
Keep a journal about questions from your life that history might be able to answer	Track thinking patterns for different math problems	Write an autobiographical essay entitled My Life to Date	Design, implement, and evaluate a one-month Be Healthy project	Try awareness techniques** from other cultures	Discuss how different physical exercises make you feel	Draw yourself from different angles in a mirror
Do a PMI* analysis of famous historical decisions	Bridge math concepts beyond school using What? So What? Now What?*	Write an autobiographical essay entitled My Life in the Future	Conduct silent reflections on pictures of the solar system	List criteria of your ideal geography or climate and find it on a map	List how things learned in shop can help in your future life	Dance the different stages of your life's journey
Discuss this question: If I could be any historical figure who would I be and why?	Use guided imagery** to see complex story problems	Analyze literature for connections to our lives today	Write about If I could be any animal what would I be and why?	Discuss this question: How would I be different if I had grown up in another culture?	Write down and analyze conversations using a computer	Create a series of sculptures to express your moods
Write an essay on mistakes from the past that you will not repeat	Evaluate your strengths and weaknesses in understanding math	Write a new poem each day for a week answering the question Who am I?	Lead a series of I Become What I Behold** exercises	Learn focusing techniques** and see how each culture uses them	Watch yourself fix a meal and note everything that goes on	Imagine yourself as each character in a play
Imagine people from the past giving advice for living today	Watch mood changes as you do math problems and note causes	Imagine being a character in a story or play—What would you do?	Practice techniques for achieving deep relaxation** (e.g., breathing)	Keep a feelings diary as you read about current events	Imagine a skill and then try to do it exactly as you imagined	Carefully observe the effects of music on you

* See Glossary and appendix C
** See Glossary

TEACHING WITH

Naturalist Intelligence

THE EVOCATIVE POWER OF NATURE FOR WRITING

A Language Arts Lesson

SECONDARY SCHOOL LEVEL

The Lesson Palette

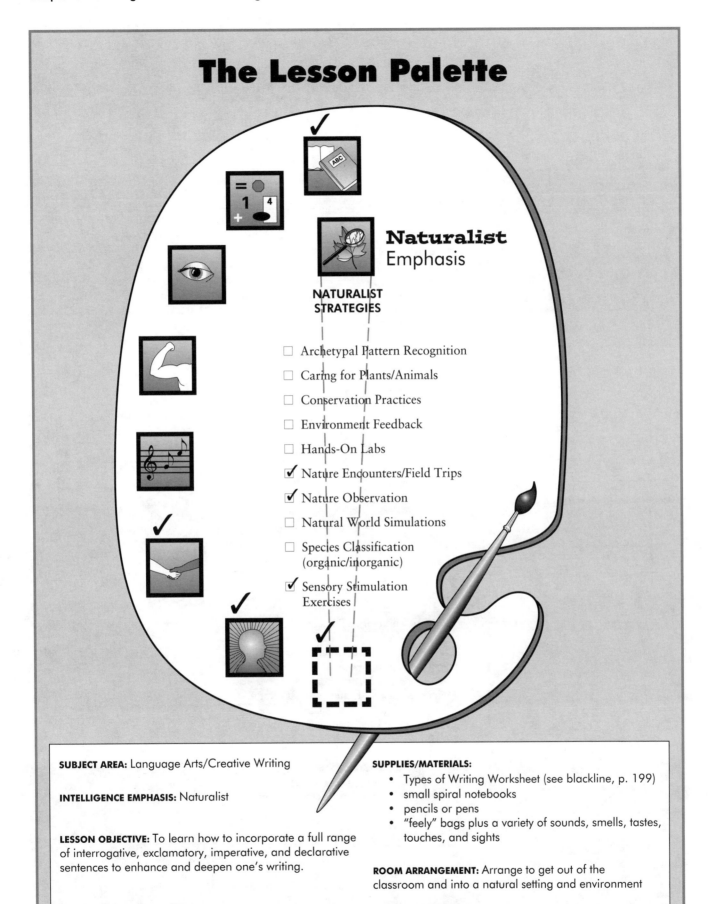

Naturalist Emphasis

NATURALIST STRATEGIES

- ☐ Archetypal Pattern Recognition
- ☐ Caring for Plants/Animals
- ☐ Conservation Practices
- ☐ Environment Feedback
- ☐ Hands-On Labs
- ☑ Nature Encounters/Field Trips
- ☑ Nature Observation
- ☐ Natural World Simulations
- ☐ Species Classification (organic/inorganic)
- ☑ Sensory Stimulation Exercises

SUBJECT AREA: Language Arts/Creative Writing

INTELLIGENCE EMPHASIS: Naturalist

LESSON OBJECTIVE: To learn how to incorporate a full range of interrogative, exclamatory, imperative, and declarative sentences to enhance and deepen one's writing.

SUPPLIES/MATERIALS:
- Types of Writing Worksheet (see blackline, p. 199)
- small spiral notebooks
- pencils or pens
- "feely" bags plus a variety of sounds, smells, tastes, touches, and sights

ROOM ARRANGEMENT: Arrange to get out of the classroom and into a natural setting and environment

THE LESSON . . .

STAGE I
AWAKEN

Awaken naturalist intelligence by immersing the self in the full sensory experience of the natural world including plants, animals, weather conditions, water, forests, inorganic matter, etc., from the microscopic world to what can be perceived with the naked eye, the sense of taste, touch, smell, sound, and the inner senses of the human spirit (e.g., being moved and touched by nature).

NATURALIST

INTELLIGENCE

Transfer naturalist intelligence to life by discussing the intelligence tools employed, finding applications for the intelligence and the content beyond the lesson or unit to other curricular areas, and finally integrating it into the task of living in the world outside of the classroom.

STAGE IV
TRANSFER

Teach for and with naturalist intelligence by using the specific tools of this intelligence and applying them to help learn the content, acquire specific knowledge, and achieve the lesson's goals and/or objectives.

STAGE III
TEACH

Amplify naturalist intelligence through practice recognizing members of a species (organic and inorganic), learning to distinguish differences among members of the same species, and understanding other neighboring species (who are similar but different). The naturalist intelligence is also enhanced in and through regular interactions with nature such as caring for or taming animals or growing and nurturing plants.

AMPLIFY
STAGE II

The Model

. . . AT A GLANCE

STAGE I
AWAKEN

- Lesson Introduction: Creative writing through encounters with nature.
- The teacher passes around several "feely" bags containing objects from nature.
- The students cannot look in the bags—only touch what is in them.
- The students guess what the object is.

NATURALIST

INTELLIGENCE

STAGE III
TEACH

- The teacher introduces the Types of Writing Worksheet to the students.
- Students go outside to a natural setting and fully experience all that it has to offer using the five senses.
- Students write about their experience using the basic types of writing.

STAGE IV
TRANSFER

- Reflect on the experience and process of being evoked by nature and trying to write about the experience.
- Reflect on the four types of writing.
- Reflect on where else the four types of sentences can be (and *are*) used beyond school.

AMPLIFY
STAGE II

- Teacher exposes students (who have their eyes closed) to a variety of sounds, smells, tastes, and touches.
- Students talk with partners about what was evoked by the experience (e.g., thoughts, associations, images, colors, other people, etc.).
- As one partner speaks, the other records what he or she is saying.

The Model *Applied*

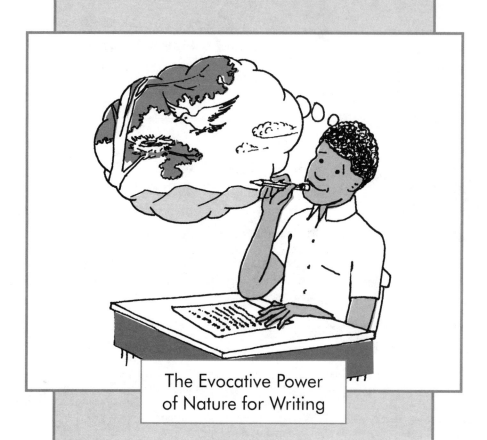

The Evocative Power
of Nature for Writing

A Language Arts Lesson with

Naturalist Intelligence

Lesson Procedures

INTRODUCTION

The natural world is full of innumerable things that can evoke the full range of our five senses as well as inner feelings, intuitions, memories, spiritual insight, and a profound sense of connectedness and unity. In this lesson students spend time in nature, allowing these things to be evoked within themselves. They then use this experience as a springboard to creative writing. The lesson focuses on incorporating the five foundational kinds of writing (declarative, interrogative, exclamatory, and descriptive) into students' creative writing. They will focus on using their naturalist intelligence to help them deepen and enrich their writing.

In addition to the naturalist intelligence, verbal/linguistic intelligence shares a secondary focus in this lesson—students will actually be writing about their experiences in nature. Throughout the lesson they will also work with a partner, so interpersonal intelligence is involved as well. Intrapersonal intelligence gets into the act, as students are asked to become introspective and be aware of nature's impact on them via the traditional five senses, but also how nature affects the inner world of the self.

The realm of the naturalist intelligence is the realm of understanding, appreciating, and enjoying the natural world. Persons who exhibit strength in the naturalist intelligence are very much at home in nature. They demonstrate expertise in recognizing and classifying the many different species (both organic and inorganic). Famous people who exemplify the naturalist intelligence include Charles Darwin, Meriwether Lewis and William Clark, James Audubon, and Carolus Linnaeus.

STAGE I

Awaken

The naturalist intelligence is awakened in and through various sensory encounters with the natural world including plants, animals, weather conditions, water, forests, inorganic matter, etc., from the

1. Tell students that since they will be using their naturalist intelligence in the lesson, you are going to spend a few minutes trying to stimulate or trigger the centers in the brain that are involved in

microscopic world to what can be perceived with the naked eye, the sense of taste, touch, smell, sound, and the inner senses of the human spirit (e.g., being moved and touched by nature).

The direct experience of nature tends to catalyze certain neural centers and networks within the human brain. Some researchers believe that certain clusters of cells within our brains are devoted *exclusively* to the recognition, appreciation, and understanding of the natural world as opposed to the world of human creation!

working with this intelligence. Tell students that you have put together several nature "feely" bags that you're going to pass around the room. (Note: Items in the bags could include a rabbit's foot, tree bark, a lump of dirt, a feather, various parts of different kinds of plants, different kinds of rocks, fur, and so on. If you have the time you could also have some "smelly" bags in which you have placed natural objects that have a distinct odor and have students encounter nature via their olfactory senses.)

2. Start passing the bags around the room. Tell students not to look into the bags. Students are to experience what is in the different bags, seeing if they can recognize them; however, they are not to speak this out loud. They are simply to know for themselves.

3. After the bags have been around the whole class, empty the bags so students can see the objects. Have students share with their neighbors what happened to them as they encountered the different objects in the bags: What got awakened or stimulated as a result of this exercise?

4. Ask several groups to share some of their observations and experiences with the whole class.

Amplify

Although the so-called famous naturalists were mentioned earlier, some less famous examples would include almost any preschooler or kindergartner and their fascination with, desire to explore, and compulsion to get dirty *in* and *with* the natural world! As we get older we tend to get further and further away from the firsthand experience with and exploration of the natural world. As we move into adulthood, we frequently spend twenty-four hours a day living and moving and having our being in the proverbial, humanly-created concrete jungle.

Nevertheless, the restimulation and possible recovery of the childhood wonder with nature (and the potential restimulation of our naturalist intelligence) is as close as the nearest natural setting, be it a national or local park, an arboretum, a botanical garden, or even a neighborhood nursery or gardening center.

The purpose of this five senses exercise is to give students a chance to practice a process for activating the senses—the very process they will use later in the lesson to enhance their creative writing.

1. Have each student find a partner that they will work with during the lesson. Remind them that the goal of the lesson is to enhance, expand, and deepen their creative writing by getting in touch with the sensory world. But first let them practice the basic process they will use in the lesson.

2. Have students arrange their chairs so they face in opposite directions but they are seated side-by-side, so that they have easy access to each other's ears for quiet conversation. Each student is to have paper and pencil.

3. Have students decide which one of them is person A; the other is person B. Instruct them to close their eyes (no peeking!). Tell them they are now going to be exposed to a variety of sounds, smells, tastes, touches, and sights.

Person A will record what was evoked (e.g., thoughts, associations, images, colors, other people, memories, etc.) in person B through the sounds, smells, tastes, touches, and sights. Person B will do the same for person A. They will switch back and forth between A and B with one person speaking, sharing what was evoked, and the other person recording what their partner is saying. (Note: The focus is *not* to guess what the sound, smell, etc. is but rather to be aware of the feelings, associations, images, etc. that are evoked.)

4. Proceed quickly through each of the five senses providing an experience first for person A then for person B. Some examples follow:

Sense	Person A	Person B
Sound	xylophone	tapping fingers
Touch	velvet	sandpaper
Smell	sage	perfume
Taste	chocolate	salted nut
Sight	weird object	mirror

After each experience, one partner speaks about his or her associations, feelings, images, memories, colors, etc. that were evoked by the experience. *Without making any comments,* the other partner is simply to record what his or her partner has said.

5. Ask several partners to share with the whole class what happened as they worked with each other: What did you discover about your five senses?

STAGE III

Teach

1. Pass out the Types of Writing Worksheet (see blackline, p. 199). Explain the different types to students and give some examples of the importance of each. Or have them come up with examples of when they use each type in communication with others.

- Declarative writing is a simple statement of fact. (For example, I'll meet you at the corner cafe.)

- Interrogative writing is a statement of a question. (For example, Should we meet at the cafe or elsewhere?)

- Imperative writing is a statement of a command to someone else. (For example, Be at the cafe no later than 11:00 a.m.)

- Exclamatory writing is an emphatic statement or one of exclamation. (For example, We had a fabulous time when we met at the cafe!)

2. Now tell the class they are going to have a chance to work with and incorporate these different types of sentences through an experience with the natural world. Give the class the following directions:

This traditional academic content part of the lesson could either be a review of previously studied information or a lesson to introduce the sentence types as new information. Feel free to utilize textbook information describing the basic sentence types (be they four or forty!).

The whole purpose of taking students outside is to expose them to nature as an evocateur of their creative writing capacities. Within our natural world are vast resources that can touch us deeply and in so doing help us enhance, deepen, and amplify our writing.

If it is impossible to take students outside into nature (which is best to fully activate the naturalist intelligence from a neurological standpoint), you must find some way to bring nature in—whether it be in a video or having actual representations of the natural world present in the classroom (e.g., you may have various nature stations that students visit during the process of the lesson).

Do not let students get too hung up on having a response in every box of the worksheet; however, make sure you encourage them to fill in as many as possible so they will have more to draw on when they get into the creative writing. In their conversations with each other, encourage the partners to stay at the feeling level as it relates to the five senses.

When they are doing their writing remind them to use the information their partner recorded on the worksheet to help them create a juicy piece!

You may point out that this is an exercise in *descriptive* writing.

a. Go outside with your partner to a *natural* spot on which you both agree. (The key is to be in a *natural* setting *not* something made by humans!)

b. As in the practice session earlier, have one partner speak while the other records. Then switch roles.

c. Once you are settled, spend a few minutes in silence just being in this place. Ask yourselves: What am I hearing? What am I smelling? What catches my eyes? What textures do I see or feel?

d. After spending several minutes of just being there, the recorder should ask his or her partner to talk out loud about what he or she is experiencing with the five senses. Record his or her sensory experience in the appropriate place on the worksheet chart and under the appropriate type of sentence. As necessary, use the questions on the worksheet to get your partner to express his or her experience of each sense in the four ways.

(Note: Students may want to focus on one sense at a time with each person speaking in the four ways back and forth and then move on to another. It is not necessary that every single box on the chart be filled. They should just do as many as possible in the given time.)

e. After each partner has completed responding to as many of the questions for the different types of sentences as possible, stop and give the Types of Writing Worksheet to your partner. Read it over, asking the partner for clarification of anything that is not clear.

f. Now take individual time to write about your experience in nature. Use the worksheet as a guide. The goal of the writing is to include sentences that express experiences from the perspective of each of the senses as well as each of the sentence type columns. Use the sensory experience and the sentence type to create an interesting and compelling piece—something that someone else will really want to read!

g. When you have completed your writing, exchange your piece with your partner. Read what your partner has written and, in turn, give feedback using the following starter phrases:

What really grabs my attention in your writing is . . .

As I read your piece I was surprised by . . .

One thing I think you could do to make this a stronger piece is . . .

If you had to give your piece to someone else to read, to whom would you give it and why?

What title would you give your piece?

Transfer

STAGE IV

The goal of the transfer part of the lesson is to help students find the relevance of the lesson for their own lives. Here we are concerned with helping them go beyond the lesson itself, into other curricular areas, and finally into their lives beyond the classroom.

The reflection on the process of being evoked by nature will help students get a better understanding of one aspect of the naturalist intelligence.

The reflection on the writing process is intended to help students see direct connections between this lesson and the use of these four sentence types to enrich their communication (both written and spoken) in all aspects of their lives.

1. Reflect with the students on the experience and process of being evoked by nature and writing about the experience using the following questions:

   - What happened to you as you allowed yourself to be impacted and evoked by nature? What was most interesting about this experience for you?

   - What surprised you? What was exciting?

   - How did this experience help you with your writing? What was most difficult?

   - What did you learn in this process that will help you in the future when you are involved in creative writing?

2. Reflect on the four type of sentences:

   - Which of the four types of sentences do you like the most? Why? Which do you dislike? Why?

   - Where (beyond school) are you aware of these kinds of sentences being used?

   - Where in your life do think the conscious use of these sentences can help you enhance and deepen your verbal and written communication?

SPIRAL ADAPTATIONS OF THE LESSON

Elementary School Level

1. Create a page of faces that show a whole range of possible feelings, such as sad, confused, angry, etc. During the amplifying stage, the partner circles the appropriate face for his or her partner as the partner reacts to the five senses experiences.

2. Keep the lesson on the speaking level rather than writing. Tell the children that when we are talking to each other, there are at least four different ways we talk: we ask questions (interrogative), we tell people what we want them to do (imperative), we explain things (declarative), and we tell about our strong feelings (exclamatory). Show a picture to go with each type.

3. Demonstrate the four ways of speaking and ask the children to point to the appropriate picture. Take the children outside and give them several nature-based scenarios to role play. Have them practice speaking in the four ways as if they were objects in

nature. (For example, speak as the plant that wants some water or as the squirrel that is wondering about how to jump from one tree to the next.)

Middle School Level

1. The awakening and amplifying levels can be used as they are presented in the lesson procedures above.

2. In the teaching part of the lesson, focus the lesson on human relations and human relating. Talk about four things we can do to improve our relating with our friends, parents, and teachers:

   - We can ask questions to make sure we understand.

   - We can tell others what we want them to do.

   - We can carefully explain and describe our own thoughts and feelings.

   - We can express our strong feelings in ways that make others take notice.

3. Take the students outside into a natural environment and present them with a potential environmental problem about the space you have chosen. Have students, in groups of three or four, prepare statements from the four ways of relating that could make a difference and resolve the problem. (For example, What are the key questions that should be asked? What are the things people should do to resolve this problem?)

TECHNOLOGY TIPS

1. Ask students to digitally record the sounds, colors, textures, objects, etc. from the natural setting. Encourage them to show what sounds, objects, etc. evoked their writing.

2. Encourage students to use presentation software to create a multimedia background. Ask students to use the background when they read their writings to the class.

3. Tell students to type their writing into a word processing program and incorporate appropriate clip art, digital photos, sound files, etc. to enhance and deepen the impact of what they have written.

ASSESSMENT TIPS

PORTFOLIOS

1. Prompt students to include all of the notes their partner took on their reflections, both reflections on the five senses exercise, and the Types of Writing Worksheet.

2. Ask students to include the writing they did about their experience of being out in nature.

JOURNALS

1. Challenge students to write which of the four types of sentences they like the most and least and explain why they like or dislike each type.

2. Encourage students to write a brainstorm list of when, where, and how each type of sentence already *is* part of their repertoire and when, where, and how they need to use each type more (or more effectively).

Look to the Past . . .

Rethink a lesson you have completed recently. How would you restructure it to teach *for* and *with* naturalist intelligence?

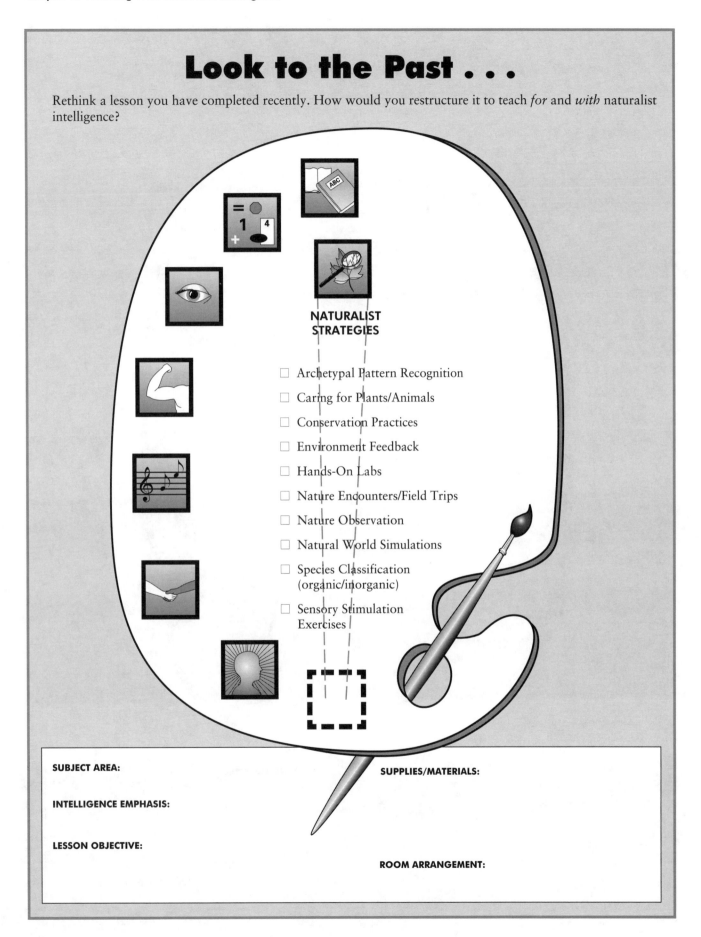

NATURALIST STRATEGIES

- ☐ Archetypal Pattern Recognition
- ☐ Caring for Plants/Animals
- ☐ Conservation Practices
- ☐ Environment Feedback
- ☐ Hands-On Labs
- ☐ Nature Encounters/Field Trips
- ☐ Nature Observation
- ☐ Natural World Simulations
- ☐ Species Classification (organic/inorganic)
- ☐ Sensory Stimulation Exercises

SUBJECT AREA:

INTELLIGENCE EMPHASIS:

LESSON OBJECTIVE:

SUPPLIES/MATERIALS:

ROOM ARRANGEMENT:

Look to the Future . . .

Think about a lesson you have coming up in the near future. How would you structure it to teach *for* and *with* naturalist intelligence?

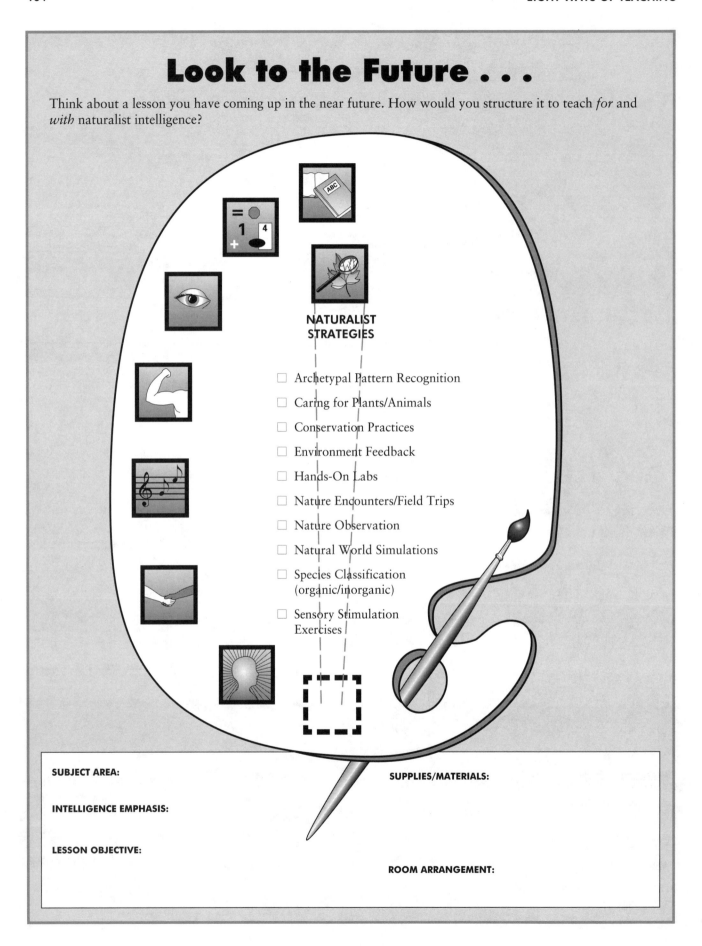

NATURALIST STRATEGIES

- ☐ Archetypal Pattern Recognition
- ☐ Caring for Plants/Animals
- ☐ Conservation Practices
- ☐ Environment Feedback
- ☐ Hands-On Labs
- ☐ Nature Encounters/Field Trips
- ☐ Nature Observation
- ☐ Natural World Simulations
- ☐ Species Classification (organic/inorganic)
- ☐ Sensory Stimulation Exercises

SUBJECT AREA:

INTELLIGENCE EMPHASIS:

LESSON OBJECTIVE:

SUPPLIES/MATERIALS:

ROOM ARRANGEMENT:

LESSON PLANNING IDEAS
Naturalist

HISTORY	MATHEMATICS	LANGUAGE ARTS	SCIENCE & HEALTH	GLOBAL STUDIES & GEOGRAPHY	FAMILY/CONSUMER SCIENCES, INDUSTRIAL TECHNOLOGY, & PE	FINE ARTS
Recognize and interpret historical trends (à la Toynbee)	Work story problems based on or dealing with patterns in nature	Re-create or simulate nature scenes from literature and poetry	Classify different foods for healthy diet planning	Create environmental representations for different cultures	Grow fruits, vegetables, and herbs and use them to prepare a meal	Compose using sounds from nature and the environment
Understand how natural events have influenced history	Use nature manipulatives in math problem solving	Write a poetic or descriptive essay based on nature experiences	Experience past scientific experiments firsthand (Do them!)	Grow and/or taste foods from various cultures	Experience (via field trips) the process of making cloth from natural materials	Recognize and re-create visual images of natural patterns
Create analogies between historical and natural events	Graph positive and negative influences on the environment	Learn and practice using the vocabulary of nature and the naturalist	Keep a diary of the natural processes of your own body	Study the influence of climate and/or geography on cultural development	Create useful objects for the home, classroom, or office using *only* natural products	Create dances that "embody" or demonstrate patterns in nature
Study how animals have affected history and historical trends	Understand the mathematical patterns of nature	Understand influences of climate and/or environment on authors	Use various naturalist taxonomies during nature field trips	Re-create multi-media experiences of the natural environments of different cultures	Play outdoor games that use natural objects and that are based on natural patterns	Design full-blown dramatic enactments of natural processes
Study the lives of famous naturalists and their impact on history	Calculate problems based on nature and natural processes	Write a creative story using animal characters and their characteristics	Use cognitive organizers to explore and understand scientific processes	Study animals, insects, etc. from different parts of the world	Create virtual reality encounters with natural phenomena on a computer	Make montages or collages incorporating natural products

Epilogue

Epilogue

The old Chinese proverb that questions whether it is better to give a man a fish for today or teach him the art of fishing to prepare him for a lifetime applies quite well to the contemporary task of education, and especially at the point of teaching *for, with,* and *about* multiple intelligences. One of the major purposes of school should be to develop as full a range of intellectual capacities in students as possible. The good news about teaching *with* multiple intelligences is that it is not an add-on to an already overfilled curricula. Teaching *with* multiple intelligences can and should be happening every day in and through whatever curricula we are teaching. However, we must keep our attention in the right place; namely, on the development of students' fullest potential as human beings. This includes their ability to perform on various standardized tests that our culture deems an important part of education. However, I believe we can have our cake and eat it too, so to speak. Students will more thoroughly learn the things we are trying to teach if we provide them the opportunity to develop the full range of their intellectual capacities and to use their multiple ways of knowing in the learning task, rather than if we only permit them to learn in the more traditional verbal/linguistic and logical/mathematical ways.

In order to be successful in this endeavor, our teaching *for, with,* and *about* the intelligences must match the pattern of the natural development and growth of the intelligences. Each intelligence begins with what Howard Gardner (1983, 1987) calls *raw patterning ability.* This stage involves the ability to perform certain simple tasks that are foundational to the operation of a given intelligence— learning certain motor skills such as walking, running, and jumping for bodily/kinesthetic intelligence or learning the alphabet and how to speak for verbal/linguistic intelligence. As the child develops, the raw patterning of an intelligence moves to a greater level of complexity in what Gardner calls a *symbol system.* Here the basic skills of an intelligence are combined in more complex patterns in order to give expressions of meaning. For example, the ability to make

SkyLight Professional Development

different tones expresses itself as a melody in musical/rhythmic intelligence or the ability to draw different shapes expresses itself in a picture with color and perspective in visual/spatial intelligence. The next stage of development builds on this symbol system stage and represents itself in what Gardner calls a *notational system*. Each of the intelligences has its own language—a language that can be taught, learned, and transmitted to others. These are things that can be recorded in some form for posterity, such as musical composition and performance (musical/rhythmic intelligence); consensus building and an understanding of group process (interpersonal intelligence); or the conscious use of inductive and deductive thought processes (logical/mathematical intelligence). The final stage of the development of an intelligence is the *vocational or avocational pursuit stage*. The mature expression of intellectual development involves its embodiment in particular career paths of societal service roles such as those mentioned in the introductory chapter to this book.

In terms of the developmental journey of the human being, the raw patterning stage is generally the earliest part of one's childhood (infancy and before school). The symbol system stage is represented by the early years of schooling (preschool, kindergarten, and the first years of elementary school). The notational system stage generally occurs in the late elementary school years, the middle school or junior high years, and early secondary schooling. The vocational or avocational pursuit stage of development can generally be associated with the late secondary and college years, as well as adulthood.

In addition to these developmental considerations, all students possess all of the intelligences at each stage of their development, although not all of them are developed to the same degree at a given time. Therefore, certain kinds of assessment activities are needed to help us paint a profile of each student's intelligence strengths and weaknesses so that we can help them design strategies for strengthening their weaker intelligences and learn how to use their stronger intelligences to enhance and deepen their learning.

In *Eight Ways of Knowing* (1998a) I proposed five experimental approaches for assessing a student's intellectual profile. Each of these suggests that the task of assessing an intelligence profile is primarily a matter of acute observation of students involved in various kinds of activities and/or learning tasks. A summary of these follows:

1. **Student Intelligence Watch.** This is a checklist of various behaviors that often manifest themselves in the classroom and may (especially if you observe them as a regular part of a student's life) indicate certain ways a student is trying to enhance his or her learning. These include such things as the student who is always getting up out of his or her seat, the doodler, the hummer, the perpetual questioner, the silent one, etc.

2. **Intelligence Skill Games.** These provide students with a choice of games to play. These could include such intelligence-specific things as Pictionary, charades, crossword puzzles, tune or music recognition, etc. It is important to observe not only which game(s) they choose, but *what they do* as they are playing.

3. **Intelligence Foci Watching.** This involves showing students a complex movie or a play in which multiple intelligence capacities are clearly portrayed and/or utilized. After the film or play, lead them in a discussion on what struck them. Notice the points—the action scenes, the musical soundtrack, colors, symbols, emotions—that captured their attention.

4. **Complex Problem Solving.** Watch *what* students do when given a problem to solve—one that they really care about solving. You can tell a great deal about their intelligence patterns as you catch them in the act of problem solving. Remember, the answer itself is not as important as *how* they approach it!

5. **Inventing.** Give students inventing, designing, or creating tasks to perform, making sure that the full spectrum of intelligence tools is available for them to use. Then, again, notice what kinds of tools they are drawn to, and again, *how* they use the tools once they have them.

Howard Gardner believes that it takes about ten hours of careful observation of students involved in activities such as these to begin sensing a profile of their intelligence strengths and weaknesses. I believe that it is also crucial to mention that this profile changes as students learn about their multiple intelligences and how to use them in daily lessons and in their lives beyond school. The observation must be ongoing. The promise, of course, is that we as teachers can find strategies for coaxing students to step beyond their limits and become all that they can be!

I wish you an exciting and wonder-filled adventure as you journey into these realms of amplified ways of knowing and being!

APPENDIX

A

Lesson Processing
Blacklines

Multiple Intelligences
Toolbox Descriptions

Verbal/Linguistic Intelligence

Creative Writing—writing original pieces without boundaries

Formal Speaking—making verbal presentations to others

Humor/Jokes—creating puns, limericks, and jokes on academic topics

Impromptu Speaking—instantly speaking on a randomly drawn topic

Journal/Diary Keeping—tracing and keeping track of one's own thoughts and ideas

Poetry—creating one's own poetry and reading and appreciating others' poetry

Reading—studying written materials on a concept, idea, or process

Storytelling/Story Creation—making up and telling stories about any topic one is studying

Verbal Debate—presenting both sides of an issue in a convincing manner

Vocabulary—learning new words and practicing using them accurately in regular communication

Logical/Mathematical Intelligence

Abstract Symbols/Formulas—designing meaningful summary notation systems for different processes or knowledge content

Calculation—using specified steps, operations, processes, formulas, and equations to solve a problem

Deciphering Codes—understanding and communicating with symbolic language

Forcing Relationships—creating meaningful connections between noncongruent ideas

Graphic/Cognitive Organizers—working with logical thought maps such as webs, Venn diagrams, classification matrices, ranking ladders, etc.

Logic/Pattern Games—creating puzzles that challenge others to find a hidden rationale or pattern

Number Sequences/Patterns—investigating numerical facts or gathering and analyzing statistics on a topic

Outlining—inventing point-by-point logical explanations for items

Problem Solving—listing appropriate procedures for problem-solving situations

Syllogisms—making *if . . . , then . . .* logical deductions about a topic

Visual/Spatial Intelligence

Active Imagination—finding connections between visual designs (or patterns) and prior experiences (or knowledge)

Color/Texture Schemes—associating colors and textures with various concepts, ideas, or processes

Drawing—creating graphic representations of concepts, ideas, or processes being studied (e.g., diagrams, illustrations, flowcharts, etc.)

Guided Imagery/Visualizing—creating mental pictures or images of a concept, idea, or process (e.g., characters in a story, a period of history, a scientific process)

Mind Mapping—creating visual webs of written information

Montage/Collage—designing a collection of pictures to show various aspects or dimensions of a concept, idea, or process

Painting—using paints or colored markers to express understanding of concepts, ideas, or processes (e.g., mural creation)

Patterns/Designs—creating abstract patterns and designs to represent the relationships between different concepts, ideas, or processes

Pretending/Fantasy—creating fun, new scenarios in the mind based on factual information

Sculpting—creating clay models to demonstrate understanding of concepts, ideas, or processes

Bodily/Kinesthetic Intelligence

Body Language/Physical Gestures—"embodying" meaning, interpretation, or understanding of an idea in physical movement

Body Sculpture/Tableaus—arranging (sculpting) a group of people to express an idea, concept, or process

Dramatic Enactment—creating a mini-drama that shows the dynamic interplay of various concepts, ideas, or processes

Folk/Creative Dance—choreographing a dance that demonstrates a concept, idea, or process

Gymnastic Routines—designing an orchestrated flow of physical movement that embodies relationships and connections with a topic

Human Graph—standing along a continuum to express agreement or understanding of a concept, idea, or process

Inventing—making or building something that demonstrates a concept, idea, or process (e.g., a model to show how something works)

Physical Exercise/Martial Arts—creating physical routines that others perform so that they may learn concepts, ideas, or processes

Role Playing/Mime—performing skits or charades to show understanding of concepts, ideas, or processes

Sports Games—creating a contest or game based on specific knowledge about a concept, idea, or process

Musical/Rhythmic Intelligence

Environmental Sounds—using the natural sounds that are related to the object, concept, or process being studied (e.g., weather conditions, geographical locations, animals)

Instrumental Sounds—employing musical instruments to produce sounds for a lesson (e.g., background accompaniment, enhancements for the teaching)

Music Composition/Creation—composing and creating music to communicate understanding of a concept, idea, or process (e.g., the stages of a cell dividing)

Music Performance—creating presentations or reports in which music and rhythm play a central role

Percussion Vibrations—using vibrations or beats to communicate a concept, idea, or process to others and the self

Rapping—using raps to help communicate or to remember certain concepts, ideas, or processes

Rhythmic Patterns—producing rhythms and beats to show the various aspects of a concept, idea, or process

Singing/Humming—creating songs about an academic topic or finding existing songs that complement a topic

Tonal Patterns—recognizing the tone dimension(s) of a topic (e.g., sounds a computer makes)

Vocal Sounds/Tones—producing sounds with one's vocal cords to illustrate a concept, idea, or process

Interpersonal Intelligence

Collaborative Skills Teaching—recognizing and learning the social skills needed for effective person-to-person relating

Cooperative Learning Strategies—using structured teamwork for academic learning

Empathy Practices—expressing understanding from someone else's standpoint or life experience

Giving Feedback—offering honest, sensitive input on one's performance or about one's opinion(s)

Group Projects—investigating a topic with others in teams

Intuiting Others' Feelings—second-guessing what someone else is feeling or experiencing in a given situation

Jigsaw—dividing the learning and teaching of a topic into distinct segments so that students can learn from and teach each other

Person-to-Person Communication—focusing on how people relate and how to improve their relating

Receiving Feedback—accepting another's input or reaction to one's performance or opinions

Sensing Others' Motives—exploring a topic by discovering why others acted in a certain way or made certain decisions

Intrapersonal Intelligence

Altered States of Consciousness Practices—learning to shift one's mood or awareness into an optimal state

Emotional Processing—becoming aware of the affective dimensions (i.e., How does it make me feel?) of something one is studying

Focusing/Concentration Skills—learning the ability to focus one's mind on a single idea or task

Higher-Order Reasoning—moving from memorizing facts to synthesizing, integrating, and applying

Independent Studies/Projects—working alone to express feelings and thoughts on a topic

Know Thyself Procedures—finding personal implications or applications of classroom learning for one's personal life

Metacognition Techniques—thinking about one's thinking (i.e., tracing the various processes and steps used)

Mindfulness Practices—paying conscious attention to one's life experience (the opposite of mindlessness or "living on automatic pilot")

Silent Reflection Methods—working with reflection tools such as reflective journals, thinking logs, learning diaries, etc.

Thinking Strategies—learning what thinking patterns to use for what task

Naturalist Intelligence

Archetypal Pattern Recognition—discovering the repeating, standard patterns and designs of nature that manifest themselves throughout the universe

Caring for Plants/Animals—completing projects that involve caring for and/or training animals, insects, other organisms, and/or growing natural things

Conservation Practices—participating in projects that care for and preserve the natural environment (including its animals)

Environment Feedback—understanding and appreciating the environment and tuning in to the natural feedback coming from the environment

Hands-On Labs—performing experiments or activities that use objects from the natural world

Nature Encounters/Field Trips—going outside for firsthand experiences in nature and/or bringing nature in via videos, objects, animals, plants, etc.

Nature Observation—participating in observation activities such as bird-watching, geological exploration, keeping nature journals

Nature World Simulations—re-creating or representing nature in some form (e.g., dioramas, montages, photographs, drawings, nature rubbings, etc.)

Species Classification (organic/inorganic)—working with classification matrices to understand characteristics of natural objects

Sensory Stimulation Exercises—exposing the senses to nature's sounds, smells, tastes, touches, and sights

Using Technology for Multiple Intelligences Teaching and Learning

In Lewis Carroll's classic, *Through the Looking Glass,* Alice remarks that things just seem to be getting "curiouser and curiouser." Alice's observation is on target when we consider the recent and continuing explosion in technology. Dr. Thomas Hoerr (2000a), headmaster of the New City School (St. Louis), believes that our most outlandish predictions about the future direction and possibilities of technology will likely be considered very conservative in twenty years. Technology is here to stay and our world is getting more technological by the minute.

In the professional development workshops I conduct, I am frequently asked how technology relates to teaching with the multiple intelligences: Can technology help students learn? Will technology change what we teach and how we teach? Can technology help students access their multiple ways of knowing?

My answer to all of these is a resounding "Yes!"

I believe that our job as teachers is to seek out software, hardware, and other applications of current technology that support multiple intelligences. I have created a preliminary set of suggestions for using current technology to enhance and deepen students' learning and to help students more fully explore all of their intelligences. I have called these suggestions the Multiple Intelligences Technology Toolbox (see the following pages). This toolbox can be used in tandem with the Multiple Intelligences Toolbox presented earlier in this book (see page 15).

The technology toolbox is not an exhaustive list of every conceivable technology application. Rather, it is a sample of ten tools for each intelligence that can jumpstart your thinking about how to use technology to awaken students' multiple intelligences and to enhance students' learning. In most cases, students do not have to be asked twice if they want to work on a computer. In fact they can teach us many things we don't know how to do! Use students' knowledge to your advantage by regularly incorporating appropriate technology into your instruction and into student learning.

Please note: Technology is progressing so quickly that by the time this revised edition of *Eight Ways of Teaching* is published, many new ideas could be added to the technology toolbox. Please add them accordingly. Boldly experiment with technology to aid you in teaching with multiple intelligences.

Multiple Intelligences
Technology Toolbox

Verbal/Linguistic Intelligence

Probably the most obvious technologies related to verbal/linguistic intelligence are word processing programs. Use these programs to teach language arts skills: definitions (e.g., electronic dictionaries), spelling (e.g., spell checkers), synonyms (e.g., electronic thesaurus), and grammar (e.g., grammar checkers—some checkers explain the grammar rules that apply to the corrections suggested).

Technology Tools:

- Word processing programs (e.g., Microsoft Word, Apple Works) with voice annotations
- Video script authoring and editing software
- Desktop publishing programs (e.g., Publisher, PageMaker; to create newsletters, books)
- Story-creation software (to compose poems, essays, letters)
- Multimedia authoring software (e.g., HyperStudio; to create media featuring the written word)
- Video, digital, or audiocassette recording hardware and software (to record or create news programs, interviews, scripting, choral reading, storytelling, formal speaking, debates)
- Internet discussion lists and forums
- Web sites (reading and interpreting information from the Web)
- Electronic reference tools (e.g., encyclopedia, dictionary, thesaurus)
- CD-ROM interactive books, e-books, and text-based software

Logical/Mathematical Intelligence

The technologies most connected with logical/mathematical intelligence are computer games, math programs, and databases. Today we see a virtual explosion of computer games. Find games that require logical/mathematical skills such as calculation, logic, critical thinking, and problem solving. You can also choose from a variety of math programs that not only drill students on math facts but also encourage them to use math operations to solve problems. Teach students how to use database programs to explore, analyze, and organize information.

Technology Tools:

- Strategy, logic, or critical thinking software
- Databases (to outline or organize ideas)
- Concept mapping tools (e.g., Inspiration, Kidspiration, OmniGaffle; to outline or organize thoughts)
- Spreadsheet programs (e.g., AppleWorks, Excel, Lotus)
- Organizational tools (e.g., calendars, PDAs)
- Online calculation tools and utilities
- Science and math software
- Statistics and online data (finding data)
- Graphing software (e.g., Graph Action, Graph Club; to show results of experiments, demonstrations, data gathering)
- Web searches (finding and analyzing data)

Note: Product names represent items available at time of printing and are included only for example. Mention of these products does not constitute an advertisement or endorsement.

Multiple Intelligences
Technology Toolbox

Visual/Spatial Intelligence

Visual/spatial intelligence is likely the easiest intelligence to address with technology, because a plethora of graphics-based software programs and packages are available. These programs include clip art libraries as well as drawing and painting, three-dimensional modeling, and virtual reality applications. Use graphics programs to develop students' creativity and visual skills. Challenge students to form mental pictures of curricular concepts.

Technology Tools:

- Drawing and painting programs (e.g., CorelDraw, iDraw, Photopaint, Illustrator, KidPix)
- Image creation, editing, and enhancement programs (e.g., PhotoShop, Fireworks, digital scanners)
- Web page creation programs (e.g., HomePage, FrontPage, DreamWeaver, Page Mill)
- Mapmaking programs and software that creates driving directions (e.g., Tom Snyder's Mapmaker, MapQuest)
- Presentation software programs that use LCD projectors (e.g., PowerPoint, Astound)
- Digital cameras, camcorders, Web cams
- Movie authoring and editing software (e.g., iMovie, Premier, QuickTime)
- Animation software (e.g., Flash, Ray Dream, GIF animation)
- Digital drawing pads
- 3-D and morphing software

Musical/Rhythmic Intelligence

I call this the auditory/vibrational intelligence, because, from a bio-neurological-cognitive perspective, this intelligence deals with more than just music and rhythm. This intelligence involves the whole realm of sound, vibration, and beats (including, of course, music and rhythm). Computer catalogs feature an increasing number of hardware and software for composing, playing, and making music, rhythm, and sound. Use this hardware and software to tap into your student's musical/rhythmic intelligence.

Technology Tools:

- Music composition software
- Reading programs that relate the sounds of letters to music
- CD recorders and burners
- Karaoke machines
- Video soundtrack creation, editing, and enhancement software and hardware (e.g., iMovie, iDVD)
- Audio recorders (e.g., Coaster; to digitize singing, musical instrument playing, sounds)
- Sound and music files or clips
- Music and sound generation and editing software (e.g., SoundMaker)
- Interactive books that include audio elements
- Percussion creation software

Note: Product names represent items available at time of printing and are included only for example. Mention of these products does not constitute an advertisement or endorsement.

Multiple Intelligences
Technology Toolbox

Bodily/Kinesthetic Intelligence

The challenge of working with technology and bodily/kinesthetic intelligence is the fact that to fully activate this intelligence the body must be in motion via dance, drama, mime, role play, physical exercise, games, etc. Most current technology requires the participant to sit in front of a computer. Obviously using computers develops fine motor skills, such as hand-eye coordination; however, computers and other technology applications can help students to become more actively involved in their learning.

Technology Tools:

- Programs or games that involve moving objects around the screen
- CDs or DVDs of live performances (e.g., musical groups, theater performances, sporting events)
- Animation programs (e.g., Flash)
- Online, video, or CD instructions for exercising, dancing, creating something
- Video productions (e.g., recording skits, dances, sports games, role plays, demonstrations of facial expressions or postures or gestures or other physical movements)
- Virtual reality applications
- Construction manipulatives or programs (e.g., Legos, Logo, Robotics)
- Digital records of physical movement (e.g., stages of performing a skill, steps to a dance, plays in a sports game)
- Software games that require contact with a keyboard, mouse, joystick, or other devices or that use PDAs (e.g., Palm Pilot, HandSpring)
- Videos that show a sequence of movements (e.g., Claymation)

Interpersonal Intelligence

We often associate working on a computer as a solitary venture—the user does not directly work with others. Therefore, to make computers more interpersonal, we must devise collaborative activities that encourage students to work together on computer-based projects. When you encourage students to work together on their computers, they strengthen their communication and cooperation skills. They not only help each other understand how computers work, they also learn how to work together via peer tutoring, mentoring, discussing, and sharing information about the concepts they are studying.

Technology Tools:

- Distance learning opportunities
- Instant messaging or chat rooms (to discuss ideas with others)
- E-mail (e.g., find pen pals in other countries)
- Web searches that include collaborative elements
- Word processing projects (e.g., round-robin writing, group editing, brainstorming, etc.)
- Listservs and forums
- Video and teleconferencing projects
- Software for making group decisions (e.g., Tom Snyder's Decision)
- Software or games that require collaboration
- Telecommunications projects or broadcasts (e.g., Flat Stanley)

Note: Product names represent items available at time of printing and are included only for example. Mention of these products does not constitute an advertisement or endorsement.

Multiple Intelligences
Technology Toolbox

Intrapersonal Intelligence

The computer is ideal for helping students build up individual skills and confidence, because computers allow students to work at their own pace and at their own ability level. While working on a computer can be a very individual task, students must create work that they can share with others. Knowing that they must share their work intensifies students' learning. When students use their intrapersonal intelligence, they also activate their other intelligences as they try to better understand themselves and what they have learned.

Technology Tools:

- Computer games or programs (that involve only one person or encourage independent work)
- Brainstorming or problem-solving software
- Instructional games (to help the individual learn specific skills or concepts)
- Personal goal-setting software
- Computer-based journals or diaries
- Electronic idea webs (e.g., Inspiration, Kidspiration)
- Self-paced software for developing a skill (e.g., vocabulary, reading skills, math operations, etc.)
- Internet research (to learn about a personal interest or hobby)
- Camcorder or video projects (to record personal ideas, thoughts, feelings, beliefs, and values)
- Multimedia portfolios (to document student's progress)

Naturalist Intelligence

The naturalist intelligence is the most difficult intelligence to tie in with technology, if you try to remain faithful to the cognitive processes involved in this intelligence. Part of the difficulty stems from the fact that the naturalist intelligence is primarily stimulated through firsthand contact with the natural world—and technology is anything but the natural world! Nonetheless, we can use technology to amplify students' encounters with nature and the knowings they receive through these experiences. Technology can also expand students' knowledge about how to relate to and care for our natural environment.

Technology Tools:

- Camcorders or digital cameras (to record events, patterns, and objects in the natural world)
- Computer-based nature logs and journals (e.g., recording observations, reflections, and insights from a field trip)
- Desktop presentation programs (e.g., PowerPoint, Astound; to report on natural trends and changes over time, such as in a science experiment)
- Microscopes and probes (to see nature up close and from the inside out)
- Digital audio recording (to capture from the natural world, the weather, animals, etc.)
- Virtual field trips to natural environments (e.g., surface of the moon, bottom of the Grand Canyon, or the rain forest)
- Multimedia simulations (e.g., natural environments, animal behaviors, weather conditions, geographical features)
- Data organization, graphing, calculation programs (to analyze empirical observations of nature)
- Web searches (to research and learn more about natural phenomena)
- Videos that show nature and how it works

Note: Product names represent items available at time of printing and are included only for example. Mention of these products does not constitute an advertisement or endorsement.

Lesson Design Palette

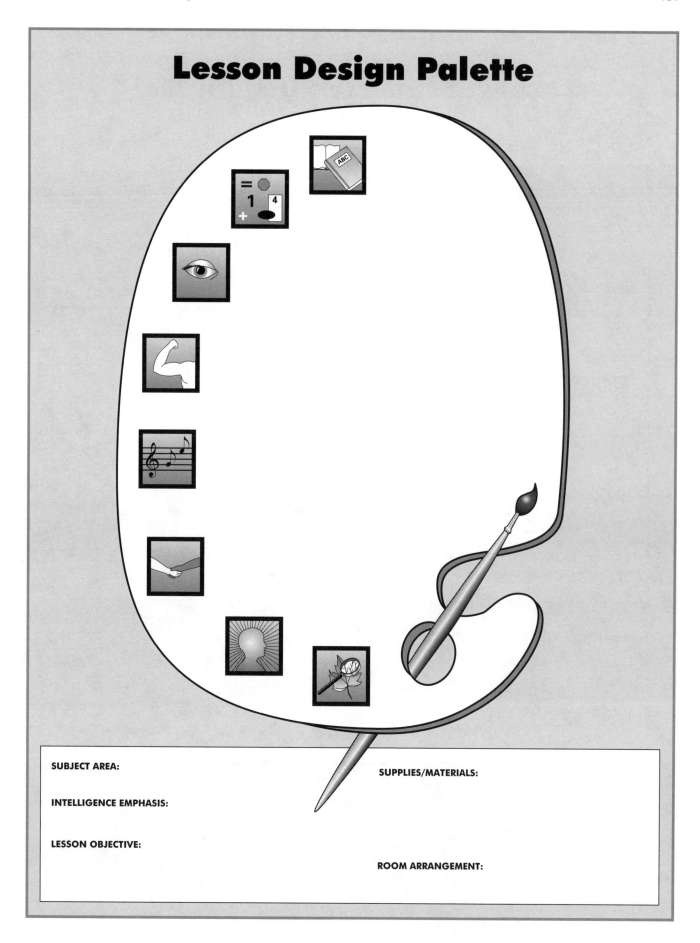

SUBJECT AREA:

INTELLIGENCE EMPHASIS:

LESSON OBJECTIVE:

SUPPLIES/MATERIALS:

ROOM ARRANGEMENT:

Lesson Plan Staging Model

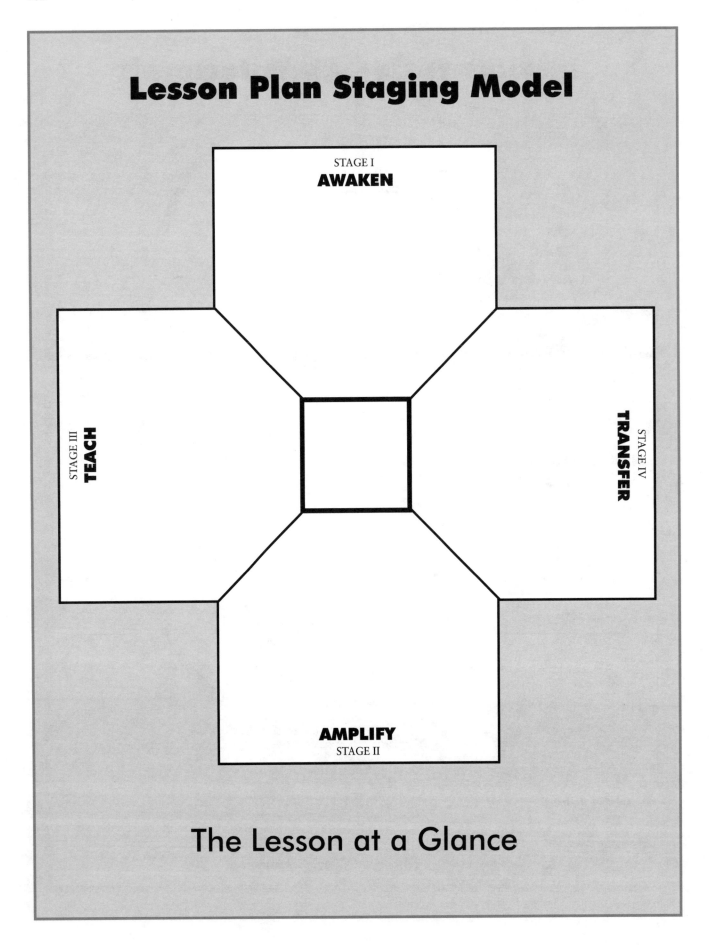

STAGE I
AWAKEN

STAGE III
TEACH

STAGE IV
TRANSFER

AMPLIFY
STAGE II

The Lesson at a Glance

Models for Student Journals

Note: Journals can involve different modes of reflecting including writing, drawing, painting, sculpting, role playing, dancing, etc.

THINKING LOGS (to process lesson content)

The main thing I'll remember is . . .
A new insight or discovery is . . .
I really understood . . .; I'm really confused about . . .
A learning I can use beyond school is . . .
Connections I'm making with other things I know are . . .

BEFORE AND AFTER SCENARIOS (to process impact of a lesson)

Analyze the impact of a unit or lesson on you using this chart.

	BEFORE THE UNIT OR LESSON	**AFTER THE UNIT OR LESSON**
Feelings about it		
Thoughts about it		
Associations with it		
Mental images/pictures		

How am I different as a result of this unit or lesson?

Models for Student Journals

Note: Journals can involve different modes of reflecting including writing, drawing, painting, sculpting, role playing, dancing, etc.

CHART YOUR MOODS (to process feelings about a period/day)

MOOD INTENSITY

10
9
8
7
6
5
4
3
2
1
0

8:00   9:00   10:00   11:00   12:00   1:00   2:00   3:00   4:00   5:00

TIME SEQUENCE

1. At the end of the day plot your different moods of the day on the graph above. (The vertical numbers represent mood intensity and the horizontal numbers time sequences.)

2. Place a mark at the high point of the day and one at the low point. Then look at the time before and after these points; think about other changes in mood. Make marks at the appropriate places.

3. Now connect the marks with a continuous curving line so that you have a visual picture of the mood changes and the affective flow of the day.

4. For each point that you have marked along the axes, jot a brief note about what was going on that catalyzed the mood shift.

5. Using colored markers or crayons, create a spectrum of colors from left to right to match the different moods you experienced.

6. Finally, think of the kind of music you would play as a background for each of the different moods of the day. Note these on the graph.

7. Try doing this every day for a week. At the end of the week lay all of your mood graphs side by side and reflect on the week. What do you learn about yourself as you look at the week in this way?

Models for Student Journals

Note: Journals can involve different modes of reflecting including writing, drawing, painting, sculpting, role playing, dancing, etc.

SNAPSHOTS OF THE PAST AND PRESENT (to process the import of a lesson)

- Write the main idea of the lesson for you: _____
- Pretend this idea had never been discovered. How would life have been different in the past? (Think of three snapshots.)

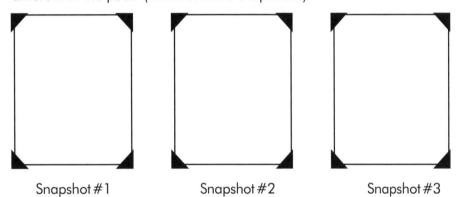

Snapshot #1   Snapshot #2   Snapshot #3

- How would life be different today without this idea? (Think of three snapshots.)

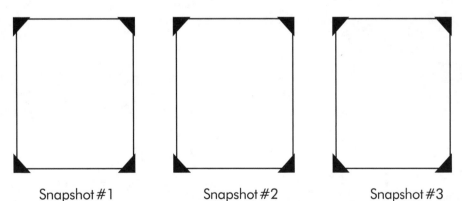

Snapshot #1   Snapshot #2   Snapshot #3

Models for Student Journals

Note: Journals can involve different modes of reflecting including writing, drawing, painting, sculpting, role playing, dancing, etc.

STEPPING STONES INTO THE FUTURE (to project future applications of a lesson)

• Write the main idea of the lesson for you: _____

• Brainstorm five ways this idea has been or is being applied in our times.

    1.

    2.

    3.

    4.

    5.

• Pretend you can step into the next century. How will this idea be applied then?

Key Ingredients for Success in Cooperative Learning

1. You must consciously bring **higher-order thinking** and reasoning to a lesson. Students must be taught how to think at higher levels and participate in lessons that challenge them to perform at these higher levels.

2. You must have a kit of strategies to **unify the teams.** You want to create a sense of "We need each other for this lesson" or what Roger and David Johnson call positive interdependence.

3. You must structure the lesson to **insure individual learning.** There should be no sloughing off on the part of the individuals just because they are in a group.

4. You must provide students enough time to **look over and discuss** both the lesson content and their cooperative behavior. As students process their lessons, they become more and more aware that they are the key to their own educational success.

5. You must carefully and explicitly **develop the necessary social skills**—the necessary skills of effective cooperation and collaboration with others. These skills include such things as listening, encouraging, taking turns, staying on task, using appropriate voice volume, etc.

Note: This blackline is provided for teacher use when teaching cooperative lessons.

Eight Ways of Teaching Weekly Checklist

Have you taught for the eight ways of knowing this week? Check yourself by listing the specific strategies, techniques, and tools you have used in classroom lessons this week.

	MONDAY	TUESDAY	WEDNESDAY	THURSDAY	FRIDAY
Verbal/Linguistic					
Logical/Mathematical					
Visual/Spatial					
Bodily/Kinesthetic					
Musical/Rhythmic					
Interpersonal					
Intrapersonal					
Naturalist					

Note: This blackline is provided as a useful tool for teachers to think through their weekly multiple intelligencies strategies.

APPENDIX

B

Lesson Procedure
Blacklines

The 6 Ss for Describing Attributes

Object: _____

Sight _____	**S**ound _____	**S**mell _____
Sense (tactile)	**S**ize _____	**S**peciality _____

Write 3 sentences telling different things that you find interesting about the object.

1.

2.

3.

See/Feel T-Chart

Object _____

What I See	**How I Feel**

Write 2 sentences:

1. Things our team saw in the object are . . .

2. My feelings about the object are . . .

3 Graphic Organizers

Attribute Web

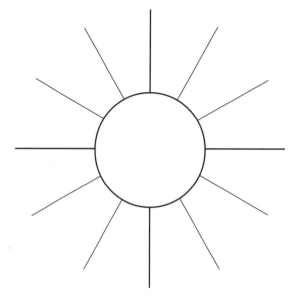

Classification Chart

Economic Attributes	Political Attributes	Social Attributes	Symbolic Attributes

Ranking Ladders

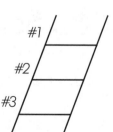

Economic   Political   Social   Symbolic

How to Make Food from Sunlight
The Amazing Process of Photosynthesis

The wonders of photosynthesis have intrigued scientists ever since the phenomenon was first recognized. The overall process—the conversion of water and carbon dioxide into sugar—has been known for more than a century. While there are still many gaps in our understanding of photosynthesis, our information is growing.

Three outside ingredients are involved to get the whole process started: (1) water, which is drawn up into the plant through its roots and stems, (2) carbon dioxide, which enters the plant through pores on its many leaves, and (3) sunlight, which is the energy source that catalyzes the whole process.

The heart of the process lies in the chloroplasts, with their light-reacting pigment. The cells of the leaf are dotted with green chloroplasts. They are shaped like tiny footballs and can turn, within the cell, to take best advantage of the light, almost like a light-sensitive radar system. The chloroplasts are stacked on top of one another and are layered with chlorophyll molecules. The chlorophyll starts soaking up or absorbing the sunlight once the chloroplasts have located it. This absorption of light energy from the sun activates or turns on the chlorophyll. The chlorophyll splits the water molecule, producing hydrogen and oxygen. The oxygen is released into the air through the pores of the leaves. The hydrogen is instantly seized by a special escort molecule and will play an important role in the next step of the process.

Meanwhile, the chlorophyll molecule starts to deactivate and return to its normal state. As this happens, further energy is released, which is used to create an energy-driver molecule called ATP (adenosine triphosphate) from certain materials already present in the plant. ATP is an energy unit that is present in all living organisms. It has the ability to supply energy to chemical reactions without itself becoming a part of the end prod-uct. This concludes the *photo* or the light-requiring part of the photosynthesis process.

The work of the chlorophyll is finished and the *synthesis* part begins. The carbon diox-ide now lines up with an acceptor module that is already in the plant. This sets the stage for a critical union to occur. The hydrogen atom, led by its escort module and powered by ATP, combines with the carbon dioxide to form a highly reactive compound called PGA (phosphoglyceric acid). The PGA molecules then combine to form sugar, which in turn is stored in the plant for food.

The machinery for this process is very complex and the whole process happens almost instantaneously; but with the electron microscope, much of it can actually be seen.

Discussion Questions
for How to Make Food from Sunlight

1. What do you remember from the reading?

2. What was surprising to you? exciting? amazing?

3. Recall and list the stages of photosynthesis. What happens first, second, third, etc.?

4. If you could have a conversation with a plant, what questions would you ask?

Physical Movement Formulas

Fold into a tent card

In 1776, America signed the Declaration of Independence. In the Declaration, America says that it is breaking away from England and will be a nation on its own. The Declaration lists the reasons the Americans decided to become their own nation.

Thomas Jefferson wrote the Declaration of Independence. John Hancock was the first person to sign it. Then fifty-seven others also signed it to show their support for the move to become free from England.

Questions:

1. What is the Declaration of Independence about?

2. Who was its author?

3. How many people signed it?

4. Why did they sign it?

Team Reflection Log

	Show #1	Show #2	Show #3	Show #4
What was the story being told?				
How did it make you feel?				
What are your questions about this event?				
Why is this story important for us today?				

4-Level Reflection Model

LEVEL # 1 HOW AM I INVOLVED?	Where and how does the issue touch my life? How does it make me feel? What are my thoughts and opinions about it?

| **LEVEL**

 # 2

 WHAT ARE THE PLUSES, MINUSES, AND WHAT DO I FIND INTERESTING? |

Positive Aspects **+**	Negative Aspects **–**	Interesting **!**

LEVEL # 3 WHAT DO I THINK COULD OR SHOULD BE DONE?	If I was in charge what would I do? What do I think needs to happen in this situation? What action(s) should be taken?
LEVEL # 4 WHAT CAN I DO NOW?	What steps could I take now (even small ones) to bring about a resolution to this issue?

Types of Writing Worksheet

	Declarative Writing	Interrogative Writing	Imperative Writing	Exclamatory Writing
	statement expressing a simple fact	statement expressing a question	statement expressing a command	statement expressing a strong emphasis
	I'll meet you at the corner cafe.	*Should we meet at the cafe or elsewhere?*	*Be at the cafe no later than 11 a.m.*	*We had a fabulous time at the cafe!*
The Sense of Smell *What odors are you aware of?*				
The Sense of Touch *What textures do you see and/or actually feel?*				
The Sense of Sight *What is catching the attention of your eyes?*				
The Sense of Hearing *What sounds are you hearing? Listen beyond the obvious. Now what do you hear?*				
The Sense of Taste *What are you tasting in your mouth?*				
Inner Feelings and Thoughts *What are you feeling and/or thinking deep inside?*				

APPENDIX

C

Graphic Organizer
Blacklines

CONCEPT MAP

CONCEPT MAP (example)

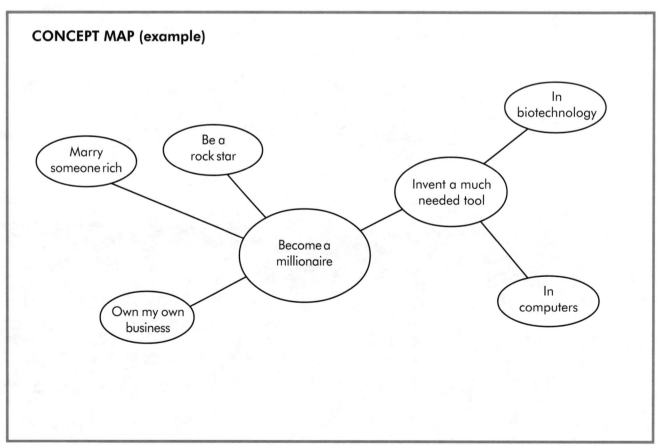

FAT AND SKINNY QUESTIONS

FAT	SKINNY
1.	1.
2.	2.
3.	3.
4.	4.
5.	5.

FAT AND SKINNY QUESTIONS (example)

FAT (requires discussion)	SKINNY (can be answered with one word)
1. Why did the colonists break away from England?	1. Who drafted the Declaration of Independence?
2. What would things be like if America were still a British colony?	2. Was George Washington involved in drafting the Declaration of Independence?
3.	3.
4.	4.
5.	5.

4 x 4 x 4 OUTLINE

I		II		III		IV	
A	1	A	1	A	1	A	1
	2		2		2		2
	3		3		3		3
	4		4		4		4
B	1	B	1	B	1	B	1
	2		2		2		2
	3		3		3		3
	4		4		4		4
C	1	C	1	C	1	C	1
	2		2		2		2
	3		3		3		3
	4		4		4		4
D	1	D	1	D	1	D	1
	2		2		2		2
	3		3		3		3
	4		4		4		4

4 x 4 x 4 (example)

On What Do I Spend My Time?

I Home		II Work		III Family		IV Self	
A the house	1 painting	A lesson planning	1 outline	A spouse	1 alone time	A reading	1 *Harper's*
	2 cleaning		2 research		2 help with bills		2 *Moby Dick*
	3 repairs		3 supplies		3 help with kids		3 newspaper
	4 bills		4 special activities		4 drive to activities		4 trade journals
B the garden	1 mowing	B grading	1 reading papers	B kids	1 drive to activities	B exercise	1 walking
	2 weeding		2 marking papers		2 cook for		2 swimming
	3 watering		3 tabulating grades		3 buy clothes		3 biking
	4 raking		4 recording grades		4 help with homework		4 bowling
C the pets	1 feeding	C teaching	1 attendance	C parents	1 talk on phone	C relaxation	1 watching television
	2 brushing		2 focusing		2 bring groceries		2 going to movies
	3 cleaning up		3 assignment		3 take kids to visit		3 sleeping
	4 taking to vet		4 monitoring		4 bring dinner		4 listening to music
D the car	1 repairs	D faculty meetings	1 preparing for	D church	1 attend Sunday	D seeing friends	1 dinner with Sue
	2 washing		2 sitting in		2 choir		2 movie with Gail
	3 filling with gas		3 taking notes		3 volunteer work		3 party at Bob's
	4 tuning up		4 discussing		4 usher		4 bridge club

JIGSAW

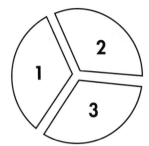

Original Group
Members divide work.

Individual Work
Members decide **what is** important and **how** to teach their fellow group members.

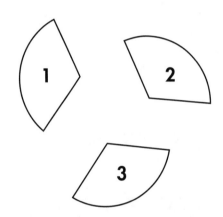

Original Group
Members teach each other.

TWO DECISIONS

#1 What to teach

#2 How to teach it

KWL GOAL-SETTING CHART

What We **Know**	What We **Want** to Find Out	What We **Learned**

KWL CHART (example)

What We **Know**	What We **Want** to Find Out	What We **Learned**
There are different parts of speech.	How to correctly use each part of speech in sentences.	Parts of speech are like a paint palette from which you can create interesting sentences.

MATRIX

MATRIX (example)

GLOBAL ISSUE COUNTRY	ENVIRONMENTAL CONCERN	HUMAN RIGHTS	CULTURAL DIVERSITY
MEXICO	Air Pollution	Homelessness	Indians
INDIA	Food Supply	Overpopulation	Religion
CANADA	Deforestation	Socialized Medicine	Language (French and English)

PMI CHART

P+	M-	I?

PMI CHART (example)   **Daughter's College Education**

P+	M-	I?
1. College sets her up for higher salaries.	1. She's not diligent with her high school studies and college is much more demanding.	1. If she took a year off between high school and college, she might be more ready for college.
2. It brings about a maturing and sense of responsibility.	2. Tight finances will force her to have a job to help pay.	2. She is very interested in drama and other cultures.
3. Tight finances will force her to have a job to help pay.		

RANKING LADDER

RANKING LADDER (example)

The Importance of the Different Aspects of Learning

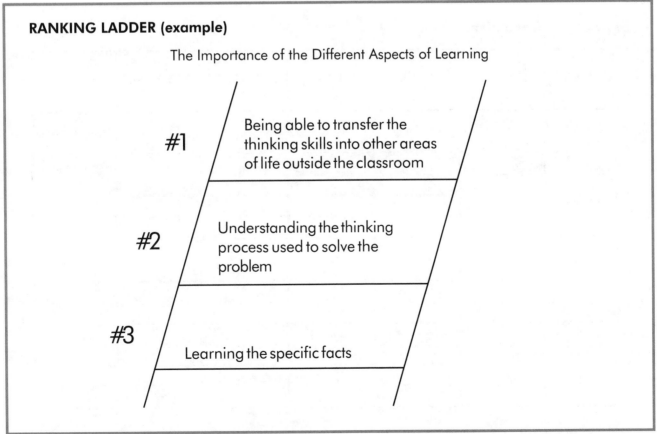

#1 — Being able to transfer the thinking skills into other areas of life outside the classroom

#2 — Understanding the thinking process used to solve the problem

#3 — Learning the specific facts

STORY GRID

STORY GRID (example)

GOOD GUY	SIDEKICK	BAD GUY	GAL	CONFLICT	SETTING	ENDING
doctor	small boy	city slicker	lawyer	man vs. nature	1800s	cliff-hanger
lawyer	farmer	land baron	gambler	ranchers vs. farmers	closet	everyone happy
Indian chief	deputy	bully	schoolteacher	town vs. stranger	Montana	serial
marshal	relative	ex-con	widow	large bank deposit lost	town	tragic
stranger	friend	gambler	little kid	man vs. self	desert	butler did it
bartender	a dog	politician	eastern cousin	good vs. evil	saloon	bad guy wins
shop owner	rancher	lawyer	bank clerk	cowboys vs. Indians	mountain	everyone dies

VENN DIAGRAM

VENN DIAGRAM (example)

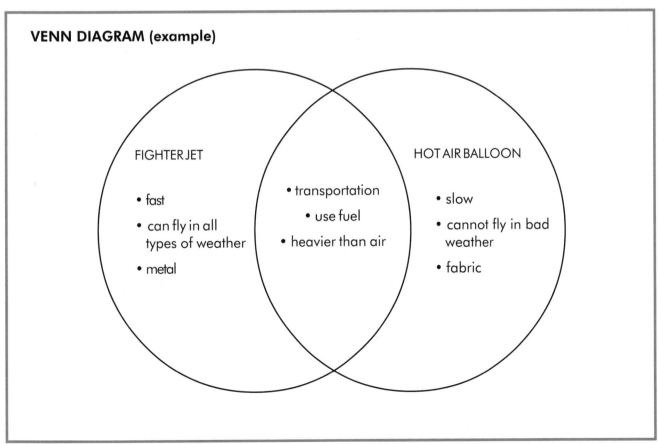

FIGHTER JET

- fast
- can fly in all types of weather
- metal

- transportation
- use fuel
- heavier than air

HOT AIR BALLOON

- slow
- cannot fly in bad weather
- fabric

WEB

WEB (example)

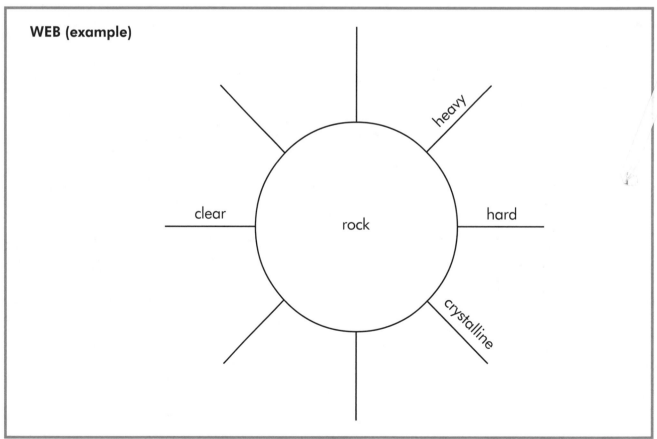

WHAT? SO WHAT? NOW WHAT?

What? (What have I learned?)

So What? (What difference does it make?)

Now What? (What can I do with this information?)

WHAT? SO WHAT? NOW WHAT? (example)

What? (What have I learned?)

Oak is harder than pine.

So What? (What difference does it make?)

Oak will burn slower than the pine will.

Now What? (What can I do with this information?)

If I want my campfire to last longer, I will use oak instead of pine.

Glossary

Glossary

amplify   to expand, strengthen, and enhance one's intelligence capacities.

archetypal pattern recognition   awareness of the many repeating and standard patterns and designs of nature that manifest themselves throughout the entire universe. *See also micro/macro pattern connections.*

attribute webbing   a thinking strategy that involves brainstorming attributes or characteristics of something using the web graphic organizer (see blackline, p. 192).

awaken   to trigger, catalyze, or assess latent intelligence capacities in the brain using specifically targeted exercises.

awareness technique   any method or tool that gives one a new perspective, expands one's thinking horizons, or alters one's self-understanding.

biofeedback   a technique for learning to control certain involuntary functions such as blood pressure, body temperature, heart rate, etc.

blackline   a master copy from which photocopy reproductions can be made.

brainstorm   to generate as many ideas as possible on a topic without evaluating or judging those ideas.

Broca's area   the area of the brain, located in the front part of the left hemisphere, that is primarily responsible for the production and understanding of language.

caring for animals   projects that involve caring for and/or training animals, insects, and other organisms.

classification chart   a graphic organizer that can help one learn the thinking skill of classifying things according to various criteria (see blackline, p. 192).

cognitive organizer   a visual diagram of a thinking pattern or process.

concept mapping   a thinking technique that begins with a central idea and proceeds to show related ideas as branches off of the center (see blackline, p. 202).

conservation practices   participation in various projects to care for and preserve the natural environment including its animals.

countermelody   a second melody in a song that is different from the main melody and yet fits perfectly with it when they are played simultaneously.

deep relaxation technique   any method that assists one in achieving a more relaxed state of being.

dramatic structure model   the classical structure of a Shakespearean play—action builds to a decisive climax followed by the results or implications of the climax.

Each One Teach One   an interactive group strategy in which each person in a group learns something and then teaches it to the others in the group.

environmental feedback   understanding and appreciating the environment by tuning in to the natural feedback coming from the environment.

fat and skinny questions   a technique for helping students stimulate further thinking. Skinny questions can be answered with a yes or no. Fat questions require thoughtful creative responses (see blackline, p. 203).

focusing technique   any method or tool that helps one bring attention and thinking to a singular point.

4 × 4 × 4 outline   a graphic organizer that can help one learn how to organize thinking through main points, subpoints, and sub-subpoints (see blackline, p. 204).

Gossip Game   a game in which something is whispered to the first person in a line of people and then is passed down the line in turn to each person, the point being to note how the final message has changed in the process.

graphic organizer   *see cognitive organizer.*

growing natural things   projects that involve growing and caring for plants, crystals, bacteria, etc.

guided imagery   a thinking process that activates one's imagination and capacity to pretend.

hands-on labs   performing experiments or activities that involve and utilize objects from the natural world.

How **I Say** *What* **I Say**   a verbal exercise in which the intended meaning of something is altered simply by the inflection, tone, and pitch of one's voice.

human graph   a thinking strategy that asks people to physically stand along a spectrum that indicates how they feel or think about an issue.

human sculpture tableau   the physical arrangement of a group of people such that postures and positions "embody" a certain idea or feeling.

I Become What I Behold   an empathy exercise that involves imagining that one can become another person, animal, or thing and, from that perspective, look back and observe the self.

inner seeing exercises   *see guided imagery.*

jigsaw   a cooperative learning strategy that involves giving each person in a group a portion of the whole to learn and then teach it to the others in the group (see blackline, p. 205).

KWL goal-setting chart   a graphic organizer that helps one assess prior knowledge and current questions for a learning task, and then to assess what was actually learned after the task is completed (see blackline, p. 206).

live painting   *see human sculpture tableau.*

matrix   a way of classifying things on a chart with certain categories across the top and others down the side of the chart; items in the chart must meet the criteria of both the top and side category (see blackline, p. 207).

metacognition   the process of thinking about and analyzing one's own thinking processes.

metacognitive processing   the evaluation of one's own thinking after the completion of a learning activity.

micro/macro pattern connections   identifying similar patterns, shapes, designs, characteristics, etc., between differing layers of the planet's ecosystem (subatomic to universe).

mind map   same as concept map except it primarily uses pictures, images, colors, designs, and patterns to express concepts or ideas.

multitracking   any physical exercise that involves performing several different actions simultaneously (e.g., rubbing the stomach and patting the top of the head while jogging in place).

natural pattern recognition identifying distinct patterns, designs, shapes, colors, etc., that belong to distinct environments or species (organic and inorganic).

nature encounters/field trips going outside for firsthand experiences in nature and/or bringing nature inside via videos, objects, animals, plants, etc.

nature observation participation in activities such as bird-watching, noting geological differences, keeping nature journals, etc.

nature simulations projects that re-create and/or represent nature in some form such as dioramas, montages, photographs, drawings, nature rubbings, etc.

New Word for the Day a vocabulary expansion practice that involves learning the meaning of a new word each day and using it in conversation during the day.

noncompetitive game a game in which the point is to have fun playing, not defeating, the opponent.

pass over *see I Become What I Behold.*

peer coaching team a cooperative group in which the members have agreed to help each other improve certain skills by giving each other positive feedback and advice.

PMI a graphic organizer that helps one learn the thinking skill of evaluation (P = pluses, M = minuses, I = interesting; see blackline, p. 208).

ranking ladder a graphic organizer that helps one learn the thinking skill of prioritizing (see blackline, p. 209).

rhythm game a game that involves recalling certain numbers and number patterns to rhythmic hand clapping and finger snapping.

sensory stimulation exercises sensory-based exposure to and participation in nature's sounds, smells, tastes, touches, and sights.

species classification (organic/inorganic) working with classification matrices to understand characteristics of natural objects.

species discrimination recognizing and understanding basic and complex similarities and differences between distinguishing characteristics of different species.

spiral adaptation altering a particular lesson so it is appropriate for different grade levels or age groups.

Stop the Action and Improvise a drama technique in which actors play a scene and the director stops the action at a random point and asks the actors to improvise the rest of the scene.

story grid a graphic organizer that contains basic information for a story (e.g., hero, heroine, villain, setting, conflict, ending) that is randomly chosen and woven together to create a final story (see blackline, p. 210).

transfer the process of making connections between one's learning and daily life.

Turn to Your Partner And . . . an interactive strategy in which two people who are seated next to each other discuss and/or process information, share feelings and thoughts, and explore ideas.

ugly Americanism rude and insensitive behavior of American tourists visiting other cultures.

Venn diagram a graphic organizer in which two or more overlapping circles help teach the thinking skill of comparing and contrasting (see blackline, p. 211).

web a graphic organizer that helps one learn the thinking skill of brainstorming (see blackline, p. 212).

What? So What? Now What? a processing technique used after one has acquired some new information. The technique uses these questions: What have I learned? What difference does it make? What can I do with this information? (see blackline, p. 213)

Bibliography

Bibliography

Alexander, F. 1984. *The use of the self: Its conscious direction in relation to diagnosis, functioning, and the control of reaction*. Downey, CA: Centerline Press.

Ambruster, B., and T. Anderson. 1980. The effect of mapping on the free recall of expository tests. Tech. Rep. No. 160. Urbana-Champaign, IL: University of Illinois, Center for the Study of Reading.

Anderson, R., and W. Biddle. 1975. On asking people questions about what they are reading. In *The psychology of learning and motivation*, edited by G. Bower. New York: Academic Press.

Arlin, P. 1990. Teaching as conversation. *Educational Leadership* 48(2).

Armstrong, T. 1987. *In their own way: Discovering and encouraging your child's personal learning style*. Los Angeles: J. P. Tarcher.

———. 2000. *Multiple intelligences in the classroom*, 2nd ed. Alexandria, VA: Association for Supervision and Curriculum Development.

Assagioli, R. 1973. *The act of will*. New York: Viking Press.

Ausubel, D. 1968. *Educational psychology: A cognitive view*. New York: Holt, Rinehart, and Winston.

Bacon, F. 1939. Of studies. In *Century readings in the English essay*, edited by W. Louis. New York: Appleton-Century-Crofts.

Bartlett, F. 1958. *Thinking*. New York: Basic Books.

Beachner, L., and A. Pickett. 2001. *Multiple intelligences and positive life habits: 174 activities for applying them in your classroom*. Thousand Oaks, CA: Corwin Press.

Bellanca, J., and R. Fogarty. 1986. *Catch them thinking*. Palatine, IL: IRI/SkyLight Training and Publishing.

———. 2003. *Blueprints for achievement in the cooperative classroom*, 3rd ed. Arlington Heights, IL: IRI/SkyLight Training and Publishing.

Benson, H. 1975. *The relaxation response*. New York: Morrow.

Berlin, B. 1992. *Ethnobiological classification: Principles of categorization of plants and animals in traditional societies*. Princeton, NJ: Princeton University Press.

Beyer, B. 1987. *Practical strategies for the teaching of thinking*. Boston: Allyn & Bacon.

Bloom, B. 1956. *Taxonomy of educational objectives*. New York: David McKay.

Bogen, J. 1979. Some educational aspects of hemispheric socialization. *Dromenon*, February.

Boulding, K. 1966. *The image*. Ann Arbor: University of Michigan Press.

Bruner, J., J. Goodnow, and G. Austin. 1956. *A study of thinking*. New York: Wiley.

Buzan, T. 1991. *Use both sides of your brain*. New York: Dutton.

Caine, R., and G. Caine. 1990. Understanding a brain-based approach to learning and teaching. *Educational Leadership* 48(2): 66–70.

Campbell, D. 1983. *Introduction to the musical brain*. Richardson, TX: Magnamusic-Baton.

Campbell, J. 1989. *The improbable machine: What the upheavals in artificial intelligence research reveal about how the mind really works*. New York: Simon & Schuster.

Campbell, L. 1985. *Tomorrow's education today.* Seattle: The Pegasus School.

———. 1997. Variations on a theme: How teachers interpret MI theory. *Educational Leadership* 55(1): 14–19.

Campbell, L., and B. Campbell. 1999. *Multiple intelligences and student achievement: Success stories from six schools.* Alexandria, VA: Association for Supervision and Curriculum Development.

Campbell, L., B. Campbell, and D. Dickinson. 1998. *Teaching and learning through multiple intelligences,* 2nd ed. Needham Heights, MA: Allyn & Bacon.

Caramassa, A., A. Hillis, E. C. Leek, and M. Miozzo. 1994. The organization of lexical knowledge in the brain: Evidence from category- and modality-specific deficits. In *Mapping the mind,* edited by L. Hirschfield and S. Gelman. New York: Cambridge University Press.

Carey, S. 1985. *Conceptual change in childhood.* Cambridge, MA: Massachusetts Institute of Technology Press.

Chi, M. 1981. Knowledge development and memory performance. In *Intelligence and learning,* edited by M. Friedman, J. P. Das, and N. O'Connor. New York: Plenum.

Chomsky, N. 1968. *Language and mind.* New York: Harcourt, Brace, Jovanovich.

Coles, R. 1990. *The spiritual life of children.* Boston: Houghton Mifflin.

Costa, A. 1981. Teaching for intelligent behavior. *Educational Leadership* (39)1: 29–31.

———. 1984. Mediating the metacognitive. *Educational Leadership* (42)3: 57–62.

———, ed. 1991a. *Developing minds* (rev. ed.). Alexandria, VA: Association for Supervision and Curriculum Development.

———. 1991b. The school as a home for the mind. In *Developing Minds, Volume 1* (rev. ed.), edited by A. Costa. Alexandria, VA: Association for Supervision and Curriculum Development.

Csikszentmihalyi, N. 1996. *Creativity.* New York: Harper Collins.

Culicover, P., and P. Wexler. 1980. *Formal principles of language acquisition.* Cambridge, MA: Massachusetts Institute of Technology Press.

Curry, L. 1990. A critique of the research on learning styles. *Educational Leadership* (48)2: 50–52.

Damasio, A. 1994. *Descartes's error.* New York: Putnam.

Dansereau, D., et al. 1979. Development and evaluation of a learning strategy training program. *Journal of Educational Psychology* 71(1).

Davidson, J. 1982. The group mapping activity for instruction in reading and thinking. *Journal of Reading* 26(1): 52–56.

de Bono, E. 1973. *Lateral thinking: Creativity step by step.* New York: Harper & Row.

Demille, R. 1976. *Put your mother on the ceiling.* New York: Viking-Penguin.

Diamond, M., and J. Hobson. 1998. *Magic trees of the mind: How to nurture your child's intelligence, creativity, and healthy emotions from birth to adolescence.* New York: Dutton.

Dickinson, D. 1987. *New developments in cognitive research.* Seattle: New Horizons for Learning.

Dunne, J. 1972. *The way of all the earth: Experiments in truth and religion.* New York: MacMillan.

Edelman, G. M. 1995. *The wordless metaphor: Visual art and the brain.* New York: Whitney Museum.

Feldenkrais, M. 1977. *Awareness through movement: Health exercises for personal growth.* New York: Harper & Row.

Ferguson, M. 1980. *The Aquarian conspiracy: Personal and social transformation in the 1980s.* Los Angeles: J. P. Tarcher.

Feuerstein, R. 1980. *Instrumental enrichment.* Baltimore, MD: University Park Press.

Fogarty, R., and J. Bellanca. 1989. *Patterns for thinking: Patterns for transfer.* Palatine, IL: IRI/SkyLight Training and Publishing.

———. 1986. *Teach them thinking.* Palatine, IL: IRI/SkyLight Training and Publishing.

Gardner, H. 1981. Do babies sing a universal song? *Psychology Today,* December.

———. 1982. *Developmental psychology: An introduction.* Boston: Little Brown.

———. 1983. *Frames of mind: The theory of multiple intelligences.* New York: Harper & Row.

———. 1987. Developing the spectrum of human intelligences: Teaching in the eighties, a need to change. *Harvard Educational Review.*

———. 1996. *Are there additional intelligences?* Cambridge, MA: Harvard Graduate School of Education.

———. 1999. *Intelligence reframed: Multiple intelligences for the 21st century.* New York: Basic Books.

Gawain, S. 1978. *Creative visualization.* New York: Bantam Books.

Gazzaniga, M. 1988. *Mind matters: How mind and brain interact to create our conscious lives.* Boston: Houghton Mifflin.

Gendlin, E. 1978. *Focusing.* New York: Everest House.

Glasser, W. 1986. *Control theory in the classroom.* New York: Perennial Library.

Graham, I. 1988. Mindmapping: An aid to memory. *Planetary Edges*, April/June. Toronto: The Institute of Cultural Affairs.

Gross, C. B. 1973. Visual functions of intero-temporal cortex. In *Handbook of sensory philosophy* (vol. II, no. 3), edited by R. Jung. New York: Springer Verlag.

Guilford, J. 1979. *Way beyond IQ.* Buffalo, NY: Creative Education Foundation.

Harman, W. 1988. *The global mind change.* Indianapolis: Knowledge Systems.

Harman, W., and H. Rheingold. 1985. *Higher creativity.* Los Angeles: J. P. Tarcher.

Hatch, T. 1997. Getting specific about multiple intelligences. *Educational Leadership* 54(6): 26–29.

Herrnstein, R., and D. Loveland. 1976. Natural concepts in pigeons. *Journal of Experimental Psychology: Animal Behavior Processes* 2:285–302.

Hoerr, T. 1996a. Introducing the theory of multiple intelligences. *NASSP bulletin* 80(583): 8–10.

———. 1996b. *Succeeding with multiple intelligences.* St. Louis, MO: New City School.

———. 2000a. *Technology and MI.* On New Horizons for Learning Web site: www.newhorizons.org/ trm_hoerr.htm. Seattle: New Horizons for Learning.

———. 2000b. *Becoming a multiple intelligences school.* Alexandria, VA: Association for Supervision and Curriculum Development.

Houston, J. 1980. *Lifeforce: The psycho-historical recovery of the self.* New York: Delacorte Press.

———. 1982. *The possible human: A course in extending your physical, mental, and creative abilities.* Los Angeles: J. P. Tarcher.

———. 1987. *The search for the beloved: Journeys in sacred psychology.* Los Angeles: J. P. Tarcher.

Hubbard, B. 1985. *Manual for co-creators of the quantum leap.* Irvine, CA: Barbara Mary Hubbard, Inc.

Institute of Cultural Affairs. 1968. *5th city preschool education manual.* Chicago: Institute of Cultural Affairs.

———. 1981. Imaginal training methods. *Image: A Journal on the Human Factor.*

Jensen, E. 1999. *Teaching with the brain in mind.* Alexandria, VA: Association for Supervision and Curriculum Development.

Johnson, D., R. Johnson, and E. J. Holubec. 1986. *Circles of learning.* Edina, MN: Interaction Book Company.

———. 1988. *Cooperation in the classroom.* Edina, MN: Interaction Book Company.

Kagan, S. 1990. *Cooperative learning resources for teachers.* San Juan Capistrano, CA: Resources for Teachers.

Kazantzakis, N. 1960. *The saviors of god.* New York: Simon & Schuster.

Keil, F. 1994. The birth and nurturance of concepts by domains: The origins of concepts of living things. In *Mapping the mind*, edited by L. Hirschfield and S. A. Gelman. New York: Cambridge University Press.

Konorski, J. 1967. *Integrative activity of the brain: An interdisciplinary approach.* Chicago: University of Chicago Press.

Laird, C. 1957. *The miracle of language.* New York: Fawcett Publications.

Langer, S. 1979. *Reflections on art.* New York: Arno Press.

Lawrence, D. H. 1959. Search for love. In *The complete poems of D. H. Lawrence*, edited by V. de Sola Pinto and F. Roberts. New York: Viking Press.

Lazear, D. 1994. *Multiple intelligence approaches to assessment: Solving the assessment conundrum.* Tucson, AZ: Zephyr Press.

———. 1998a. *Eight ways of knowing: Teaching for multiple intelligences*, 3rd ed. Arlington Heights, IL: SkyLight Training and Publishing.

———. 1998b. *The rubrics way: Using MI to assess understanding.* Tucson, AZ: Zephyr Press.

———. 1999. *Pathways of learning: Teaching students and parents about multiple intellligences.* Tucson, AZ: Zephyr Press.

———. 2000. *The intelligent curriculum: Using MI to develop your students' full potential.* Tucson, AZ: Zephyr Press.

Lederer, R. 1987. *Anguished English.* New York: Dell Publishing.

Loye, D. 1983. *The sphinx and the rainbow: Brain, mind, and future vision.* Boulder, CO: New Science Library.

Lozonov, G. 1978. *Suggestology and outlines of suggestology.* New York: Gordon & Breach.

Machado, L. 1980. *The right to be intelligent.* New York: Pergamon Press.

MacLean, P. 1977. On the evolution of three mentalities. In *New dimensions in psychiatry: A world view* (vol. 2), edited by S. Arieti and G. Chrzanowski. New York: Wiley.

Markley, O. 1988. Using depth intuition in creative problem solving and strategic innovation. *Journal of Creative Behavior* (22)2: 85–100.

Martin, A., C. L. Wiggs, L. G. Ungerleider, and J. W. Haxby. 1996. Neural correlates of category-specific knowledge. *Nature* 376: 649–652.

Masters, R., and J. Houston. 1972. *Mind games*. New York: Delacorte Press.

———. 1978. *Listening to the body: The psychophysical way to health and awareness*. New York: Delacorte Press.

McTighe, J. 1987. Teaching for thinking, of thinking, and about thinking. In *Thinking skills instruction: Concepts and techniques*, edited by M. Heiman and J. Slomianko. Washington, DC: National Education Association.

McTighe, J., and F. Lyman. 1988. Cueing thinking in the classroom: The promise of theory-embedded tools. *Educational Leadership* (45)7: 18–24.

Monroe, R. 1985. *Far journeys*. Garden City, NY: Doubleday.

Neisser, U. 1976. *Cognition and reality*. San Francisco: Freeman.

Nhat Hanh, T. 1988. *The miracle of mindfulness*. New York: Beacon Press.

Nielsen, J. 1946. *Agnosia, apraxia, and aphasia: Their value in cerebral localization*. New York: Hoeber.

Orff, C. 1978. *The schoolwork*. Translated by M. Murray. New York: Schott Music Corporation.

Perkins, D. 1986. *Knowledge as design*. Hillsdale, NJ: Lawrence Erlbaum Associates.

Pert, C. 1997. *Molecules of emotion: Why you feel the way you feel*. New York: Scribner.

Piaget, J. 1972. *The psychology of intelligence*. Totowa, NJ: Littlefield Adams.

Pribram, K. 1971. *Languages of the brain: Experimental paradoxes and principles in neuro-psychology*. Englewood Cliffs, NJ: Prentice-Hall.

———. 1974. *Holonomy and structure in the organization of perception*. Stanford, CA: Stanford University Press.

Progoff, I. 1975. *At a journal workshop: The basic text and guide for using the intensive journal*. New York: Dialogue House Library.

Rico, G. 1983. *Writing the natural way: Using right-brain techniques to release your expressive powers*. Los Angeles: J. P. Tarcher.

Roe, A. 1953. *The making of a scientist*. New York: Dodd, Mead.

Rosch, E., C. Mervis, W. Gray, D. Johnson, and P. Bayes-Braem. 1976. Basic objects in natural categories. *Cognitive Psychology* 8: 382–439.

Rosenfield, I. 1988. *The invention of memory: A new view of the brain*. New York: Basic Books.

Rourke, J. 2001. Why is Mona Lisa smiling? *Principal Leadership* 2(3).

Rubado, K. 2002. Empowering students through multiple intelligences. *Reclaiming Children and Youth* 10(4): 233–235.

Russell, P. 1976. *The brain book*. New York: E. P. Dutton.

———. 1983. *The global brain: Speculations on the evolutionary leap to planetary consciousness*. Los Angeles: J. P. Tarcher.

Samuels, M., and N. Samuels. 1975. *Seeing with the mind's eye: The history, techniques, and uses of visualization*. New York: Random House.

Schmeck, R., ed. 1988. *Learning strategies and learning styles*. New York: Plenum Press.

Shone, R. 1984. *Creative visualization*. New York: Thorson's Publishers.

Silver, H. F., R. W. Strong, and M. J. Perini. 2000. *So each may learn: Integrating learning styles and multiple intelligences*. Alexandria, VA: Association for Supervision and Curriculum Development.

Slavin, R. 1983. *Cooperative learning*. New York: Longman.

Snowman, J. 1989. Learning tactics and strategies. In *Cognitive instructional psychology: Components of classroom learning*, edited by G. Phy and T. Andre. New York: Academic Press.

Springer, S., and G. Deutsch. 1985. *Left brain, right brain*. New York: W. H. Freeman.

Steiner, R. 1925. *Music in light of anthroposophy*. London: Anthroposophical.

Sternberg, R. 1984. *Beyond I.Q.: A triarchic theory of human intelligence*. New York: Cambridge University Press.

———. 1986. *Intelligence applied: Understanding and increasing your intellectual skills*. San Diego, CA: Harcourt, Brace, Jovanovich.

Sternberg, R., L. Okagaki, and A. Jackson. 1990. Practical intelligence for success in school. *Educational leadership* (48)1: 35–39.

Striker, S., with E. Kimmel. 1982–1990. *The anti coloring book*. (Series.) New York: Holt.

Sylwester, R. 2000. *A biological brain in a cultural classroom: Applying biological research to classroom management.* Thousand Oaks, CA: Corwin Press.

Taylor, C., and F. Barron. 1963. *Scientific creativity, its recognition and development.* New York: Wiley.

Teele, S., and T. Armstrong. 2000. *Rainbows of intelligence: Exploring how students learn.* Thousand Oaks, CA: Corwin Press.

Vaughn, F. 1986. *The inward arc.* Boulder, CO: The New Science Library.

von Oech, R. 1983. *A whack on the side of the head: How to unlock your mind for innovation.* New York: Warner Books.

———. 1986. *A kick in the seat of the pants: Using your explorer, artist, judge, & warrior to be more creative.* New York: Perennial Library.

Vygotsky, L. 1986. *Thought and language.* Cambridge, MA: Massachusetts Institute of Technology Press.

Wagmeister, J., B. Shifrin. 2000. Thinking differently, learning differently. *Educational Leadership* 58(3): 45–48.

Walsh, R., and F. Vaughn, eds. 1980. *Beyond ego: Transpersonal dimensions in psychology.* Los Angeles: J. P. Tarcher.

Walters, J., and H. Gardner. 1985. The development and education of the intelligences. In *Essays on the intellect.* Alexandria, VA: Association for Supervision and Curriculum Development.

Warrington, E. 1994. The conceptual abilities of pigeons. *American Scientist* 83: 246–255.

Warrington, E., and T. Shallice. 1984. Category-specific semantic impairments. *Brain* 107: 829–854.

Weber, E. 1999. Uniting to introduce multiple intelligences teaching approaches. *NASSP Bulletin* 83(604): 57–68.

Weinstein, M., and J. Goodman. 1980. *Playfair.* San Luis Obispo, CA: Impact.

Wilber, K. 1980. *The atman project.* Wheaton, IL: Quest Books.

———. 1983. *Eye to eye: The quest for the new paradigm.* Garden City, NY: Anchor Books.

Winocur, S. L. 1986. *Zooley.* IMPACT (improve minimal proficiency by activating critical thinking) program. Huntington Beach, CA: Phi Delta Kappa.

Wolfe, P. 2001. *Brain matters: Translating research into classroom practice.* Alexandria, VA: Association for Supervision and Curriculum Development.

Index

Index

Advisory council game, 129
Amplifying intelligence, 38, 39, 216
  bodily/kinesthetic, 94, 95, 98
  interpersonal, 124, 125, 128
  intrapersonal, 138, 139, 142–44
  logical/mathematical, 62, 63, 66–67
  musical/rhythmic, 110, 111, 114
  naturalist, 154, 155, 158–59
  verbal/linguistic, 48, 49, 52
  visual/spatial, 78, 79, 82–83
Archetypal pattern recognition, 216
Art. *See* Fine arts
Assessment tips, 41, 43
  for bodily/kinestetic intelligence,
      102
  for interpersonal intelligence, 131
  for intrapersonal intelligence, 146
  for logical/mathematical intelli-
      gence, 70
  for musical/rhythmic intelligence,
      117
  for naturalist intelligence, 162
  for verbal/linguistic intelligence, 55
  for visual/spatial intelligence, 87
Attribute web, 66, 70, 192, 216
Audubon, James, 157
Awakening intelligence, 38, 39, 216
  bodily/kinesthetic, 94, 95, 97–98
  interpersonal, 124, 125, 127–28
  intrapersonal, 138, 139, 141–42
  logical/mathematical, 62, 63, 65–66
  musical/rhythmic, 110, 111,
      113–14
  naturalist, 154, 155, 157–58
  verbal/linguistic, 48, 49, 51–52
  visual/spatial, 78, 79, 81–82
Awareness technique, 216

Before and after scenarios, 183
Biofeedback, 216
Biology lesson. *See also* Science lesson
  elementary school adaptation for,
      86–87
  middle school adaptation for, 87
  at secondary school level, 77–90
Blacklines, 216
  graphic organizer, 202–13
  lesson procedure, 190–99
  lesson processing, 172–88
Bodily/kinesthetic intelligence, 5, 7,
      93–105
  amplifying, 94, 95, 98
  assessment tips for, 102
  awakening, 94, 95, 97–98
  elementary school adaptation of,
      101
  lesson palette for, 93, 103, 104
  lesson planning ideas, 105
  for literature lesson, 127, 129
  secondary school adaptation of,
      102
  teaching, 94, 95, 99–100
  technology tips and tools for, 102,
      179
  toolbox for, 15, 37, 173
  transfering, 94, 95, 100–101
Brain. *See also* Left brain operations;
      Right brain operations
  Broca's Area of, 2, 51, 216
  musical centers of, 114
  triune, 2
  views of, 3
  whole, 1–2
Brainstorming, 53, 65, 66, 128, 142,
      145, 216

Broca's Area of brain, 2, 51, 216

Can You Guess My Attributes? game,
      65–66
Can You Guess My Classification
      Scheme? game, 66
Can You Guess My Rank Ordering
      Rationale? game, 66
Can You Guess What I Am? game, 51,
      54
Caring for animals, 216
Cerebral cortex, 97
Charades, 97–98
Chart your moods, 184
Classification Chart, 67, 70, 192, 216
Cognitive organizer, 216
Communication games, 127–28
Complex problem solving, 170
Concept mapping, 202, 216
Conservation practices, 216
Consumer sciences. *See* Family/
      consumer sciences
Cooperative Learning, Key Ingredients
      for Success In, 187
Countermelody, 216
Cultures
  analyzing another, 68
  appreciating another, 68
  understanding other, 61–73
Current events lesson. *See also* History
      lessons; Social studies lessons
  elementary school adaptation of,
      145
  interpersonal intelligence in
      teaching, 141
  intrapersonal intelligence in
      teaching, 137–49

middle school adaptation of, 145–46

at secondary school level, 142–49

verbal/linguistic intelligence in teaching, 141

Curriculum axis, 40

Declarative writing, 159

Deductive thought processes, 4

Deep relaxation technique, 216

Descriptive writing, 160

Diaries. *See* Journals

Discussion questions, 115, 194

Dramatic structure model, 216

Each One Teach One, 217

8-in-1 lessons

designing, 14, 16–17

impact on learning, 17–18

making time for, 19–20

planning strategy for, 13–23

structuring, 18

timing, in using, 18–19

Eight Ways of Teaching Weekly Checklist, 43, 188

Elementary school

adaptation of biology lesson for, 86–87

adaptation of current events lesson for, 145

adaptation of geometry lesson for, 101

adaptation of language arts lesson for, 161–62

adaptation of literature lesson for, 130

adaptation of social studies lesson for, 69–70

history lesson at, 109–20

science lesson at, 20–23, 45–58

Environmental feedback, 217

The Evocative Power of Nature for Writing, 153–65

Exclamatory writing, 159

Exploring Natural Objects (science lesson at elementary school level), 45–58

Family/consumer sciences

bodily/kinesthetic lesson planning ideas for, 105

interpersonal lesson planning ideas for, 134

intrapersonal lesson planning ideas for, 149

logical/mathematical lesson planning ideas for, 73

musical/rhythmic lesson planning ideas for, 120

naturalist lesson planning ideas for, 165

verbal/linguistic lesson planning ideas for, 58

visual/spatial lesson planning ideas for, 90

Fat and Skinny Questions, 203, 217

Feuerstein, Reuven, 2

Fine arts

bodily/kinesthetic lesson planning ideas for, 105

interpersonal lesson planning ideas for, 134

intrapersonal lesson planning ideas for, 149

logical/mathematical lesson planning ideas for, 73

musical/rhythmic lesson planning ideas for, 120

naturalist lesson planning ideas for, 165

verbal/linguistic lesson planning ideas for, 58

visual/spatial lesson planning ideas for, 90

Focusing technique, 217

Forming a Personal Advisory Council (literature lesson at middle school level), 123–34

4 x 4 x 4 outline, 204, 217

4-Level Reflection Model, 144, 145, 198

worksheets for, 142, 144

Fraction and decimal equivalents, 24–28

Frontal lobes, 127

Geography. *See* Global studies and geography; Social studies lessons

Geometry lesson. *See also* Mathematics lesson

with bodily/kinesthetic intelligence, 97

elementary school adaptation for, 101

at middle school level, 93–105

secondary school adaptation for, 102

Global studies and geography. *See also* Social studies lessons

bodily/kinesthetic lesson planning ideas for, 105

interpersonal lesson planning ideas for, 134

intrapersonal lesson planning ideas for, 149

logical/mathematical lesson planning ideas for, 73

musical/rhythmic lesson planning ideas for, 120

naturalist lesson planning ideas for, 165

verbal/linguistic lesson planning ideas for, 58

visual/spatial lesson planning ideas for, 90

Gossip Game, 127–28, 217

Graphic organizers, 192, 217. *See also specific*

blacklines for, 202–13

Growing natural things, 217

Guided imagery, 217

Hands-on labs, 217

Health lessons

bodily/kinesthetic lesson planning ideas for, 105

interpersonal lesson planning ideas for, 134

intrapersonal lesson planning ideas for, 149

logical/mathematical lesson planning ideas for, 73

musical/rhythmic lesson planning ideas for, 120

naturalist lesson planning ideas for, 165

verbal/linguistic lesson planning ideas for, 58

visual/spatial lesson planning ideas for, 90

History lessons. *See also* Current events lesson; Social studies lessons

bodily/kinesthetic lesson planning ideas for, 105

at elementary school level, 109–20

interpersonal lesson planning ideas for, 134

intrapersonal lesson planning ideas for, 149

logical/mathematical lesson planning ideas for, 73

middle school adaptation for, 116

musical/rhythmic lesson planning ideas for, 109–20

naturalist lesson planning ideas for, 165

secondary school adaptation for, 117

verbal/linguistic lesson planning ideas for, 58

visual/spatial lesson planning ideas for, 90

Hologram, 2, 4

How Am I Involved and What Can I Do? (current events lesson at secondary school level), 142–49

How Does It Feel To Be a Circle?(geometry lesson at middle school level), 93–105

How I Say *What* I Say, 128, 217
Human graph, 217

I Become What I Behold, 217
Imperative writing, 159
The Incredible Journey of Photosynthesis (biology lesson at the secondary school level), 77–90
Inductive reasoning, 4
Industrial technology
    bodily/kinesthetic lesson planning ideas for, 105
    interpersonal lesson planning ideas for, 134
    intrapersonal lesson planning ideas for, 149
    logical/mathematical lesson planning ideas for, 73
    musical/rhythmic lesson planning ideas for, 120
    naturalist lesson planning ideas for, 165
    verbal/linguistic lesson planning ideas for, 58
    visual/spatial lesson planning ideas for, 90
Inner seeing exercises. *See* Guided imagery
Intelligence. *See also* Bodily/kinesthetic intelligence; Interpersonal intelligence; Intrapersonal intelligence; Logical/mathematical intelligence; Multiple intelligences; Musical/rhythmic intelligence; Naturalist intelligence; Verbal/linguistic intelligence; Visual/spatial intelligence
    enhanced and amplified, 2
    as multiple reality, 4
Intelligence foci watching, 170
Intelligence-focused lesson planning strategy, 35–44
Intelligence skill games, 170
Interpersonal intelligence, 5, 7, 53, 123–34, 169
    amplifying, 124, 125, 128
    assessment tips for, 131
    awakening, 124, 125, 127–28
    elementary school adaptation of, 130
    for geometry lesson, 97
    for history lesson, 113
    for language arts lesson, 157
    lesson palette for, 123, 132, 133
    lesson planning ideas, 134
    for science lesson, 51
    secondary school adaptation for, 130–31
    for social studies, 65
    teaching, 124, 125, 129

in teaching current events, 141
    technology tips and tools for, 131, 179
    toolbox for, 15, 37, 174
    transfering, 124, 125, 130
Interrogative writing, 159
Intrapersonal intelligence, 5, 7, 137–49
    amplifying, 138, 139, 142–44
    assessment tips for, 146
    awakening, 138, 139, 141–42
    elementary school adaptation of, 145
    for language arts lesson, 157
    lesson palette for, 137, 147, 148
    lesson planning ideas, 149
    middle school adaptation for, 145
    for science lesson, 51
    teaching, 138, 139, 144
    technology tips and tools for, 146, 180
    toolbox for, 15, 37, 175
    transfering, 138, 139, 145
Inventing, 170

Jigsaw, 205, 217
Journals, 41, 43, 70
    for bodily/kinesthetic intelligence, 102
    for interpersonal intelligence, 131
    for intrapersonal intelligence, 146
    for logical/mathematical intelligence, 70
    models for student, 183–86
    for musical/rhythmic intelligence, 117
    for naturalist intelligence, 162
    for verbal/linguistic intelligence, 55
    for visual/spatial intelligence, 87
Journey of metamorphosis, 20–23

KWL Goal-Setting Chart, 206, 217

Language arts lesson, 153–65. *See also* Literature lesson
    bodily/kinesthetic lesson planning ideas, 105
    elementary school adaptation for, 161–62
    interpersonal lesson planning ideas for, 134, 157
    intrapersonal lesson planning ideas for, 149, 157
    logical/mathematical lesson planning ideas for, 73
    middle school adaptation for, 162
    musical/rhythmic lesson planning ideas for, 120
    naturalist lesson planning ideas for, 165
    verbal/linguistic lesson planning ideas for, 58, 157

visual/spatial lesson planning ideas for, 90
Learning logs. *See* Journals
Left brain operations, 1–2. *See also* Right brain operations
    in bodily/kinesthetic intelligence, 97
    in interpersonal intelligence, 127
    in logical/mathematical intelligence, 65
    in musical/rhythmic intelligence, 113
    in verbal/linguistic intelligence, 51
Lesson palette, 36, 181
    for bodily/kinesthetic intelligence, 93, 103, 104
    for interpersonal intelligence, 123, 132, 133
    for intrapersonal intelligence, 137, 147, 148
    for logical/mathematical intelligence, 61, 71, 72
    for musical/rhythmic intelligence, 109, 118, 119
    for naturalist intelligence, 153, 163, 164
    for verbal/linguistic intelligence, 47, 56, 57
    for visual/spatial intelligence, 77, 88, 89
Lesson Planning Ideas Chart, 44
Lesson planning ideas for teaching with
    bodily/kinesthetic intelligence, 105
    Interpersonal intelligence, 134
    intrapersonal intelligence, 149
    logical/mathematical intelligence, 73
    musical/rhythmic intelligence, 120
    naturalist intelligence, 165
    verbal/linguistic intelligence, 58
    visual/spatial intelligence, 90
Lesson plan staging model, 182
Lesson procedure blacklines, 190–99
Lesson processing blacklines, 172–88
Limbic system, 127
Lion Hunt, 128
Literature genre, 29–32
Literature lesson. *See also* Language arts lesson
    elementary school adaptation for, 130
    at middle school level, 123–34
    secondary school adaptation for, 130–31
Logical/mathematical intelligence, 4, 7, 53, 61–73, 168, 169
    amplifying, 62, 63, 66–67
    assessment tips for, 70
    awakening, 62, 63, 65–66
    elementary school adaptation of, 69–70

for geometry lesson, 97
lesson palette for, 61, 71, 72
lesson planning ideas, 73
for science lesson, 51
secondary school adaptation of, 70
teaching, 62, 63, 68
technology tips and tools for, 70, 177
toolbox for, 15, 37, 172
transfering, 62, 63, 69

Mathematics lesson. *See also* Geometry lesson
bodily/kinesthetic lesson planning ideas, 105
interpersonal lesson planning ideas for, 134
intrapersonal lesson planning ideas for, 149
logical/mathematical lesson planning ideas for, 73
musical/rhythmic lesson planning ideas for, 120
naturalist lesson planning ideas for, 165
verbal/linguistic lesson planning ideas for, 58
visual/spatial lesson planning ideas for, 90
Matrix, 69–70, 207, 217
Memory storage, 2, 4
Metacognition, 217
Metacognitive processing, 217
Metaintelligence, 9
Micro/macro pattern connections, 217
Middle school
adaptation of biology lesson for, 87
adaptation of current events lesson for, 145–46
adaptation of history lesson for, 116
adaptation of language arts lesson for, 162
geometry lesson at, 93–105
literature lesson at, 123–34
math lesson for, 24–28
social studies lesson for, 61–73
Mind map, 217
Multiple Capacities Summary Wheel, 16
Multiple intelligences
teaching *for, with,* and *about,* 1–9
technology toolbox for, 177–80
toolbox descriptions, 172–75
using technolgy for teaching, 176
Multiple Intelligences Capacities Wheel, 6, 8, 51
Multiple Intelligences Toolbox, 14, 15, 16, 37
Multitracking, 217
Musical/rhythmic intelligence, 5, 7, 109–20, 169

amplifying, 110, 111, 114
assessment tips for, 117
awakening, 110, 111, 113–14
lesson palette for, 109, 118, 119
lesson planning ideas, 120
middle school adaptation of, 116
secondary school adaptation of, 117
teaching, 110, 111, 115–16
technology tips and tools for, 117, 178
toolbox for, 15, 37, 174
transfering, 110, 111, 116
Musical talent, 114

Naturalist intelligence, 6, 7, 53, 153–65
amplifying, 154, 155, 158–59
assessment tips for, 162
awakening, 154, 155, 157–58
elementary school adaptation of, 161–62
language arts lesson with, 153–65
lesson palette for, 153, 163, 164
lesson planning ideas, 165
middle school adaptation of, 162
for science lesson, 51
teaching, 154, 155, 159–60
technology tips and tools for, 162, 180
toolbox for, 15, 37, 175
transfering, 154, 155
Natural pattern recognition, 218
Nature encounters/field trips, 218
Nature observation, 218
Nature simulations, 218
Neo-cortex, 127
New Word for the Day, 218
Noncompetitive game, 218
Notational system stage, 169

Pass over. *See I Become What I Behold*
The Past Is Alive With The Sound of Music (history lesses at elementary school level), 109–20
Peer coaching team, 218
Personal Advisory Council, forming, 123–34
Physical education
bodily/kinesthetic lesson planning ideas for, 105
interpersonal lesson planning ideas for, 134
intrapersonal lesson planning ideas for, 149
logical/mathematical lesson planning ideas for, 73
musical/rhythmic lesson planning ideas for, 120
naturalist lesson planning ideas for, 165

verbal/linguistic lesson planning ideas for, 58
visual/spatial lesson planning ideas for, 90
Physical movement formulas, 98, 195
PMI (pluses, minuses interesting), 142, 218
interesting) Chart, 208
Portfolios, 41, 43, 70
for bodily/kinesthetic intelligence, 102
for interpersonal intelligence, 131
for intrapersonal intelligence, 146
for logical/mathematical intelligence, 70
model for creating student, 42
for musical/rhythmic intelligence, 117
for naturalist intelligence, 162
for verbal/linguistic intelligence, 55
for visual/spatial intelligence, 87
Positive interdependence, 127
Project Zero, 4

Ranking ladders, 67, 192, 209, 218
Rank ordering, 67
Raw pattering ability, 168
Raw patterning stage, 169
Rhythm game, 218
Riddles, 51–52
Right brain operations, 1–2. *See also* Left brain operations
in bodily/kinesthetic intelligence, 97
in interpersonal intelligence, 127
in logical/mathematical intelligence, 65
in musical/rhythmic intelligence, 113
in visual/spatial intelligence, 81
Role-playing, 70

Science lesson
bodily/kinesthetic lesson planning ideas, 105
at elementary school level, 45–58
with interpersonal intelligence, 51
interpersonal lesson planning ideas for, 134
intrapersonal intelligence for, 51, 149
logical/mathematical intelligence for, 51, 73
musical/rhythmic lesson planning ideas for, 120
naturalist intelligence for, 51, 165
verbal/linguistic intelligence for, 45–58
visual/spatial lesson planning ideas for, 90
Scientific thinking, 4
Script-writing assignment, 115
Secondary school

adaptation of geometry lesson for, 102

adaptation of history lesson for, 117

adaptation of literature lesson for, 130–31

adaptation of social studies lesson for, 70

biology lesson at, 77–90

current events lesson at, 142–49

language arts lesson at, 29–32, 153–65

See/Feel T-Chart, 53, 54, 55, 191

Self-transcendence, 128

Sensory stimulation exercises, 218

6 Ss for describing attributes, 190
worksheet for, 52, 54, 55

Snapshots of the past and present, 185

Social studies lessons. *See also* Current events lesson; Global studies and geography; History lessons

elementary school adaptation for, 69–70

interpersonal intelligence for, 65

logical/mathematical intelligence for, 61–73

for middle school level, 61–73

secondary school adaptation for, 70

verbal/linguistic intelligence for, 65

visual/spatial intelligence for, 65

Species discrimination, 218

Spiral adaptations of lesson, 41, 218

Spiral curriculum, 41

Stepping stones into the future, 186

Stop the Action and Improvise, 218

Story grid, 210, 218

Student intelligence watch, 169

Symbol system, 168

Teach for/with intelligence, 38, 39

Teaching intelligence
bodily/kinesthetic, 94, 95, 99–100
interpersonal, 124, 125, 129
intrapersonal, 138, 139, 144
logical/mathematical, 62, 63, 68
musical/rhythmic, 110, 111, 115–16

naturalist, 154, 155, 159–60
verbal/linguistic, 48, 49, 53–54
visual/spatial, 78, 79, 83–86

Team Reflection Log, 116, 197

Technology tips and tools, 43
for bodily/kinesthetic intelligence, 102, 179
for interpersonal intelligence, 131, 179
for intrapersonal intelligence, 146, 180
for logical/mathematical intelligence, 70, 177
for multiple intelligences, 176, 177–80
for musical/rhythmic intelligence, 117, 178
for naturalist intelligence, 162, 180
for verbal/linguistic intelligence, 55, 177
for visual/spatial intelligence, 87, 178

Temporal lobes, 2

Thinking logs, 183

Thinking pattern games, 65–66

Through the Looking Glass (Carroll), 176

Transfering intelligence, 38, 39, 218
bodily/kinesthetic, 94, 95, 100–101
interpersonal, 124, 125, 130
intrapersonal, 138, 139, 145
logical/mathematical, 62, 63, 69
musical/rhythmic, 110, 111, 116
naturalist, 154, 155
verbal/linguistic, 48, 49, 54
visual/spatial, 78, 79, 86

Triune brain, 2

Turn to Your Partner And . . ., 218

Types of Writing Worksheet, 159, 160, 199

Ugly Americanism, 218

Understanding Other Cultures (social studies lesson at middle school level), 61–73

Venn diagram, 70, 211, 218

Verbal/linguistic intelligence, 2, 4, 7, 45–58, 168, 177
amplifying, 48, 49, 52
assessment tips for, 55
awakening, 48, 49, 51–52
for history lesson, 113
for language arts lesson, 157
lesson palette for, 47, 56, 57
lesson planning ideas, 58
for literature lesson, 127
middle school adaptation of, 55
secondary school adaptation of, 55
for social studies, 65
teaching, 48, 49, 53–54
in teaching current events, 141
technology tips and tools for, 55, 177
toolbox for, 15, 37, 172
transfering, 48, 49, 54

Visual/spatial intelligence, 2, 4–5, 7, 77–90
amplifying, 78, 79, 82–83
assessment tips for, 87
awakening, 78, 79, 81–82
biology lesson, 77–90
elementary school adaptation of, 86–87
for history lesson, 113
lesson palette for, 77, 88, 89
lesson planning ideas, 90
for literature lesson, 127, 129
middle school adaptation of, 87
for social studies, 65
teaching, 78, 79, 83–86
technology tips and tools for, 87, 178
toolbox for, 15, 37, 173
transfering, 78, 79, 86

Vocational or avocational pursuit stage, 169

Web, 65, 212, 218
attribute, 66, 70, 192, 216

Wernicke's area, 2

What? So What? Now What?, 213, 218

Whole brain, 1–2